Praise for "My Healing

"Within no time I got engrossed in Charlie
story of adventures and travel, experience and learning, suffering and
growth, that would easily do for at least three lives; told in a smooth,
humorous and unassuming way as if it was nothing out of the ordinary.

"What an exceptional background of learning and personal development
to a gifted natural healer! I feel honoured for having been one of the first
readers."

Frieke Karlovits, Austria

"Such an honour to read Charlie's inspirational, courageous, beautifully
scribed and heart-centred journey of his life so far. This will be a life-
changing book for so many of us daring to be true to our life's
purpose. Highly recommended."

Emma Taylor, The Bay Horse Speaks

"Reading Charlie's story gave me a fascinating insight into a culture I
know very little about. His descriptive writing drew me right into the
book, and made me feel as though I was experiencing the events."

Sally Logan

"I hope this tale of the search for meaning and finding your calling
touches others with its courage, humility and generosity."

Nick Taylor, Coach to the four time consecutive winner of the 'Sunday
Times Top 100 Best Companies to Work For'

My Healing Journey

from healing to horses to wholeness:
a story of self discovery

Charlie Holles

Published by Charlie Holles
First printing: 2014.
ISBN-13: 978-0-9928797-0-9

British Cataloguing Publication Data
A catalogue record of this book is available from The British Library.

Also available on Kindle from Amazon

This book is dedicated to my beloved, late parents, Troy and Jane Holles.
Their love and support was always unflinching and unconditional.

Contents

Acknowledgements

Everyone mentioned in the book has helped me on my journey, as well as many others not in this story. My writing coach Alison Thompson has kept me inspired and focused when I have faltered. My test readers, Nick Taylor, Emma Taylor, Frieke Karlovits and Sally Logan gave me great encouragement and honest, constructive feedback.

With the exception of the animals referred to and my Uncle John, all names are pseudonyms.

Prologue

A little boy lies on the grass in his garden looking up at a cloud-flecked sky. In his serious, childish way he wonders: "What is up there? Is there a great big wall up there? I don't understand how the sky can go on forever. But we have a big wall round the house where we live and outside of the wall there are the fields and woods, the road. So if there is a big wall up there then there must be something on the other side. Oh, I just don't understand. It makes my brain feel funny."

Then he drifts. He is very still, lying on a soft green carpet. No flicker of muscles in his arms or legs. His body merges with the ground beneath and then his awareness stretches out to become one with the huge trees surrounding him; with the birds; with their song. He is no longer in his body nor aware of it. There is no separation between him and what is all around; between him and what is far away. He is still and at peace. No longer wondering about that giant wall up there but at one with all. In bliss.

I was perhaps nine or ten when I lay on the grass, musing in this way. Before the world of adolescence sucked me in I could quite naturally feel the energy of the universe. Most children can and do. Yet they are told not to let their imaginations run away with them. The animals, spirits and faeries they see are just silly. I used to have a little friend, a rabbit, and I walked around holding him by the paw. When my mum washed my hands before a meal, I had to wash one hand first and then swap the bunny to that hand before washing my other hand. I am told that this was a serious ritual for me. The bunny was part of my life. Who is to say he was not there; that he was just a fantasy? Society and family pressure; school and the scorn of older 'wiser' boys and girls slowly crush that fragile connection to our essence. Yet so little truly separates us from all else in the universe. The difference at the DNA level between our physical body and a stone, a flower, an elephant is infinitesimal. We are genetic cousins to all life. So of course we can feel connected.

As I lay on the grass looking up and pondering the unanswerable riddle, the immensity of the question slowly bent my brain, short circuiting the logical left brain. Then I could flow into my creative right brain; flow within and then outward, ever outward.

The essence of the experience was bliss: peace and love. That is the essence of the universe. The essence of healing energy is love. It was a healing. Though in my childish way I had no intellectual understanding of what was happening, I could feel it and it felt good. It was the beginning of my healing journey, which continues to this day and will continue till I die and beyond.

I know that this experience of the energy of life, of the dance of that energy set me on my life path. It has led me through a myriad experiences. All of them have been essential to my growth. Many have been tough, traumatic, even life threatening. Yet there truly is no good or bad. I am deeply saddened when I hear people say such things as 'life's a bitch'. Life is a blessing; every single thing that happens to us. It is simply our choice as to whether we see the blessing in all. In the midst of pain it may be hard to see the blessing. Yet as my mother used to say, 'every cloud has a silver lining'. I would add 'look for it' then; even in the pain we can feel joy.

In common with most children, as I grew into adolescence I moved a little further from the awareness of that primordial energy. Still I would feel it when walking out alone. We lived on the edge of what was then a very small town. Beyond the big old house in which my parents rented a flat were open fields leading up a gentle slope towards more open common land that was in part quite heavily wooded. As I walked up the fields on overcast and autumnal days, the wind howled quite eerily. I loved it. I felt that stillness within; within the wind; within me.

I went to a school that put a premium on sporting performance and I was only averagely gifted in this way. My scholastic achievement, though above average, was not at the very top. So I felt pressure and over time I became very competitive as a sportsman and worked hard at my studies. Naturally this took me deeper into the world created by man; deeper into society and further from my source. That too is part of life's journey for most of us.

What I had felt when merging with all around me as a little boy stayed with me, deep within. It manifested itself as a sense of wonder that I never lost. Even as a fiercely competitive sportsman (and I was that) I could still feel the wonder. The sport I chose at school was rowing. Demanding, both of physical strength and endurance, I gave it my all. I trained with almost obsessive dedication. Yet even when I was in a boat in midwinter out on ice-strewn waters under a leaden sky, I would wonder at the beauty of the chop of blades in the water. The streaks of bubbles racing along the hull of the boat; the feel of the wood of the oar in my hands: all seemed somehow magical, mystical, special. I always retained an intense awareness of my body and all things physical.

It is in the physical that our awareness of the spirit is rooted. Being spiritual has nothing to do with being airy fairy, in floating away to 'lala' land. We have a body and we are part of a physical universe. At our essence we are pure energy but the gateway to it is through our physical senses.

Why a healing journey? Our healing is our journey back to full awareness of the energy of life. It has nothing to do with cleansing ourselves of sin. We are born perfect. An old Buddhist teacher whom I once followed used to say that even the most wicked act was done from 'twisted love'. Not easy to apply that to a mass murderer, but perhaps we should.

My healing journey has been rich and exciting; painful and joyous. It has been mine and I would change nothing. Why should I wish for anything different? I might as well wish not to have been born. Within everything have been the seeds of my growth. Life is not a bed of roses, nor should we expect it to be. That kind of thinking is rooted in a sense of entitlement. That thinking is destructive because it prevents us from experiencing the beauty of each moment.

The first chapter begins in the flower power era of the late sixties. It follows a sequential path highlighting key milestones on my journey. Much happened between those high moments, of course. Those times in between were like incubation periods but they would make for tedious reading.

If you are a healer I hope it will help you to go deeper into your calling. If you are just starting on the journey of life I hope that it may give you strength when all around seems dark. If you are in darkness, know that it will pass. That is easy to say and not always what we want to hear but we are not alone. One thing I have learnt is that though ultimately I am solely responsible for my life and my choices, yet I can receive so much help, support and love from my fellows. What I am still learning to do is to reach out to others. Reaching out is not weakness but a sign of strength, because it requires us to put aside the ego. I am still in awe of the love in men's hearts. When I let go of my ego and just come from my heart, it allows others to open their hearts too. It is as if it gives them permission to let their love flow. Perhaps some of my experience and the lessons I've learned will resonate with you; help you to see and understand more clearly the challenges in your life.

Something that is important to remember is that we are each on a unique and personal journey. So much of the time we compare ourselves with others. Society encourages that and most of us have a tendency to compare and then to judge ourselves. Having first felt that connection with the universe it has taken me till my mid sixties to finally acknowledge my true purpose. That might seem a long apprenticeship. I think that sometimes, and had I made different choices in the past, then I might have reached this point sooner. And yet....by the same token I believe that we have a journey which we each have to follow. I remember once a Buddhist teacher said to me that two men may knock on the doors of enlightenment. Both are good men. One is swiftly shown the light while the other has many lessons still to learn. One is not better than the other; it is simply that one has more to work through, perhaps because of lessons as yet unlearned in this life or from a past existence.

I believe that the most important thing in life is to find our true purpose before we die. Shakespeare said: *"First to thine own self be true, then thou canst not be false to any man."* Really finding oneself allows one to live a life of real integrity. The saddest thing is to die with the music unsung, still locked within our hearts. I hope that you find your purpose and that you sing the song in your heart.

Chapter 1: Meeting the Guru

In my final year of school, I failed to get into Oxford University where my father and an uncle had studied. But recalling my Oxford interview I would certainly not have offered me a place. I was very immature. Then I failed entry to another six universities. Was the universe trying to tell me something?

Off I went for three years into the big wide world. My father was pleased that I was considering following in his footsteps in business. My dear old mum taught me a couple of things she thought were important in looking after myself. She showed me how to sew a button onto a shirt and how to darn a pair of socks. Does anyone still do those things today? Then she presented me with something my grandfather had been given when he went off to the Second World War. It was a little sewing kit, complete with assorted spare buttons, thread, darning wool, needles, pins, a thimble and a pair of mini scissors. It was in a little cloth case, embroidered with flowers. Most of the contents were new but there was one item which had survived from my grandfather's day. It was a small amount of heavy brown sewing thread, made by Garnock of Scotland. I still have the kit and I have deliberately not used much of that thread, which must now be over seventy five years old.

The first place I headed for was Amsterdam. I spent around nine months there working with one of my father's business agents. At the time I thought that a career in business was what I would pursue. I worked with a company that imported into Holland and distributed a range of glass and pottery. In the end I decided this was not my career path but I had a great time. I guess I first developed a taste for exploring other cultures and countries in my early teens. At age thirteen I went with my family to Australia where my father had taken a job. Back in 1960 it was still possible to travel by boat (not just as a cruise) to reach a destination. Stopping at different exotic places on the way – Port Said, Aden, Bombay, Colombo and several Australian ports before reaching Sydney – was an exciting journey.

Amsterdam was another chapter in my voyage of discovery. The architecture and the all-pervading presence of the canal system was something new for me. The houses along the canals loomed high, seeming to overhang the water from either side, especially on the narrower canals. I made friends with an artist who sketched my portrait. Of course he lived in an apartment at the top of a house, with a small balcony that had a wonderful view over the canal and the rooftops beyond (the archetypal artist in a garret). Rooftop vistas in cities are magical as they transport me far from the noise and bustle of the street level. Needless to say much of our time was spent drinking good coffee and putting the world to rights.

Having been a keen oarsman at school I found a rowing club and continued my sporting passion. I was lodging with a family in the outer suburbs and the journey in to the club, on the river Amstel, involved several changes of tram. Trams were also new to me and I had a lot of fun 'tram hopping' with a time limit ticket to get to the club. It was a brutally cold winter and training out on the river was hard work. We also used to paddle up some of the small tributaries with sweeping views over the flat and frozen landscape so typical of the Netherlands.

The house I stayed in was a tiny apartment, with my widowed landlady and her two sons squeezed into very small rooms. She was a small, very thin and extremely fastidious lady. She used to peel grapes carefully with a knife and fork. I have never seen that since. I had a fold out bed in a part of the living room that could be partitioned off with a concertina door for the night. Every morning I had a wonderful breakfast of coffee and bread and chocolate chips. I'm not sure it was a very healthy breakfast but it appealed to my sweet tooth.

The older son was an avid volleyball player and we had long discussions about the merits of our respective sports. He thought I was slightly mad to choose something that involved being out in such harsh winter conditions. It was hard to learn the language simply because so many Dutchmen speak near fluent English. Still, I did manage to speak a little and in fact I found it a relatively easy language, somehow quite close to English in its fairly loose grammatical structure.

During 1965 a group of anarchists, led by Luud Schimmelpennink, started the White Bicycle Scheme to reduce pollution and promote more use of bikes. White painted bikes were left around the city for anyone to use and simply leave somewhere when you finished with them. The scheme didn't last long as the bikes were either stolen or confiscated by the police. I did use them occasionally in the centre of the city, which, together with the trams, made for great adventures around this beautiful city as I discovered my new found independence after leaving home.

I returned to England with no firm plans, having decided that I didn't want to pursue the kind of work I had done in Holland. Then I had the idea of spending time working on a kibbutz in Israel. I knew little about them other than that quite a lot of youngsters like me were heading off to spend a few summer months on them. Mostly they were agriculture based so the work would be physical and healthy. The kibbutz was something radically different to anything I had experienced. The communal style of life and the closeness to the earth in which the residents lived really struck a chord in me.

First I went to Tel Aviv and sought out an office that organised visitors like me. I chose Kibbutz Ginegar in the north, fairly close to Nazareth. I hopped on a bus to Haifa and then headed inland to Ginegar. It was early spring and getting a lot warmer there than I was used to back home. I got off the bus at the kibbutz gates on an empty dusty road with no idea of what to expect other than knowing that it was fairly small, about 500 or so members, with an economy based on cotton, fruit growing and a herd of dairy cattle. Over to the left I could see the cotton fields. Inside the boundary of the kibbutz everything was rich and green in contrast to the arid road and surrounds. There was a short walk to the main buildings and beyond them the land climbed a hill to individual accommodation, toilets, shower blocks and the swimming pool. I glimpsed the fruit orchards, which consisted of mainly orange, apple and pear trees. My first work assignment was in the orchards.

I was warmly greeted and shown to my room. Rooms were basic but adequate and shower and toilet facilities were communal. Many people don't know that the kibbutz system evolved out of necessity. As Jewish refugees travelled to Palestine mainly from Eastern Europe during the early twentieth century, they would arrive with very little in the way of possessions. With socialist and Zionist ideals as their inspiration, people would group together to establish small agriculture-based communities. Jobs, possessions and even the care of children had to be shared. Hence the system evolved. Children, for example, slept in and were raised in children's houses. They knew their parents of course and would spend time with them but most of the rearing was done by surrogate mothers. There is much evidence to suggest that this caused a lot of psychological problems though I was not aware of that at the time.

What amazed me was such a different and communal way of living. Everything that the members received was simply by seniority through age. So initially, single people had a small private room. A normal wage was not earned; rather each person received a small cash allowance for use on visits to the city. Then as one's turn came round you would be entitled to other luxuries such as a record player or a radio. Clothing was given out as needed. Since most laundry was done by the communal laundry, there was no need for individually owned washing machines, though some people had a small one. We were treated in the same way with a rather smaller allowance but all we needed in the way of food, clothing, medical care, basic toiletries and stamps for mail home.

All meals were served in a big communal dining hall and there was no shortage of excellent cuisine, much of which was home produced.

Breakfast was a boisterous gathering with the young volunteers. Many were from the USA with a few from England, Australia and a handful from other European countries.

Once we had eaten our fill we headed off to the orchards. Although our labour was a help, some of our supervisors despaired of those of us who were not careful enough in picking and so damaged the fruit. Then there was the business of taking breaks. Many of us were not used to the heat so we frequently stopped for water and to sit in the shade, which caused some of our supervisors to get a bit irate. Mostly it was pretty good natured. Barefoot under the trees, hot even in shorts and t-shirt, we lived a lifestyle so different from England. Sometimes we visited another kibbutz for an evening. The hospitality of the residents was unbounded. Many of the older, founding members of the kibbutz had suffered immense hardship in Eastern European countries and they were happy to share their simple lifestyle with us. I made some very good friends amongst the residents and I would often join them in their private rooms for an evening coffee.

We usually spent the afternoons after work at the swimming pool and then often danced under warm evening skies. I enjoyed the Sabbath, which runs from sundown on Friday till sundown on Saturday. We gathered for the evening meal with everyone dressed in fine clothes and started with singing. After a long hot week, Saturday was a blissfully lazy day often spent at the pool. Good food and company; no worries over the future; exploring other cultures and different ideas; it was an idyllic time. Of course I fell in love and was besotted with an Israeli girl who was spending a short time on the kibbutz while doing her military service. Though around my age she was much more mature and she led me a merry dance, seeming to encourage my tentative advances and then playing hard to get! Having only brothers and going to an all boys' school had not given me much understanding of the fair sex and I suffered a serious broken heart, but then one often does at that age.

After the other visitors left at the end of the summer, I was the sole foreigner there. This gave me a unique opportunity to get to know the people, their customs and lifestyle much better. I was offered some Hebrew lessons, which I took up. I have a natural affinity for languages but this was quite a challenge. The script is different; it is written from right to left and no vowels are used – apart from when one is learning. One judges what the written word is from the context in which it appears. Vowels in the form of dots beneath a consonant are used only for children or immigrants learning the language. Most of the adult residents spoke English, which made learning harder for me. However, I did take up a challenge given me by a friend who taught at the kibbutz primary school. Apparently the children were curious to see me as the sole foreigner there during the winter. She asked if I would like to give a short talk, in Hebrew, to her class telling them a little about England. I did so with considerable trepidation. Though my talk was in pretty basic and halting language, none of the youngsters laughed and I think they enjoyed the novelty even if it was not really very informative for them.

For most of the winter I worked with the dairy cattle. They were kept in big pens open to the air, but contained. At 5.30 every morning we gathered for a hot drink before going out to the pens. Milking had already been underway for an hour and Mordechai, responsible for the dairy herd, would join us, always painfully bright and cheerful for that hour. His catchphrase to us was *"Morning light to you"*. He was short and wiry, with a big head and receding hair, and he was always full of bounce. I think he spoke five or six languages, which was common. During the winter I got to know him well, and his Argentinean wife and their two little girls. Though I was not quite as bright as he was I loved the early morning energy, working while still dark. The cows that were not yet being milked would be slumbering quietly; great warm brown mounds of gentle energy.

I used to get into the pens barefoot to bed them out with straw and I had no fear of their size or strength. I found them very tactile. One or two in particular I felt drawn to and they always recognised me. There is no doubt that my feeling for animals began to develop more deeply there. I had always loved the cats that my parents had kept but something about the cows touched me at a level I had not felt before.

Mordechai took me under his wing and taught me to drive the big tractor and trailer used to bring in the straw bales. There were two distinctive groups working with the herd. One was those who did the milking. This happened three times a day and one shift was finishing as I started work. The other group was those of us doing the rest of the care of the animals. The milkers definitely thought they were superior but I revelled in the kudos I imagined I gained from driving the tractors. Quite often I would go into the milking parlour at the beginning of my shift and dip a ladle into the vats filled with still warm fresh milk. It was a great treat.

One of the milking team was a girl around my age. I spoke to her a little and years later I happened on an amazing coincidence concerning her......but more of that later. Perhaps my experience talking to the school children aroused an interest in teaching. When I returned home I decided I would like to teach and with my passion for sport I decided to train as a Physical Education teacher. This was also partly inspired by a friend of my parents who had been my PE teacher at school. I applied successfully to go to Loughborough College, which was then the foremost college for PE.

I arrived at Loughborough College in September 1968. Strutting around in our African Violet tracksuits (not purple please) we thought we were the only students on campus who mattered. Of course we were the only ones the girls would fawn over!

Although my time in Holland and Israel had opened me to new ideas, I had still developed pretty traditional values from my upbringing and public school education, and I took those with me to college. During my first term I ordered and read the Financial Times. Hmm, not sure what that was about. But the pink pages on which it was printed certainly made me stand out, which was probably why I did it.

But all changed when I met the hippies in my second year. There weren't many amidst a sea of sweating, muscle-flexing PE students. Just a small band of them tucked away in a rented house at Middleton Place. Even the street name was breathed in hushed or even scandalised tones. It was a quiet house that they had found to rent together instead of living in halls or college-approved digs.

Strange things happened there. Many of them were vegetarian. They slept on mattresses on the floor instead of beds. They burned incense sticks, smoked marijuana and there were even men and women living under the same roof. Some of them were actually living together! After a 1950s childhood and a pretty conventional conditioning my world was about to change.

'Drugs and sex and rock and roll' was the mantra of the flower power era and I was catching the tail end of that. Well, I was a pretty shy guy and I didn't do so well on the sex but I sure made up for it with the other two. We were exploring new territory against a backdrop of nature. Our socially accepted drug is alcohol but man has used many different drugs throughout history. Many wisdom traditions have taken psychedelic drugs as part of their ceremonies to reach heightened states of awareness. Following in the footsteps of people like Dr Timothy Leary and Aldous Huxley, we experimented with psychedelic states of mind. We were young and naïve but we truly believed we could turn the world on to love and peace in this way. Trips to nearby Charnwood Forest were almost sacred to us as we explored these altered states of mind.

Pacifism and flower power were our badges. We could be brutally insensitive in writing off the deeds of our parents; rebelling against what they stood for. We forgot how privileged we were in being able to live as rebels because they, at that same age, had fought for freedom in the Second World War. Sometimes I think back to the offhand way in which I rejected my parents' values and what they had worked so hard to give me. But hey, that is the right of youth – although I later saw how cruel it was. Thankfully I made my peace with my parents well before they died.

The natural world, the woods and fields were our refuge and inspiration. Charnwood was an ancient forest, though much reduced in size from years past. Once within its boundary there was an almost Tolkien-like feel, as if the Ents might suddenly appear. Paths twisted tortuously between great thick trunks. Rocky outcrops made good seating for looking towards the edge of the wood and glimpsing the gently sloping fields beyond which taller buildings on the student campus could be seen pushing upwards. The athletics club used to run there too, as I had done in my first year, and there were occasional strange meetings of shaggy-haired hippies and African Violet-clad athletes, each eyeing the others disdainfully.

At times the Ents did indeed seem to be there. It would be easy to brush these experiences off as delusional and simply drug induced but there was no doubt that I was reaching through a veil to another level of awareness. We treated the drugs as a sacrament and it was a tradition within the group that on one's first 'trip' one would be accompanied by one of the more experienced hippies. Now that might sound pretentious but it was not at all. It was all part of the journey into exploring our consciousness and realms beyond our normal daily existence. We took it seriously. I don't believe now that this offers a real long term way to live in tune with our true nature. Though many people still do experiment with different substances I believe that they are damaging to our health, both physically and mentally. Nevertheless it acted as a catalyst to awaken my sense of spiritual yearning and it was fun in the context of the time.

We all lived on student grants so money was not plentiful. Sharing a house as my friends did at Middleton Place was a good practical arrangement and fostered a sense of community. Of course it was also a tribe and membership was by invitation. James lived there and I had chatted with him at college though I didn't know him well as he was in different groups to me for study purposes. He invited me round because, as he later told me, he thought that I was perhaps a little different and might be open to discovering something of the lifestyle he and his friends led there. I'm not sure what gave him that notion but that was my introduction to marijuana.

What I experienced in Charnwood Forest evoked memories of what I had felt as a little boy lying on the grass looking at the sky and wandering out on solitary walks. It was as if the experiences of my childhood were coming back and reaching through the clouds around me to tap me on the shoulder. It was a reminder that, deep inside, I was still seeking richer meaning to my life. I really yearned for something that was within me, though I was not quite sure what it was. I guess it was a kind of awakening. Many of my companions felt the same.

And then......

"Hey man, you gotta get the Knowledge. Go to London, to one of these ashrams and ask for Knowledge. It's mind blowing!" The Divine Light Mission had hit the west.

The boy guru had arrived in the west. Thirteen years old with a chubby, cherubic face and a broad smile, he captivated many of the flower children. What was Guru Maharaji's mysterious Knowledge? Well, I had to find out, so I hitched down to London. It was so easy then to find 'a pad to crash' for a few days. Just being adorned in beads, long hair and flared trousers was enough to gain entry to some communal house, even if the link with anyone in the house was pretty tenuous. Back at Middleton Place people thought nothing of waking to find some stranger curled up in a sleeping bag on the floor.

So it was in London that I sought one of these ashrams. I found one and tried to talk to one of the guru's senior disciples, a mahatma. The house was full of young folk floating around in blissful states (now naturally induced). I had hitched to London with a friend and we were made welcome and offered floor space to pitch our sleeping bags. We sat outside the door of the Mahatma's room in anticipation of receiving this mystical initiation. Every time he emerged, a young Indian not much older than us, we begged him for this Knowledge. Looking back it seems a mighty disrespectful way to have sought initiation to the mysteries of the universe. But we were assured that it was the way to demonstrate our sincerity, without which he would not deem us worthy. So we sat patiently, launching into a tirade of exhortation every time he appeared. In the end the poor man caved in, though I suspect he was rather enjoying the game and indeed the power that we were investing in him through this strange process.

The ashram was a hurly burly of activity during the day: people coming and going; food being prepared in a tiny kitchen for tens of visitors and residents; piles of shoes at the front door as 'bare feet in the house' was the rule; bodies overflowing from the 'satsang room' where talks were given. Yet the room my friend and I were ushered into for the Knowledge ceremony was almost in another world. Even allowing for the atmosphere created by the incense burning and the altar on which the guru's picture sat (all appealing to the hippie in me) there was something special in there. I experienced the same fathomless depth of peace that I had felt as a little boy looking up at the sky and while I was on the kibbutz with the cattle.

What was the initiation? Was the atmosphere I felt there a genuine energy emanating from this teacher? Was it simply the result of expectation building up? Certainly Guru Maharaji was a master of psychological games and he knew how to manipulate crowds. I think there was something of this but I do believe that the mahatma was very sincere and he was very powerful in the teaching that he gave us before imparting the meditation techniques.

Four simple meditation techniques, which were not the exclusive prerogative of this boy guru, though I did not know that at the time. They were taught in other Hindu traditions too. To be truthful, after the hype of the chase the capture was a letdown. Was that truly the Knowledge? And yet.....I know that I was drawn a little closer to my source.

So many people have said in different ways that our life is about the journey and not the destination. It is in the journey that we grow and learn; experience pain, love and joy. If we think we have arrived then we are missing the point and we have stopped growing. We have lost the wonder of each magical moment. For sure I was looking for the big hit (rather like a drug), the explosion of awareness, but inside I knew things don't work like that. It was another step on the road. I had set out on a path of spiritual seeking, which is a lifetime journey. It has taken many years to curb the impatience and the desire for instant enlightenment. Now as I am older I do feel that I am living much more in the moment; enjoying the journey without any expectation; just allowing the universe to give me what is right for me in this moment. At my age I guess it is about time that happened!

"Hey, you must get into the Word and listen to Pink Floyd on headphones!" I remember James excitedly saying this to me. We infused the Knowledge into our lifestyle back in Loughborough. The Word was one of the four techniques revealed in the Knowledge ceremony. It was a sacred secret, not to be revealed to others. That was the sole job of the mahatma. I realised later that this secrecy was a way to create a sense of exclusivity. Thus the guru exerted control over us. At the time many of us were blinded by our spiritual yearning. We wanted to believe. There was also quite a lot of ego: the need to be different from the other students, from our parents' generation, from the wider world. Youth often falls into this trap, which is why young people can become caught up in movements they later regret. Mind you, the need to belong to a particular tribe is common to most people in some way or another. At least most members of my Loughborough tribe were gentle and loving.

Part of the commitment to this pathway was to attend satsang meetings. These were simply gatherings where devotees – called 'premies', meaning lovers – got together to share their experience of meditation and to express their devotion to the master. They were held in small, local ashrams, sometimes in bigger halls, maybe in London, where Alexandra Palace was a chosen venue if the guru was there. In 1971 he did indeed come to the west.

We integrated our new found spiritual practice into our hippie lifestyle. It became fun. Jammed into my old green Ford Zephyr estate car (I was one of the few students with a car) we trekked off to Leicester or

London to satsang, often with ten bodies squeezed into a car designed for about six. Amazing how many you could get into the back section designed for luggage. I hate to think what would have happened had we been stopped by the police, but we never were. We led charmed lives.

When I look back I believe that the guru was a fake. Perhaps that is harsh, as I think he may have been genuine in the beginning, but he became corrupted by the adulation given him here in the west. But everyone we meet can be our teacher. We can learn from every experience. Within the context of the movement, there was immense appeal in the trappings of all things eastern. The Beatles had been drawn to that and had made their pilgrimage to India. Certainly there was corruption in the movement. Not everybody was a manifestation of love and light. Flowing kaftans and beads often masked charlatans and rogues. Yet the majority of us truly wanted to feel love. Unfortunately this heartfelt desire laid many of us open to exploitation.

If Guru Maharaji himself was coming to visit, or even one of his mahatmas, huge amounts of money were spent in preparation. The local community would collect money to rent a house; even buy a house in some cases. Then people would be persuaded, often with considerable pressure, to completely redecorate inside, all in white. A bedroom for the exclusive use of the master would be furnished; a satsang room prepared; a kitchen equipped and all basics provided. Often the master did not even come after all this work had been done.

There was a young English ex-hippie who was given the name of Mahatma Sahasya. During a visit to London some members of our local sangha (community of premies) were instructed by him to rent and prepare a house in Loughborough. Such was our devotion or gullibility that it was duly done. A female devotee volunteered to act as house mother — in effect a glorified slave. In the end Sahasya was the only person who made use of it. He spent two or three months living royally at our expense and often asked to be provided with marijuana, even though this was something he should have given up.

Many people are incredulous when they hear this. Were we stupid? Could we not see we were being duped? As I later found out, my parents and other family members were very concerned at my involvement. But that is the nature and the power of brainwashing, which is exactly what it was. That is exactly how well-meaning and sincere people get sucked into groups and sects. Certainly it was the start of a rollercoaster ride for me as I spent the next four or five years heavily involved. Even when I began to see through the masks it took another two or three years to extricate myself fully. Yet I don't regret it. I have not always seen the value, at the time, of tough experiences. However, in the long run, the valuable lessons always come through. Absolutely everything has within it the seeds of learning and growth. What doesn't kill us makes us stronger.

Meditation is something about which many people still have misconceptions. One doesn't meditate to achieve but rather simply to be. Most of humankind is concerned with doing, achieving, acquiring and having things. Of course that has a place. We live in a material world and very few are suited to a monastic life of self-imposed austerity – though part of me is drawn to that. But we meditate in order to experience stillness. The still, small voice of God speaks within. We turn within to a silent space and as the furious activity of the mind becomes quieter, we may step through a doorway into a different awareness. In this state there is no time or space as we understand it. There is no separation between us and all creation. We can feel directly the energy that underpins the universe, which is our essence. To feel it is to know pure love. This is the core of the teachings of all the masters who have walked the earth since time began. Sadly we often interpret and twist those simple truths to our own ends and then we fall prey to dogmatic hate.

Middleton Place was an end of terrace house with a small untidy garden. We had our own satsang there in the shade of a straggling tree. Endless mugs of tea, sometimes home-made bread – baking was a joy I had just discovered – and a few 'joints' accompanied our musing and philosophising. We seldom used the front door so visitors just walked down the side of the red brick house and appeared in the garden. Nobody was turned away even if we hardly knew them. The funny thing was that we all thought that our clandestine lifestyle was not seen by anyone else. Not so, as I discovered when chatting to some of the younger tutors at college. They knew exactly what we were up to, as indeed did the local police. At that time, in some smaller towns at least, the drug scene was quite small and pretty new and the attitude of the authorities was one of laissez-faire. We were judged harmless, though had there been trouble in the town with any of us no doubt things would have changed. I know many people at the time who did run foul of the law yet we seemed to have guardian angels watching over us. We floated along in a blissful state: playing in Charnwood Forest; getting stoned to the sound of bands like Pink Floyd, King Crimson and Captain Beefheart; imagining that we were on the cusp of turning the world on to love and peace. It was fun.

By now most of us had graduated college and thoughts of the future beckoned. I spent a lot of time buzzing around on a little motorbike. It was a small machine, only 125cc, but it gave me a certain image or so I thought. Unfortunately on one occasion I sabotaged that image when I drove down the side of the house and round into the garden with a girl, whom I hoped to impress, riding pillion. I lost control of the bike and over we went. Only pride was bruised fortunately but that was the last I saw of her!

So what to do? I was not drawn to pursue a career in teaching though that was my qualification. The rigidity of the system did not appeal from what I had seen during my periods of teaching practice. A trip to India beckoned. The Beatles did it; a couple of friends, fellow premies, had done it. I would too. I would make a pilgrimage to the source of the teaching I was following and I would do it in style on a motorbike. Ever the romantic, I had ideas of buying a big bike and, dressed in black leather with yellow satin liners (yellow was my colour), I would ride off to the east with hair flowing in the wind. I did make the trip but not quite in that style.

Chapter 2: Overland to India

A forlorn figure, standing on the roadside with snow settling on my shoulders.... The beginning of March 1973 was bitterly cold when I set off on my overland trip to India. I had realised that it would take a while to earn enough cash to buy a good motorbike so heading off with a rucksack on my back and trusting to the benevolence of other travellers seemed the better way to go. I had a sleeping bag, a lightweight tent weighing a couple of pounds complete with poles, and a little over two hundred pounds in cash. It was going to be an adventure for sure.

I took a ferry over to Holland and landed with heavy snow falling. Hitching a ride back in those days was usually pretty easy, and so it proved through the Netherlands. Germany was a bit harder. I imagine the sight of a soaking wet young lad with a bulky rucksack put drivers off stopping. I managed to get as far as Munich and decided to get a train from there to Athens.

Things are undoubtedly different now. However, back then you bought a ticket to your destination city but the route you took was up to you. So you might pick up the train at Munich and get in a carriage marked for Milan. Then if you felt like swapping carriages at a particular station, that was fine. So the trick of it was to find a carriage that was fairly empty to allow for stretching out to sleep, even if it was not in the direction of your final destination. The drawback was that you might wake in the middle of the night to find your carriage unhitched from the train because it had reached its destination. You were sleeping soundly while the engine and the rest of the carriages steamed off into the distance. Fortunately I avoided that scenario.

Since the destination of the carriage was only marked on the outside, you had to jump off at a stop and run up and down to find a carriage you wanted. Then you hopped on board again, bagged a good seat and settled down once more to watch the scenery drift by.

Borders have changed since then but I wound my way through what was then Yugoslavia, Bulgaria and on to Athens. I had travelled a bit after leaving school but so many things were still new and exciting. Even down to the fact that most policemen wore a pistol at their belt. In Britain this was not the case but it was the norm everywhere I went. I remember two burly Yugoslav policemen invading my carriage and rousing me from my slumbers, none too gently. All they wanted was to see my passport but being on my own and somewhat nervous, I wondered if they were going to find something to object to. Fortunately not.

Rail is a wonderful way to see a country; much better than road transport. The line through Yugoslavia was spectacular, hugging river banks and hillsides. Local travellers used the train too. It was not just long distance adventurers like me so there was the chance to meet the natives in each country. The lack of a common language made in-depth communication difficult though I could speak some basic German and French, which often proved useful. But I have always found that a friendly smile and the willingness to use sign language can go a long way in getting on with people.

From Yugoslavia I headed through Bulgaria. Both were very poor countries. People boarding the train were mostly shabbily dressed, sometimes with chickens in cages, yet they were cheerful and often ready to share some simple food and the fun of the journey. Of course there were other young adventurers too. Many of them were also bound for India. It was one of the places to go and the overland route was popular then and still relatively safe. The route from Europe through Turkey, Iraq and Iran was not then as war torn as it has since become. It could be hairy, as I later found out, but some of the east–west prejudices that have become entrenched over the last thirty years or so were not as prevalent then.

So at last the train reached Athens. The roads in Athens are something else – or they were. I had been there once before but only briefly to pick up a ferry to Israel. Now I could stay as long as I wished if I could stay alive while crossing the road! I had been warned about that. I swear that the Greek drivers accelerated even harder when they saw a pedestrian dare to put a foot forward onto the road. But what a change of ambience. Northern Europe was cold and law abiding. The Eastern European countries were poor and had a feeling of being a little wild. Greece was different. It had that Mediterranean ambience: warm, chaotic, slightly anarchic but underpinned by a long history as one of the major civilising influences in the world.

The Greeks are open and friendly and I had a great few days warming my bones after the cold trek through Europe. From there I wanted to start hitching again. I had not intended to use the train and it had taken more of my limited funds than I had planned. So I looked at the map and planned a rough route to Istanbul. I had no idea where or how I might eat en route so I took some basic provisions – bread, cheese, a couple of cucumbers and some oranges. I was sure I could fill my water bottle pretty much anywhere.

I was also looking forward to trying out my tent. I was a keen camper and the idea of pitching canvas out in the Greek countryside really appealed. I guess it could have been dangerous but somehow I just never used to consider things like that. Foolish maybe, or naïve; or was it just that I have always had a basic feeling that most people are good and can be trusted? I know there are travellers who have terrible tales to tell and I have been in tricky situations myself. But on the whole I believe that going out with trust as your badge brings out the best in others. People might now call that the 'Law of Attraction' - you get back what you put out.

So I was on the road to Istanbul at last. Students hitchhiking around northern Europe were common and usually it was pretty easy. When I was at college some guys would have a weekend hitching competition. Leaving the UK on a Friday afternoon, the idea was to see how far you could get simply holding out your thumb on the roadside before turning back for home on a Sunday morning. Greece was not quite so easy.

Maybe that was in part because there were far fewer cars on the country roads. Back then there weren't as many big long distance trucks there as in northern Europe. Nevertheless I managed a combination of small lorries, a tractor and a donkey cart. And I got to pitch the tent out in the wilds. Luckily as well as being lightweight it was erected in moments because my first stop saw me putting it up in heavy rain, though that cleared by the morning so I could enjoy a sumptuous breakfast of bread, cheese and cucumber washed down with cold water.

It's not far from Athens to Istanbul, around 400 miles, which I covered in about four days. I think the donkey cart slowed me down but the experience of that ride was worth it. Istanbul is a real mix of cultures. It is the gateway between Europe and Asia, with influences of both abounding. It was an essential watering hole on the hippie trail to the east.

You were guaranteed to meet fellow long-haired and bearded youngsters in any cheap hostel, but the real meeting point was the Pudding Shop. This was the nickname given to the Lale Restaurant, and with good reason, because the puddings and sweetmeats were something special. It was in the Sultanahmet area of the city, home to the famous Blue Mosque. In fact the Pudding Shop still stands today.

It had a board outside where you could post messages, leave requests and see offers of lifts. It was there I found the Magic Bus that later took me to Afghanistan.

I had seen something of the beauty of Islamic architecture in Jordan a few years before but the Blue Mosque is nothing short of stunning. The main dome and six minarets are a truly arresting site and of course it gets its name from the blue tiles on the interior walls.

Istanbul was really the starting point of the hippie trail. Most of the travellers there were either heading east or were on their way back from India. I met some really interesting folk. There was a young American Vietnam veteran who had spent time in Thailand during his war posting. Now discharged from the army, he was heading back to Thailand to live, making a long and slow overland trip. He spoke in glowing terms of the gentleness of the Thai people and the beauty of their land. Meeting people like this began to make me look anew at what we had in our western culture. For someone to make such a move seemed to me at that time like a pretty radical thing to do. I met him only once but I sure hope he reached his paradise.

The seasoned travellers on their way home looked distinctly different from those of us still heading out. Most were considerably thinner. This was a result of a pretty basic diet in India and often due to the ravages of dysentery. Of course they had tales to tell that kept the new adventurers on the edges of our seats – advice and warnings, mystical tales and promises of exotic things to come. Many were distinctive by being dressed in a variety of Indian clothing, lungis, loose tops or baggy trousers. No wonder most of the indigenous people along the hippie trail did not know what to make of us.

Then I heard about an easy way to get some ready cash – sell my blood! You could get five pounds (a lot of money then) for a pint of blood, so I decided to boost my cash reserves. Someone in the Pudding Shop gave me directions to the clinic. It was in a shabby part of the city, off the beaten track. As I climbed an outside staircase to a balcony that led to the entrance I did have some misgivings, but the lure of some extra money was too much. Obviously they knew the drill with yet another young traveller. It's a miracle I didn't contract hepatitis as the general conditions were none too clean. But I survived and I was a bit richer.

So what was the Magic Bus? There was a good choice of modes of transport available at the Pudding Shop. The old VW camper van was popular. It was the archetypal travelling van in the early seventies – probably because it was pretty much the only one of its type and being German, it was very reliable and it was easy to access the rear placed engine if things went wrong. Often a driver would have a spare seat or two so you could team up with someone for all or part of the trip east. The arrangements were loose and easy going. You could hop off a camper anywhere you felt like it, if you had paid your share to that point. One particular American guy, John and I kept bumping into each other at different points along the way right through to New Delhi as we swapped transport and stayed a few days in an interesting place.

John was older than I was. He had graduated university and he was taking a good time out before settling down. In fact he had travelled to the east before so it was useful to chat and get advice on things. He advised me of something that had never occurred to me before. He said that most cheap accommodation would have a clasp on the bedroom door where you could fit a padlock in order to be secure. Even if you were given a key for the room, the proprietor would have a duplicate. He advised me to buy a good padlock, which I did, so that I could be surer of my own security. Of course it would not stop a determined thief but it would prevent opportunist theft. Of course most of the advice was shared as we sampled the tasty puddings and strong black coffee in the Lale Restaurant.

The Magic Bus was......well, magic! It was an ex English public service coach that two tough, hard-bitten English guys had bought and were using to ferry people back and forth between Istanbul and New Delhi. They didn't always fill it right up but they seemed happy to set off as long as they had around fifteen passengers. It was comfortable, secure and cheap enough so I booked a place. They introduced themselves as Joe and Mike. If you had the money, you could ride with them. They made only one stipulation. Anyone caught with any drugs or seen along the way with any shady local characters would be thrown off the bus – no question nor query and no chance of being allowed back on board. It sounded harsh but they had their reasons and later they did just that in Iran.

MY HEALING JOURNEY

Having got enough passengers to cover their costs – I think they did it for the adventure as much as to earn anything – they set a date for leaving. So early one morning, with the sun only just appearing, a mixed bag of eager adventurers from several countries gathered outside the Pudding Shop. A last cup of thick black Turkish coffee and we set off on the next leg of our journey east. We were now heading into more exotic realms than most of us had experienced. I was having a ball on the way but I was also excited about heading towards the home of my guru. That, after all, was the main point of my trip: to explore more deeply the spiritual pathway I had embarked on in Loughborough. At the same time we only have the present moment as our reality and I was certainly enjoying the moment.

We were a pretty mixed bunch of passengers. There was a young French couple, several Americans, an Australian and a couple of English women. It was the first time that I had come across women travelling alone in that part of the world. Although they had teamed up for this ride, they were in fact making the trip independently. They were seasoned travellers and both were as tough as nails but even so it seemed pretty risky to me.

Joe and Mike had been doing the run for about eighteen months so they knew the ropes. They took regular turns at the wheel and quite often they would swap around with no need to stop the bus. They had perfected a technique whereby the one being relieved kept his foot on the accelerator while allowing the other to slide into the driving seat. Then they did a quick change of foot on the pedal. They weren't big on socialising with us. I think they saw us mainly as a meal ticket to fund their slightly piratical lifestyle. Still, they did a good job and fortunately they could handle the vehicle, as we discovered later.

Driving through central Turkey just a couple of days into the journey we stopped late afternoon at a small village. It spread along either side of the road for maybe half a mile or so. There was a single guest house that I suspect had taken root to cater for the growing number of people doing the India trek. A few years earlier I doubt it had been much more than a large house belonging to an extended family. Several passengers slept on the bus but one American, Guy and I decided we would take a real bed for the night.

After checking in we ambled along to a small tavern come eating house. It was still early evening and some food was our main concern. Candles and a gas lamp struggled to light the interior as the pitch black of night wrapped around us. This was deep in rural Turkey and though mine host did have a few more words of English than either of us had of Turkish, it was mainly sign language that got us by. As I have usually found in poor places off the beaten track, most folk are friendly and welcoming. Of course they see western travellers as a meal ticket and you learn to be firm about prices and business arrangements. The initial bargaining and haggling is really something of a game. Once the ground rules are established, everyone relaxes and becomes friends.

Over in a corner a group of local men were sitting round a table. They were obviously having a good time and they were fairly well lubricated. As they spotted us, they beckoned us to join them. That was too good to turn down. I love to meet the real people when I am travelling and it really doesn't seem to matter if you don't have much language in common. Smiles, nods, sign language and maybe a glass or two of the local hooch make for pretty good communication.

My buddy and I showed them our passports to try and indicate where we came from. We both had the impression that they were local woodcutters. Maybe that wasn't actually what they did but it was obviously the end of a hard day and they seemed to be celebrating something and they wanted us to join them. I have always been amazed by how generous the poorest of people are. We paid for our food, of course but they insisted we drink with them at their expense. And they wanted us to do it in style. They placed glasses of beer in front of us, insisted we drink the head of the beer, and then they topped the glass up with ouzo. Ouzo is more common in Greece but it is drunk in Turkey too. It is an anise flavoured spirit, usually drunk neat or with a little water. Adding it to the beer made for a wicked concoction. The food we ate did not do a lot to soak up the alcohol so by late evening we were definitely ready to head for bed. It had been a great evening and if not a lot of verbal communication had taken place, we had shared a warm camaraderie. Luckily it was only five minutes back to our beds. Once there, we realised that we were sharing the lumpy mattresses with hefty bed bugs but thanks to the beer and ouzo cocktails we went out cold as soon as we hit the beds and the bugs had an uninterrupted feast.

It is easy to be very critical about western countries and to get carried away about how wonderful the people are in less developed cultures. I've always found the whole range of humanity wherever you are. However, I think it is true that as we accumulate more in a material sense we can fall prey to becoming grasping and protective of what we have, with an unwillingness to share. I have seen that in me but when I just share without thought of return or what I will gain, most people respond and show their best qualities.

There was nowhere open for breakfast the next morning so we were glad to vacate our beds to the bugs and board the Magic Bus again. By now we were driving through mountainous terrain with steep drops to one side of the road and snow above us. Our drivers usually preferred to stop in villages or small watering holes that they knew, so if this meant continuing to drive long late hours to find such a place, they did that. At one point we were not so far from the border with the then USSR, though that seemed like something of a detour. But hey, we didn't worry about things like that. Anyway, it was getting pretty late and they were planning to drive through the night. High in the mountains, on a narrow road, we came round a bend and had to make a hasty stop. The road ahead was blocked solid with an articulated truck that had jack-knifed because of a blown tyre. Nothing could be done till it was shifted so we were resigned to wait things out.

It was freezing, at least ten below zero, with a crystal clear sky and a near full moon. For a while I went outside and just stared in wonder at the landscape. There was a distant howl of wolves that helped to create an eerie beauty. Magic moments like that give our lives a rich texture and I still see the scene vividly in my mind. With the rigours of the journey and the conditions on the bus, it was easy to just get into survival mode – eating, watching one's health and the security of one's passport and money. The beauty of an experience like that was that it brought me right into the present moment. Because it was so still outside, I slipped easily into an inner stillness. The adventure and the challenges of these exotic places were ever present of course, but within all that was an inner oasis of calm that my meditation practice was all about.

But it was cold and after a while the biting night air seeped through my down jacket, so I climbed back aboard the bus. Thankfully they were keeping the engine ticking over, which maintained some heat on board. I clambered to the back where my seat was and dozed fitfully. Perhaps an hour later a tractor came and shifted the truck far enough for us to squeeze past and resume the drive.

Leaving Turkey, we drove through Iraq for a short stretch but we didn't get much time to explore it. Our next border crossing took us into Iran. This was at a time some six years before the overthrow of the Shah of Iran. It was certainly a vastly different culture to anything I had seen before, though maybe rural Jordan shared something with it. There were no difficulties at the border. With the way things have developed politically since then, I fear it would be rather different today. As was usual at most of these border crossings the police took all our passports in a batch and disappeared into an office to inspect them at their leisure. How long this took was entirely at the whim of how they felt.

An hour or so later they were returned to Joe and Mike – with the exception of the passports of the American contingent. That was a common occurrence. Unfortunately for the Americans, it was always assumed they were wealthier than the rest of us and a bribe was expected to get the necessary stamp on their passport. There was no way round it so a few extra US dollars were handed over to the police and, smiling broadly, they stamped the passports and handed them back.

Iran is a big country and long dusty roads lay ahead. I think our two intrepid drivers had suffered bad experiences there because they were particularly forceful in reminding us of the 'no drugs on the bus' rule. Anyway, we left the checkpoint and headed east. We were driving at a good speed on our second day in when there was a huge bang and the bus skidded wildly, almost leaving the road. Maybe it had happened before or maybe it was just skilful reactions but we came to a halt safely, with a blown rear tyre having left a great streak of melted rubber on the road behind us.

We were on a long, flat stretch of road with open, uninterrupted terrain to either side. To the north we could see hills rising quite high. As luck would have it we were a short walk from a cluster of houses. There was a two storey house set back from the road, three or four low dwellings and what looked like a big shed. I think our two intrepid guides had contacts in most of the way stations en route. They found someone to help with the tyre change, though I'm sure they could have managed alone, but their friend also produced a spare for us so using the one we had would not leave us bereft of a spare wheel. It seemed that the shed had probably been equipped with some basic spares for such events, with the increasing number of travellers plying the route. Maybe Joe and Mike had even organised spares along the way at strategic spots. Looking back I wonder they did not have several spare tyres on board, but then again many of us were travelling with remarkably little provision for contingencies. The rule of the day seemed to be 'have basic pack, will travel'. It seemed to work for us.

While this was happening the young French couple broke the rules. They disappeared to the upstairs floor of the building just back from the road. A couple of hours later when we were ready to resume the drive, they reappeared. Waiting for them at the door of the bus with their bags were Joe and Mike. They were being thrown off right there. It seems that they had been smoking with the local hash supplier. The hippie trail was giving trade to local entrepreneurs and they had committed the cardinal sin of visiting him. Even if they were clean of any hashish Joe and Mike said that they would have been seen and that gave every excuse for the word to be passed to a local policeman – possibly even by their smoking companion. We would likely be stopped and fined at the very least – or maybe worse.

No amount of tears from the pair or arguments from the rest of us would sway our drivers. They had warned us and they put themselves and the rest of us first. So off we went leaving a very forlorn pair standing by the roadside. What would happen to them? At least the girl had her boyfriend, without whom she might well have been at considerable risk. But he didn't look like the toughest guy I had met so I just prayed it would work out fine. The atmosphere on the bus was sombre, but that was it.

When we reached Tehran, Joe and Mike gave us a few days' respite. We all needed a break, not just from the physical demands of travelling but we were all still feeling a bit low about the French couple. Can you imagine my joy on our second day there when I saw the French couple in a café? They had managed to hitch a ride quite safely and were still on course for India. We celebrated together of course.

I had been exploring Teheran with two companions from the Magic Bus. We were waiting at a bus stop to get back to our cheap hotel. It was hardly the most auspicious place for what happened next. It was the end of March and Teheran was getting quite warm. The city was dry and dusty. The journey had been hard. I was probably not eating very well. Did all this contribute to my suddenly having an out of body experience? Quite without warning I was floating above the three of us, clearly able to see myself standing below with the other two. Often there are rational explanations for such events: hunger or fatigue causing hallucinations and so on.

Did it really happen as I believed? If so, why and what, if any, was the significance? What I have felt on those occasions (this has not been the only one) has been a quality or realness that convinces me they were not imagination or hallucination. To someone who discounts such things that sounds pretty woolly. It is all I can offer and I am not here to persuade but simply to share what has happened to me. It was hardly a huge spiritual revelation but it happened, of that I am sure. What I have come to believe over the years is that once we begin a path of spiritual searching, there will be constant little reminders prompting us to remember that our lives are about more than just the world in front of us. Certainly that has been the case for me.

Our few days in Teheran seemed to refresh everyone. We had arrived in the Iranian capital feeling somewhat jaded but as we gathered again to resume the trip, everyone was happier. I think people were lifted by hearing that the young French couple had survived their ordeal. Even Joe and Mike seemed relieved, even if they pretended not to show it. The stretch from Teheran to the Afghan border was more than half the Iranian leg of the journey but it flew by. Our drivers seemed keen to get out of the country so we did the long late drives and the 'change the wheel while driving' trick to get along quicker.

Afghanistan was a name to evoke wonder and mystery. I knew little of the place other than that it was mountainous, landlocked and had never been conquered by any invading army. Most recently the British had tried and failed miserably in the colonial days. It had a reputation for fierce warrior tribesmen who gave no quarter and certainly the travellers' tales I had heard suggested it was not a place to venture too far off the beaten track. Crossing the border was easy without any bribes needed. Though the stories of the place were daunting, Joe and Mike seemed much more relaxed and there were no warnings about being ejected from the bus.

A few miles past the border checkpost we made a tea stop. It was basic, not even a hut but just an open fire heating the water and a few chairs, though mostly we squatted or sat on the floor. Joe and Mike's fears of any of us being involved with drugs in any way appeared not to apply to Afghanistan. It was a pretty lawless place with little central organisation. Smoking marijuana was not seen in a bad light and there was no organised police network that would come into operation as might have happened in Iran when the French couple were thrown off the bus. So when someone offered us a water pipe with a large piece of hashish burning, several of us happily had a smoke, though not Joe and Mike. When I look back to those times I see how naïve and innocent we were. Foolish as well perhaps, but it was all part of the flower power era.

Once we all felt refreshed we headed on to Herat. This is an ancient city, occupied by Alexander the Great, and there are still the remains of a citadel he built there. Being on an ancient trade route it is the gateway to Afghanistan for anyone coming from Iran. It was the centre to which agricultural produce from the surrounding area was sent. As with the rest of the country there was the usual stark contrast between the dust, poverty and mud huts of many residents and the splendour of old Islamic architecture in the form of the mosques. Being situated on the Harirud River, it was more verdant than the scenery through which we had driven. It is sad that our view of the country now is coloured by what we hear in the news and the image presented by the Taliban. There is so much ancient culture in the region, even though much of it has been lost. For example, Herat contains the tomb of the famous fifteenth century Persian poet, Nur-ud-din Abdurrakhman Jami. He was outstanding as a poet even in a time of supreme literary achievement.

From Herat there are two possible roads to reach Kabul. The northern road runs pretty much parallel to the border with what were the Soviet states. It goes up through the city of Mazar-e Sharif and then winds south to the capital. We heard wild tales of people taking that route and coming to a sticky end and indeed some luckless traveller was supposed to have been murdered there recently. Maybe truth or maybe exaggeration, but we took the southern road that goes down to Kandahar through slightly less rugged terrain and then heads north to Kabul.

I hopped off the bus in Kandahar. I had paid my dues to that point and I wanted to explore a little on my own. It was good to slow down and just hang out for a while. And what a new experience it was. The full burkha, as worn by women in Afghanistan, was not something I had seen before. It all helped to create a very other-worldly atmosphere. This is another city built by Alexander the Great in an area with some of the oldest known human settlements. As the country's second city with an airport not long built when I was there, it is the most important trade centre. Though the city itself is quite arid, good irrigation of the surrounding area produces excellent fruit crops, especially grapes and pomegranates. When I was there recent harvests had been poor and there was not an abundance of food. Indeed spinach and rice in varying forms seemed to be the staple food, along with long thin naan bread made with wheat and oil. But that didn't matter. It was just fun to explore. Things are probably different now but forty years ago very few people there spoke English so again sign language was the way to get by.

I always feel that I have been watched over when travelling. I have never been robbed nor had my pockets picked. I have always taken basic precautions and at all times my passport and any valuables were on me in a money belt secured under my clothing. But I have never returned to my room (usually in cheap dives) to find my possessions rifled or stolen. Treat and view people with respect and openness and I believe that the same is returned. I did find myself feeling rather alien as I wandered the dusty streets down little alleys but I never felt unwelcome. Perhaps that was because the young hippies on their way to India were still a source of wonder and amusement.

After a few days I bumped into a couple of American guys who had a VW camper. They were heading on to Kabul and they offered me a ride. They insisted that we would not stop overnight to sleep in the bus unless it was in a village. They had been warned against parking up in the countryside, for fear of being robbed or worse.

I'm not sure whether their fears were justified and it made for a hard drive. The upside was the fun of driving through the night. I've been at the wheel of a car myself doing that as well as being a passenger when once I drove to Morocco with my youngest brother. There is something entrancing about watching the sun set, watching the colours in the sky turning golden, rusty brown and then black. Against the arid backdrop of the country we were driving through, followed by the clear and star-specked sky with the moon glinting, any fatigue was a price well worth paying. Of course I wasn't driving so I could sleep fitfully. The inside of those old VW campers was always noisy but somehow the still and quiet of the night pervaded. Sunrise in such terrain is truly wonderful. At first anything in the landscape is just a dark outline. Then the growing light slowly picks out rocky outcrops and peaks. First the tops slowly turn orange and pink; the shadows seem to melt downward as the lower slopes of the peaks become illuminated; just dark patches are left at the very bottom till finally everything is bathed in full sun.

Kabul brought a great surprise when we checked in to a cheap hotel. Also staying there was John, with whom I had shared black Turkish coffee and travellers' tales at the Pudding Shop. He had made his way on a succession of local transport and hitched rides and we had a ball swapping experiences. I made a point of showing him the padlock I had bought at his insistence. So I was a good apprentice.

As the temperature was warming up I began to jettison some of my heavy clothing: a thick jacket and some patchwork, multicoloured, flared leather trousers. I had acquired the trousers back in Loughborough and even made some alterations to them on an old treadle sewing machine. They were part of my badge of office as a bona fide hippie but I didn't really need them and I found someone who gladly took them.

So with the weather getting better I decided to get some lighter clothing, personally made. I found a tailor in the city who measured me up for a pair of shalwar (baggy trousers that fit tight at the ankle) and a top that came down to the hips. The material was exquisitely fine to the touch, white with yellow embroidery at the neck. I placed my order after being carefully measured and was assured it would be ready in a couple of days for a price that was next to nothing by western standards. The young chap insisted we celebrate the transaction with a smoke and tea. His English was pretty good and he plied me with questions about my homeland. As human beings we really do suffer from very stereotyped views of other peoples and cultures. As usual he had the oft held assumption that any western traveller was wealthy. Although the money I had set off with was worth far more then than it would be now, two hundred pounds was hardly great wealth.

True to his word, a couple of days later my tailor had the clothes waiting for me. I'm sure that I presented an incongruous sight dressed in Afghan trousers and top with long hair flowing over my shoulders but I felt good.

Always on the lookout to stretch my funds I had found another place to stay which was a bit cheaper than where I had first checked in so I moved. A day later I went back to my previous place to meet up with my American buddy, who was still there. The proprietor got really annoyed with me, accusing me of treachery for moving out of his place without having actually left Kabul. I guess the paltry amount I was saving was fairly insignificant to me but not to him. He was seriously angry so I decided to meet with John outside the guest house the next time.

This 3500-year-old city is also built in a river valley and, being close to the Khyber Pass into Pakistan, it has always been of considerable strategic importance. Against a backdrop of snow-clad mountains, the narrow streets and beautiful Islamic architecture was entrancing if not quite as beautiful as Herat and Kandahar. I was beginning to think of moving on. Pakistan was the next leg on the way to my Indian destination. I checked out buses and found one that would take me to Islamabad in Pakistan, going through the Khyber Pass. Just that name evoked romantic images. Britain has had a long connection with that whole region through the Imperial conquest of India. My maternal grandfather was in the Educational Service in India and my mother was born there so I have always had a feeling of connection and an interest in the whole sub-continent of India and Pakistan.

The bus drive through the pass was absolutely spectacular. It is just over thirty miles through wild and steep mountains. The flowers, poppies in particular, that lined the roadside, in some cases as far as the eye could see, created a lush red carpet. The driving was somewhat more reckless than that of Joe and Mike on the Magic Bus. That was something I would get used to right through to and in India. The rule of the road seemed to be to sit in the middle of the road, drive flat out, sit on the horn and hope that the oncoming driver chickens out! At some points it was too narrow for vehicles to pass one another. Several buses that could be seen over the edge of the road, crushed on the rocks below, gave a hint that things didn't always work out but we survived.

Strangely enough, Lahore was the first and only place where I experienced general hostility from several people. I guess it was racial prejudice, perhaps inspired by my appearance, and I was shouted at and jostled in the street. I wanted to get on into India anyway so this prompted me to get a bus ticket to New Delhi after just a couple of days. In addition I was beginning to suffer from a stomach upset, so I reckoned that it would be good to head for Guru Maharaji's ashram where I hoped to rest up. With my insides in the state they were, I was forced to use whatever unsavoury toilets were on offer whenever the buses stopped. But it was all part of budget travel in that part of the world. I was wary of drinking untreated water and the buses were stiflingly hot. Most places where we stopped I bought a bottle of Fanta orange to slake my thirst, which I think did no good to my rebelling digestive system.

Delhi couldn't come too soon. When my family and I had travelled to Australia by boat when I was a child, we had made a stop at Bombay so this entrancing land was not completely new to me. On that first visit in 1960 we had just a couple of days in port pursuing tourist activities that didn't really reveal the true India. This was different. I was there alone; always a great way to meet people and at an age when I could explore wherever I chose. I have been to India a number of times and right from that first visit as an adult I have always felt very secure and safe. Of course there are danger spots and things to be aware of. I'm sure too that some people do resent the British occupation yet on the whole I have always felt a lot of goodwill towards us and I loved Delhi from the first.

New Delhi defies words to describe it adequately. It is noisy and dirty; heaving with humanity; filled with elegant colonial buildings juxtaposed with awful poverty and it entrances me. Building sites are a revelation. The scaffolding usually consists of bamboo poles tied together and often the labourers are women carrying bricks or containers of cement on their heads. The roads are a battle for survival that make the roads in Athens look like a kid's playground. Buses overflow with people hanging off the side and clinging precariously to the luggage piled on the roof. Rickshaws and tuk-tuks battle for what space is left by the buses or taxis and of course there are cyclists too. The tuk-tuks are little motorised scooters. They are really little more than a small motorbike with a cab grafted onto the back behind the driver. Designed to seat maybe two or four people, you can guarantee that several more will be squeezed into most of them.

Then there is the fee. The golden rule is to barter and thrash out what you will pay before you start. If you wait till the end of the journey the driver will certainly grossly overcharge you. By then it is too late to bargain as any attempt to do so at that stage is likely to cause unpleasantness with the owner calling on the locals standing around to support him and there is only going to be one outcome to that. How do you know what to offer against the fare you are asked for? You just go lower. The driver will never accept a figure that is completely unfair for him so you start the barter game – and a game it is – and hope to end up paying a fair deal.

After the rigours of the journey and the relatively poor diet this was a chance to eat a little better and to indulge myself. The Indians have a sweet tooth and all sorts of syrupy delicacies are available. One of my favourites is galub jamun, which are cheese-based balls soaked in syrup. Together with a glass of chai….just too tempting. I loved watching the chai wallahs at their work. The liquid, usually milk or maybe with a little water, is brought to the boil and while simmering the tea is thrown in and then sugar added. It is kept hot and scooped out into glasses as needed. It is surprisingly refreshing in the heat and usually has spices added, which vary in different parts of the country.

It was over a glass of chai that I got chatting with a German fellow who was on his way home. He had been wandering around northern India for nearly six months. His advice on how to deal with the hygiene and food conundrum was simply to eat and drink everything. He reckoned that was the best way for your body to build immunity to any bugs it might encounter. I wasn't entirely sure about that so I continued to try and take some precautions but I'm not sure they worked too well – as I later experienced.

He very generously gifted me one of his lungis so I could keep cool and dress in local style. A lungi is a rectangle of cloth that wraps around the waist and hangs to the floor, though depending on the style in which you wrap it, you can wear it anywhere from nearly floor length to just around the knees. It was a beautiful deep pinkish colour made from very soft material and though it is now very thin and getting threadbare, I still have it to this day, forty years on. I still wear it around the house in the hot weather.

My guru's ashram was beckoning. The ashram was in Hardwar, north of Delhi on the upper reaches of the River Ganges. It is one of the seven holiest places for Hindus and is the venue for the huge Kumbh Mela festival that's held every twelve years and visited by thousands of Hindus from all over India. The ashram was started by my guru's father who was the founder of the sect. It was something of a family business. In reality it was all rooted in Hinduism with some added extras to make it stand out as being something different. At that time I was still too closely involved to view things as objectively as I later would.

It was easy to find a bus from Delhi to Hardwar and though there were no dangerous mountain roads en route, I had to contend with the usual breakneck driving. I was beginning to get used to it. After a while the nonchalant attitude of the Indian passengers seemed to rub off on me. My rucksack was thrown up onto the roof rack along with other bags and, relieved of that encumbrance, I tucked myself into a seat and watched the scenery roll by. The 125 mile journey to Hardwar takes you into the lower foothills of the Himalayas and the scenery becomes much softer and greener than around Delhi.

The ashram was situated just outside the town. I stood outside the gates, almost hardly believing I had finally made it. It had been a long hard journey, full of adventure and new experiences. I had enjoyed it all and I was in a very different place, emotionally, to when I had left the UK. This was where I wanted to be and yet I felt some trepidation. I had visited ashrams back home and I knew something of how they were run but I had never stayed in one. What would it be like? What revelations, if any, would I experience? Would it reinforce my beliefs or prick a bubble? I walked up a long paved pathway lined with rose bushes and arrived at the kitchen area. Someone sent a messenger to the office to announce that another western devotee had arrived. By now they were used to a growing number of westerners coming by to join the Indian premies living there. I was made welcome by the old man who was the senior mahatma running the place. He was very gentle and aware that the rigorous schedule they followed might be a little hard for some of us. There were about half a dozen western devotees there and we were given small rooms where we could be a little independent of the main community. Nevertheless, we were encouraged to attend morning meditation, starting at 4.30, which was followed by devotional singing. There was one fellow from the USA who had been staying several weeks who was the 'go to guy' for the newer western visitors who were uncertain of anything. He did his own thing and appeared to take little part in the general routine of the ashram but I preferred to take part in as much as possible. That seemed to me the best way to immerse myself in the experience of the ashram; the best way to tune in to what Guru Maharaji was offering.

I always love the early morning. If you catch the early morning energy, it seems to set you up for the day. Though it was still dark and sleep clung to my eyes, the hard floor of the meditation hall and the relative cool at that hour helped to wake me up. Following the singing was a period of service, which was simply work done in dedication to Guru Maharaji. The usual job at that hour was to go into the extensive rose gardens and pick flower heads. These were put in baskets that were taken and sold in the bazaar in Hardwar. They were bought by Hindu pilgrims to be cast into the waters of the Ganges.

Breakfast followed, which consisted of chapattis (the flat unleavened Indian bread) dipped in chai, and maybe a little cold rice and vegetables from the night before. Lunch was fresh cooked rice, subji (vegetables) and chapatti and supper was more rice, subji and chapatti! No catering to fussy palates in the ashram. There was no such luxury as a dining room. We simply squatted outside the kitchen under an awning with our plates. The cooks then came round and dished out our food from the big cooking pots. It was during meals that we were closest to the Indian devotees. Often during the work periods, the westerners were grouped together. None of the Indians, with the exception of the senior mahatma, spoke more than rudimentary English. However, they showed real warmth and affection towards us and the cooks were always concerned that we were getting enough food.

The ashram was built close to the river. Mother Ganges is such a huge part of life in northern India. From its source high in the western Himalayas it flows 1500 miles right across the north of the country to pour into the sea far to the east past Calcutta. It is worshipped as a great mother. People wash in it: their bodies and their clothes. It is fished and used for the irrigation of crops. Pilgrims come to bathe in it to become cleansed. They cast rose petals in it and lighted candles on clay dishes are set afloat.

I swam in it while I was in the ashram. There was a little track that led out of the ashram grounds just a short distance to the bank of this mighty mother river. At that point it was quite wide and though fast flowing in the middle, the edges had only gentle currents. It was a quiet spot. I was beginning to feel the deep peace of this oasis of calm that was the ashram amidst the bustle of India. I loved to meditate on the bank and then to just sit watching the life of the river flow by: small boats, or sometimes the carcass of some beast (maybe a cow or goat). That is part of what meditation helps us to do: to find a still place inside from which to observe the bustle of life with some degree of detachment. I would slip into the water, swim out just a short way, where the current was still gentle, and float a little way down stream before heading back to my patch. The only company I had was a snake that used to lie along a branch above me. We didn't bother one another and he never seemed frightened of me.

I wasn't able to communicate verbally with most of the simple and largely uneducated Indian devotees. I could not understand the satsang and teachings, which were in Hindi, though the senior mahatma did give the westerners some teaching in English. But I felt what was behind it and the rituals were familiar from my having spent time at UK ashrams. The peace and tranquillity that enveloped the place was palpable. Some of the western devotees would occasionally slip out of the front gate to get a glass of chai from a little stall on the roadside. Even though we were only yards from the ashram and it was well away from the bustle of the town, it just felt so different to step outside the gates. It was like stepping out of one world into another. I knew the feeling that was so easily attained and experienced within the bounds of the ashram was what I wanted to feel within at all times. I believed – and still do – that we can attain that level of awareness constantly. That is not to say that we should live as a hermit in a cave. We don't need to do that in order to know that peace. We just have to find a way of contemplation or meditation and a way of living that enables us to be tuned in at all times. A metaphor often used in satsang was of the lotus flower. It has roots that go deep into muddy water where it thrives, yet the flower head itself rises above and does not touch the water. For me the spiritual life is not about being separate from the everyday world, or thinking one is different or superior to others. We are living in and so rooted in this world. However, we can choose to live by different values and aim to rise above the pressure and pain that engulfs so many people. If we can do that, it also helps us to give more love to other people.

The old mahatma told us that there was a festival of the guru's devotees being held a little way south on the River Yamuna in the direction of Delhi so a few of us headed down there. The Indians have an amazing facility to organise big gatherings – full of noise and bustle, with children running around, food being cooked and life just happening – which, at the same time, contain a core or kernel of deep peace and tranquillity.

A considerable number of people were squeezed into quite a small area by the river. The focal point was the satsang stage with flowers and an altar with Guru Maharaji's picture. He would not be there in person. In fact I did not get to see him while I was in India but that mattered not. I felt all I needed to feel. The area around the stage was tidy and kept in order by premies charged with security duties. The further one moved from the stage the more the chaos and bustle grew. There was little need for shelter with the warmth of the night, though some people had makeshift covers thrown up. Myriad fires burned and people willingly shared their meals with us. Most of them were getting used to seeing western devotees and somehow they were really pleased (almost flattered) that we too should have adopted their guru. Several times I found some little child take my hand and drag me over to a family group where I was motioned to sit and join them for food.

By now I was suffering quite badly with dysentery, which was not much fun in the situation of the festival. I found an ayuverdic doctor there who gave me something that helped, though it did not clear completely till I got back to the UK. The festival lasted three days so where to go next? I had heard people talking of the beauty of Rishikesh, which was a few miles further upstream from Hardwar on the Ganges. It is in the foothills proper of the Himalayas and I wanted to see something a little more mountainous. I hopped on a bus, trusting my life once more to the hands of yet another wild driver. There was enough distraction on board with every seat taken by whole families and umpteen kids, and great interest in me as a foreigner, so I was able to ignore the fact that the driver was weaving his way through traffic like some aspiring Formula One driver. Anyway I was becoming quite the seasoned traveller.

The river is still quite wide in Rishikesh but just above the town it is a little narrower and faster flowing. That is where I found a beautiful place to stay. It was easy to team up with other travellers and even though I love to meet the locals when I am abroad it is also good to share the journey with new friends where you have a stronger cultural connection.

Brenda from the USA had been at the ashram in Hardwar, though not when I was there, and she had arrived in Rishikesh the same day as me. We met at a chai stall near the bus station so we went off to find somewhere to stay. We discovered a guest house with grounds that backed down to the river. It was perfect. We bathed at the edge of the waters and spent time stretched out on the rocks in the sun. There were beautiful walks up along the river, and monkeys chattering in the trees. They really are some of nature's greatest lovers of mischief and they can be quite fierce too. People often said that in hot countries like that it was wise to shake out one's shoes before putting them on in the morning to ensure no unfriendly creature was inside. One morning there was an anguished scream as one of the other European visitors was stung by a scorpion, probably hiding in a shoe. Fortunately it was not lethal but still a very painful sting.

It was interesting talking to Brenda. She had made her pilgrimage with much the same desire in mind as me. She was seeking affirmation of what she had felt when connecting with the Divine Light Mission back home. She was a similar age to me. As I had felt, she too had gone deeper into the experience of meditation. Looking back, I do not think our experience was as deep as we thought. To a degree we were seduced by the trappings and the Indian aspect of the whole thing. Nevertheless we had both gained some new spiritual understanding. After all, the spiritual journey is a lifelong one and at any point one can only have realisation and understanding appropriate to the level one has reached. That is what I love about it. The experience and understanding goes deeper every day. If I see more now, this does not devalue what I saw then. Now it is simply more and when I was younger I would not have been able to see with the eyes I now have.

The ayuverdic pills were helping to keep things at bay but my dysentery was not really improving. I began to think of returning home but I did not have the energy for a trek back overland. The only option was to get some money transferred to a bank in Rishikesh so I could buy an air ticket. It was not too difficult to arrange and all I had to do was wait for it to arrive. That was when I first experienced Indian bureaucracy at its most frustrating. It was almost certain that bureaucratic ways were taught to them in the days of the British Empire. Mind you, I think it would be true to say that they were also very willing students of this arcane art.

At the bank they told me to come back in a few days to see if my money was there. Now in this present technological era such a transfer would be very quick. I didn't expect a miracle but when I returned there was no sign of the cash. Each time I went in over several days, I was given the same answer – *"There is nothing here yet."* It was always accompanied by that typical Indian wave of the hand and shake of the head and a smile of course. But it was still a negative. Eventually I began to push a little harder. Rather than just accepting this response I insisted on seeing a more senior official. In the end I discovered it had been there for a few days already. I think there must be an unwritten rule that delays should be part of any transaction or procedure.

So at last, armed with the money I was able to book an Air India flight from Delhi back to London. All that remained was to take a bus down to Delhi and find my way to the airport. My pilgrimage was drawing to a close. One thing I was looking forward to on getting home was being able to eat anything without having to worry about the hygiene or how it had been cooked.

Although airline food is normally notorious for being pretty tasteless, in fact what we were given on board was wonderful: real Indian cuisine. It was a longer flight than would be the case now, with a refuelling stop in Beirut. This was only a few weeks after Israel had raided the Lebanon in an attack believed to be retaliation for the Munich Olympic massacre of Israeli athletes the summer before. The stop was strictly for fuel with the doors locked and everyone confined on board. I'm sure that in normal circumstances safety would demand disembarkation before refuelling but that is how it was. The atmosphere at the airport was tense and there were tanks surrounding the perimeter. I was very relieved when we took off again. I had been away for about three months and I arrived home to pouring rain. Well at least I could feel at home in England.

My pack was a lot lighter by then, having jettisoned all my warm clothing on the journey. I could have done with some of it that day though, as I stood by the roadside trying to hitch a lift, dressed in my shalwar and top. I headed for my parents' house in Buckinghamshire. With two younger brothers who also lived somewhat unconventional lifestyles, they were used to our unpredictable comings and goings. I didn't want to impose on them for too long but it was a welcome port of call while I adjusted to being back in the UK.

Had my journey given me what I was seeking? I felt very committed to the pathway of meditation that Guru Maharaji was teaching and at that time I still believed that he was who he claimed to be: the enlightened perfect master of the time. I had no desire to go into teaching, which the majority of my fellow students from Loughborough had done. In terms of my life, I simply saw myself earning enough to live while pursuing my path as a devotee. This latter was my focus. In hindsight I can see that it was a very naïve way to view things. Fortunately in the seventies it was easy to find a job and a place to live, whether bedsit or flat, unlike today. In addition I had the premie network to tap into. This meant that I could live wherever took my fancy, knowing that I could pay my way. Then once settled with accommodation and work I would plug into the local premie community.

While I was at my parents' house I made contact with the guru's followers who were living and holding satsang meetings in nearby Hemel Hempstead. Through them I met some premies living in Bristol. I didn't know Bristol but they invited me to stay at their house for a while till I found a place of my own. One of my dear friends from college was teaching there as well so it seemed like a good place to explore.

So what had really happened and what had I learnt in India? With the wisdom of hindsight it would be easy to be cynical. I was one of many youngsters who were seduced by the charms of this charlatan who relieved us of quite a lot of money as we financed his travel and lifestyle. I could easily be accused of having wasted my training as a teacher, forsaking everything to live a very casual lifestyle in which the most important thing for me was my spiritual path or my naïve view of how to pursue it.

I have always paid my way and I never lived on benefits or handouts. It was not that I was using a spiritual quest as an excuse for a free ride. I simply felt that I could not immerse myself, at that time at least, in the conventional lifestyle many expected of me. So my experience in India was profound – not in the sense that I had discovered a really valid vehicle in Guru Maharaji's teachings for a life of inner discovery, although I did think that at the time. I believe that I did have glimpses of a more heightened consciousness. I was still at a level in spiritual development where I needed some of the external trappings that went along with the Divine Light Mission. Later I would see it differently. However, as I have come to see in getting older, every step I have taken, every experience I have had, every person who has touched me, all have been the catalysts that have helped me to go deeper within. My journey in this life is about the inner journey, although it is the outer journey that is the teacher.

On the road to India and while I was there, I experienced love and friendship that transcended the boundaries of culture and language. I began to glimpse the stillness within our hearts; the stillness that is our true nature. It was just the beginning and I would go through many painful twists and turns as a member of Guru Maharaji's Divine Light Mission. But at that time it was right for me so I am grateful.

Chapter 3: A Novice Healer

Well sir, the tests show you have a nasty case of amoebic dysentery. Oh the joys of travelling in the east. Even after moving to Bristol the problems I had picked up in India took a bit of shaking off. The medication I was given didn't help. Luckily I still had some of the ayuverdic medicine I had been given in India. I took that and along with a good diet and time, things finally settled down. Still, I was having a good time exploring Bristol. I had found a rented house to share with a very dear friend from college and a colleague of his from the school where they were both teaching. My friend Hugh had decided to go into teaching after graduating and he was doing an excellent job.

I had slipped into a 'premie lifestyle'. I had plugged into the local community and I attended satsang regularly at the Bristol ashram. It was quite a big community and I began to make friends. Interestingly enough it consisted of far more than just shiny-eyed hippies. There were a fair number of older and professionally qualified people. It seemed that the guru had a way of catching a wide variety of people. It was easy to find work in those days and I was driving a three ton lorry for a building contractor, delivering materials to his sites. It suited me well because once out of the yard I was really my own boss. Provided I delivered to each site and got back to the yard by the late afternoon, all was fine. The old boy who was the foreman and my immediate superior was pretty easy going. Mind you, I did stray a bit because if my route took me near my house I would sometimes drop in for a break and a smoke. Unfortunately I was spotted by one of the more senior staff, who happened to be around where I lived when I made one of these detours.

I got hauled into the office and questioned. There was no point in playing innocent so I confessed, and I thought that would probably get me sacked. But he had a strange request: he said he would keep quiet if he could visit the house one evening with a friend. Initially I was non-plussed but then I realised he was obviously having an affair and wanted somewhere for a secret tryst. Well I said yes, to save my neck, but fortunately he never took it up and I also kept the job. That was probably as well as I'm not sure my two housemates would have liked the idea.

My sojourn in Bristol was a strange interlude. The job paid my way in the house and it was good to be with Hugh again. We had been very close at college, sharing many adventures. In fact we are still very good friends some forty-five years after meeting. It has been a precious friendship. We were young hippies together; we have watched one another growing and exploring different spiritual pathways; we have been through years when we have hardly seen each other. Yet there is a special and unbreakable bond between us. We respect the differences, yet at root we are on the same path. We are both searching for the deeper meaning in life yet still enjoying the journey. It is a privilege to have him in my life.

Outside of what we shared as friends, my focus was on my meditation practice and being a part of the guru's community there. No matter what we do in life, whether it is our spiritual practice, religious belief or our social pursuits, it is natural that we want to be with like-minded people. Sadly there are too many divisions in the world that keep people apart and cause them to judge each other. We often have too much need to be part of a tribe, and that can cause separation. At that time I was very committed to my practice and I fear that it did cause me to feel different. That is not good but I was immature. Over the years that has changed. Now I am better able to see what we all have in common at a deeper level. Of course I still prefer the company of some people to others and we need to spend quality time with like-minded folk. However, now I put up far fewer barriers than I used to. A little wisdom does come with age.

I decided to move back nearer to London and went to stay with the premies I had met in Hemel Hempstead in their shared house. We even had our own satsang meetings there and of course bigger gatherings in London were within easy reach.

"Hey Charlie, when you were massaging my shoulders, my headache just went." My friends in the house often asked if I could give them a shoulder or neck massage when they were feeling a bit stiff after work. It came naturally to me but something more was happening. This was totally new to me. I had heard of spiritual healing though I associated that with evangelical type Christian groups. Was that what was happening? I didn't really understand it but I began to experiment. Sometimes I would just lay my hands on someone's head or hold my hands over their eyes. Their pain would be relieved.

If you talk to people now about energy healing or perhaps Reiki, many will have heard of it even if they have not experienced it. In the mid seventies it was hardly known. I was curious to explore and I found a lady to visit in London who advertised herself as a 'hands-on' healer. As much as anything I went just to experience what she did, rather than to ask her much. I think I was too shy to do that. Yes, I felt something when I saw her and she worked on me. It was still hard to grasp what was happening and I had no points of reference to work with, but I realised I had stumbled on a gift that I had.

I continued to help when I was asked. Gradually I began to do more than just massages for stiff necks and the relief of headaches. I recall my father asking if I could help with some pain he had in his upper back, around the right shoulder. He said that he could feel a lot of heat from my hands even though my hands were not even warm to the touch. I have since learnt that this is quite common with many healers, but at the time I found it mind-blowing.

I'm not sure that I made a connection between the emergence of my healing gift and the meditation I was practising back then. Over time, however, I have seen that for me they are linked. Meditation in some form, which is the practice of inner listening, is essential to my journey as a healer. Why is that? As a healer I am a channel for energy that comes from a universal source. I do now use the word 'God', though not in the way most religious people do. To that extent it is not me that heals although I do have a part to play. To deny that I have a gift or a power is a kind of inverted ego trip. It is important to accept my part but without pride. In order for the energy to flow unhindered, it is necessary to get me, 'Charlie', out of the way. I do that through meditation because it connects me to the still, small voice of God within. In that state the petty ego is naturally quietened; clarity prevails; energy flows.

While I was in Hemel Hempstead I did some voluntary work with MIND. Although the mental health charity was established in 1946, it was still quite young and each local branch was — and still is — largely autonomous. I was interested in this area of health, which was then largely misunderstood. The Hemel branch was very small and did little other than run a weekly social club for people who had been discharged from a psychiatric unit or who were in some kind of out-patient care. We met for a couple of hours one evening, drank tea and coffee, ate biscuits and danced to current pop tunes. I distinctly recall that the favourite tune for dancing to was a song called 'Going to Barbados' by Coconut Airways. Looking back it was a dreadfully racially clichéd song. But back then we did not have the awareness we have now and it was great to dance to. It was almost a precursor to an experience I would have many years hence. It showed so clearly that mental, emotional or physical disease can hit anyone and we are all essentially the same despite whatever troubles we are having. We just need love — and that is all I tried to give when we were 'bopping' around to Coconut Airways.

I like a fairly quiet existence. Although the life of a total recluse is not suited to many people in the modern world, it is something I have considered. But without going to that extreme I do need my own quiet space and I have always needed that. The house in Hemel was fun but too many different personalities and the consequent difficulties didn't agree with me.

I bought a little cottage in neighbouring Buckinghamshire. In those days it was so much easier to find a mortgage than now. There didn't seem to be the same requirements for salary levels and everything else people face now. All of a sudden I became a home owner. The cottage was in a small village called Pitstone, nestling at the foot of the Chiltern Hills. It was an ancient village recorded in the Doomsday Book of 1086 under the Anglo Saxon name of Pincelestorne, which meant 'Picel's thorn tree'. I didn't know this when I discovered and bought the cottage but I believe there was an ancient energy that drew me there.

Just outside the village was a cement works that I passed each day. The grey dust of the production process coated the factory buildings and the surrounding road and verges. It cast a somewhat surreal atmosphere, like something from an apocalyptic movie. As the village stood in a flat area, the cement works could be seen clearly from my cottage, standing like a brooding sentinel.

I still drove in to work in Hemel Hempstead each day, employed as a gardener for the local council. When I was tucked in behind the wheel of my little yellow, three wheeled Reliant Robin, it felt rather like being strapped into the cockpit of a plane. It was small and quite low to the ground and gave a sensation of speed far greater than I was actually doing, as I drove along the quiet country roads. It was a funny little vehicle with a fibre glass body. Due to the three wheels it was classified along with motorcycles. The insurance and running costs were tiny and I puttered along the country lanes with not a care in the world.

I went to satsang meetings when I could but I was also beginning to explore more things on my own account. I had such a feeling of peace as I drove into the village each evening. When I look back I don't feel I got the most I could have from being there. I didn't fully appreciate the ancient energy of the village and the surrounding landscape. The area had a slightly bleak and windswept feel; it was quiet and not heavily populated. It was not so far from where the Great Train Robbery had taken place a decade earlier and that whole part of Buckinghamshire felt quite remote although fair sized towns, such as Aylesbury, were actually quite close.

The cottage needed renovation and I did a lot myself with some help from a jobbing builder who used to do work for my parents. I began to discover the joy of working with my hands, which later led me to set up my own building business. It was an end of terrace cottage with a tiny garden and an outside toilet. I planted a chamomile lawn instead of grass. Chamomile has an apple-like scent when crushed so lying on the lawn in the summer produced an exquisite smell. As I stepped out of the back door there was a high brick wall to the left with a great buddleia hanging over and shading my garden. To the right were the gardens of the neighbouring cottages. At the bottom of the garden, which was about twenty feet long, was an old wooden shed. My neighbours were older and very quiet, seldom appearing so I felt very private when I used to lie out on the chamomile in the summer, enjoying the apple scent.

Autumn brought lush crops of wild blackberries, which I picked in large bowlfuls. I am not a skilful cook but I have always enjoyed baking, so blackberry and apple crumbles and pies were the order of the day. If I could give them away – all the better. I recall my youngest brother and his wife coming over and going away with a freshly baked pie. The still and peace of the village was perfect for me. I would arise at five to meditate for an hour and a half before driving in to work and at that early hour there was seldom a car on the road. It was idyllic. I can look back to certain periods of my life and feel that the veil between me and the 'infinite' was very thin; that I was somehow very close to the 'source'. It's strange because it was a very quiet time. I had a very simple routine. Nothing especially exciting was happening, which was in complete contrast to my college days or my trip to India. Maybe that is just the point. Enlightenment (not that I am claiming that) is not about seeing stars and floating off into the cosmos. There is a saying in Zen Buddhism that 'Before enlightenment you chop wood and carry water. After enlightenment you chop wood and carry water'. It is just about a shift in awareness and part of that is surrendering and letting go of the pressures that usually control us. I believe I was in such a state of mind during this period.

There really seemed little in my life that needed to change but I was restless. Probably I was not ready to simply be in that quiet still state of mind. I could claim that I have always sought to keep moving and exploring for good positive reasons. To an extent that is true but I also have a tendency to just jump around from one situation, job or even country to another on a whim. That has certainly given me some hard lessons. As I get older I realise that in a way there is nowhere to go. We have it all within. But even now I have to be aware of this habit. Nevertheless, exploring new things is always stimulating and back then at least I believed that I needed to keep changing my external circumstances. I decided to join one of Guru Maharaji's ashrams here in the UK.

I applied to the organisation and I was accepted. Now the hard part, certainly for my family, was that this was a life of poverty, obedience and chastity. Every possession I had, including my house, was sold and the money donated to the Divine Light Mission. That was pretty serious stuff but I was certain that it was what I truly desired to do. I was giving over the reins of my life, on an external level, in order to find the inner goal that I sought. It was a drastic step, as my subsequent experience proved, but I have always thrown myself headlong into whatever I have been pursuing. Though I am less headstrong now, I still get the most out of things by being very committed.

So my house went, along with all my possessions, including a beautiful kayak I had built when I was at college. Taking off to go solo camping by the sea and surfing the waves in my boat, along with my life of tranquillity, was being consigned to the past. Where would I go? Would the guru truly be with me on this headstrong journey? Well I would soon find out. My destination was an ashram in West Bromwich, which was not somewhere I would have gone of my own volition because it seemed to be neither a rural nor a city environment and I preferred one or the other.

I arrived at the ashram on a grey day in the late summer. It was a small semi detached house in a quiet suburb with pleasant leafy roads. Little did I know what lay ahead or I would probably have beaten a hasty retreat. I was greeted by the house mother, who was a gentle, very devoted and sincere girl. The house father proved to be rather different and abusing of the power of his position. In theory these two young people were in supportive, caring roles as well as being administrators. It did not take long to see some of the abuses of power that took place in the Divine Light Mission.

The house mother performed a full time and really selfless role. In fact she worked herself to the bone. The rest of us, mixed males and females, had to get a job and every penny we earned was given to the ashram or in effect the Mission. Because I was qualified as a teacher I was instructed to find a teaching post. This proved quite easy. West Bromwich is situated just a few miles north west of the city of Birmingham. There were plenty of schools around and I found a post being advertised in one nearby as an assistant PE teacher with some English classes, which fitted my qualification exactly. It was towards the end of the school summer holiday that I attended the interview. Certainly the area looked a bit rough and the school itself was not very pretty but it was a job. I had no inkling of the horrors to come.

Meanwhile I slotted into ashram life. Till the school term started I helped with various chores around the house. Most evenings, after the other residents had got in from work I was assigned to the jumble round. As well as wages and salaries donated, we worked at raising money in as many other ways as possible. The ashram used an old van that had belonged to one of the residents, Tom, to drive around the local area collecting any old jumble people wanted to be rid of. This ranged from clothes, books and the like to old furniture. The ashram rented a small shop where most of the items were offered for sale and in addition regular jumble sales were held in places such as church halls. Tom was a great, gentle giant of a man, dark complexioned and strong. We made a good pair for lifting some of the donated furniture into the van. He was very devoted to the guru and the lifestyle we had chosen. He also had a lovely sense of humour and I enjoyed the time we spent together as he drove the lumbering van around the suburban streets, with me hanging out of the nearside of the cab keeping an eye out to see which households had left items of jumble out for us to collect.

We had no private life. We slept on mats on the floor, squeezed into one of two bedrooms or even the hall or upstairs landing. A wake up bell rang just before six and after fighting one's way to the bathroom for a cursory wash, there followed a period of meditation, then breakfast and off to work. Other than clothing we had no personal possessions. For a short while the buzz of being there carried me through but such a lifestyle is really not for me.

I did get a chance to practise my emerging healing skills. Tiredness and stress affected many of the people in the house. So shoulder massages and soothing their headaches was something I was often called on to do. The house father took a slightly dim view. He was the sort of guy who was of the opinion that you should just put up with any pain and stress all for the sake of our 'higher calling'.

As we moved into autumn and my teaching post loomed, I took to rising half an hour before anyone else and going out for a short walk. We were not quite prisoners but the house father did ask me my reasons for doing this. I simply said that I needed some fresh air to help me keep awake during the morning meditation period. It was the only chance I had for some private time and it was therapeutic to kick through the fallen leaves as I strolled along in the pre-dawn grey light. Although I felt that ashram life was a discipline that would help me go deeper into my spiritual practice, it really cut against the grain of the person I am. There are times when we need to do things that are a challenge. It is only in getting out of our comfort zone that we grow. However, it is also important to recognise who and what we are. Some things may be too much and so are counterproductive. Learning and growth may be a challenge but it does not have to make you feel miserable. Doctors will often say that you can't expect your medicine to taste nice – but there is a limit.

Then school started and I went through six weeks of hell. Having been to the interview out of term time, I had no idea what the place was like. It was a tough school in a rough area, it had a huge staff turnover, and the female teachers usually walked around in pairs. That sums up the atmosphere there. I had been given no preparation for what I faced in the classroom either at college or by the staff at the school. I was thrown to the wolves. The difference is that at least wolves make a quick kill without torture and taunting of the victim.

During my third year in college I had done a course in contemporary dance. It was a little out of the ordinary at what was a very traditional physical education college. In fact most of the other students looked at the six of us who did this as being cissies. Macho attitudes were much more prevalent then. I decided to do some dance work with my pupils. Oh dear! After the first class I was greeted with comments like *"Are we going to be flowers today, teacher?"* In a place like that, once my reputation was set, there was not much I could do about it. Keeping discipline consumed all my energy and actual teaching seemed to run a poor second in both my PE and my English classes. In English, my college course had introduced us to ideas of creative writing and I was keen to try these out as well. Bad mistake! There was a tiny handful of pupils interested in what I was offering but for most it was just more silly stuff.

In a nutshell, I 'blew a gasket'. In despair, I went to see the deputy head just before half term. His response was that I was doing well in that I was keeping fairly well on top of discipline and had not had any riots. That really didn't help and I was hugely relieved when the half term break arrived. The break coincided with a Divine Light Mission festival in London. All the members of the ashram piled into an assortment of vehicles and headed off to the capital. We were shunted around different ashrams and communal premie houses to sleep over a long weekend. It was there that I felt I could take no more.

One of my fellow devotees in the house where I was sleeping happened to be a doctor, a general practitioner. Perhaps because we shared the same birthday I struck up a bond with him and shared my woes. He took over as he could see I was suffering complete mental exhaustion. I really believe he was a guardian angel sent to me. He arranged my resignation from the school on medical grounds and moved me to a recuperation ashram. When I look back on that, though I did not see it at the time, the need for such an ashram should have sounded some warning bells for me.

There is an old saying that *"If something doesn't kill you, it will make you stronger"*. Throughout my life I have found love and peace in some of the direst situations and this was no different. I was put on a brown rice diet – brown rice with some sesame spread, water and nothing else – in this new ashram to help me detoxify. The house mother was gentle and understanding. There was no fixed schedule for me to follow. I could sleep and rest as I wanted. I shared what was happening to me with her. I felt a peace, a stillness and a love there that had been missing during my stay in the house in West Bromwich. I was able to go out for walks as we were right on the edge of Hemel Hempstead – funny that I was back in that area again. The ashram was beautiful. It was an apartment in an old house, with great high ceilings, set in a large garden. I found solace in the woods nearby and indeed I experienced tree energy in a way that I had not known since my childhood.

All beings are simply energy at root. So is a tree any different? Why should it be? Many people believe that every living thing on the planet has consciousness, even down to the rocks of the earth. The reason we cannot see that or may not believe it is because these beings are vibrating at such a slow rate that they seem to be inanimate. Pantheism, after all, includes the belief that all beings have awareness. I believe that. I discovered one particular tree in the company of which I felt great healing energy. Of course the cynic will say that I was ill and in a mental state that caused me to experience delusions. That is one interpretation. How I see it is that my stressful experience had broken open a barrier and allowed me to reach through to another level of awareness. All my normal and familiar crutches were ripped away and all that was left was my internal connection to universal energy. It was similar to when I lay on the grass as a little boy and looked upwards, pondering the unanswerable question of what lay beyond the sky; it helped me to go beyond the logical mind to experience a different level of reality.

Buddhists achieve this kind of breakthrough by focussing on what they call a koan. This is a riddle that defies logic, such as *"What is the sound of one hand clapping?"* By meditating on that for long enough they can achieve sudden flashes of enlightenment. Maybe this was my koan and that is what happened to me with my tree. I was in a state of mind that somehow bypassed the norm. When I stood by it and touched it, I was filled with healing energy and peace. It might seem I had paid a big price to gain such an experience but if that is what I needed at that point in my life, I accepted it. The peace and quiet and the rather tedious brown rice diet seemed to work. Once I felt fit enough to leave, I stayed with some friends nearby for a short while and then made my way down to Bristol once more. In terms of the places I was living, I seemed to be shuttling up and down between Bristol and the Buckinghamshire / Hertfordshire area for a few years.

Although I still considered myself a follower of the guru the chains that bound me to the whole movement were beginning to loosen. The experiences I had been through had been enough to suggest that not all was well within the movement, even if the basic message was one that I wanted to embrace. I still believed that meditation was an important part of my life but I was prepared to explore other forms.

This period in Bristol brought big changes and exciting new experiences. As always seems to be the case I was in for a rollercoaster of a ride. When I look at how hard it is for so many youngsters to find work today I realise how fortunate I was then as finding a job was easy. From when I first learnt to swim as a boy I loved the water. It was a sport in which I did well at college, though I was not in the top echelon competitively. During one of my spells in Hemel Hempstead I had trained as an Amateur Swimming Association instructor and I had worked in that field while I was there.

Now in Bristol I decided to go into this again. There were no immediate openings for exactly what I wanted but attached to the main municipal pool in the city was a laundry and someone was needed there. It was not quite what I had in mind initially but I thought that once my foot was in the door I might be able to advance my cause, as the same gentleman managed both the pool and the laundry. I spent most of my day amidst piles of bright orange boiler suits and overalls. Most of the laundry's clients were other council departments and orange was the main colour they wore. So I started the day by shoving heaps of filthy boiler suits into giant washing machines before putting them through dryers, to be followed by pressing them with great steam press machines.

It was over the next few years in Bristol that I began to make more use of my healing gift and to explore different healing modalities. While in the laundry I got chatting with another young fellow who worked there. I'm not sure exactly how the conversation got round to it but he mentioned having some trouble with one knee and I offered to do something for him. So we found a quiet corner at the back of the laundry where he could sit during our lunch break. It felt rather clandestine and I did wonder what would be thought if we were discovered. I simply laid my hands on his knee. I had complete faith that something would happen and it did. He felt the pain lessen and he was able to walk much more easily. I have come to feel that having simple faith in what I do is one of the keys to healing. Yes, I have trained in many modalities; I keep open to working with other healers to glean new inspiration and ideas. Yet the three most important things are to keep myself 'empty'; to feel unconditional love for my client; and to just have faith that it will work. Healing is beyond the rational mind. It is really beyond particular techniques. It is about opening up to something beyond me. That requires faith, but not in a religious sense (though perhaps in a spiritual sense): faith that it will work despite me.

Fortunately it was not long before I got the chance to work poolside and after a while I was transferred to another municipal pool in the Horfield area of the city. I loved the work there, which gave me face-to-face contact with the public; I enjoy any people-based work. Again little opportunities kept coming up to do small healings on staff members. I was the head attendant on one shift and my opposite number was a gnarled, late middle aged fellow with a cigarette constantly in his lips, except when he was poolside. It was an old fashioned swimming pool with changing cubicles down either side, from which you stepped straight out onto the poolside. Clothes were put on hangers and handed in to the locker room for safekeeping. The second person on the shift was mainly responsible for the locker room. My colleague here was a sprightly local lady who knew all the Horfield gossip. This was still only the late 1970s and healing was not something that most people had even heard of, let alone understood. Yet I have no doubt that my path through life was constantly bringing me into contact with folk who would either teach me or allow me to practise my gift. Both of them asked for my help with various aches and pains. These were just simple everyday people going about their lives. I guess they trusted me because I made no pretentious claims but just offered to help. They trusted me and in the love and acceptance they showed me, they gave me more than they will ever know and I am truly grateful to them.

Then, courtesy of a spilt baked potato, I found romance. Just across the road from the pool was a café where I used to go for lunch sometimes. There was a young lady working there who was quiet and not as extrovert as the other waitress, who tended to flirt with everyone. One day as she served my baked potato she spilled it onto the table (not the floor fortunately). Well one thing led to another: we started dating, she moved in with me and in due course we were married. In contrast to my somewhat impetuous nature she was much more level headed. By then I was drifting away from my Divine Light Mission involvement and her different view point on many things helped me to see Guru Maharaji from a rather more balanced stand point. I had known in my heart for some while that he was not what he claimed and that the organisation was deeply corrupt. However, when you have invested so much energy, passion, time and indeed money it is not easy to extricate yourself from something like that. She was the helping hand I needed. There were times while we were together that I did not always show my appreciation for her wise and balanced counsel. My pride and ego often got in the way but she was the perfect foil to my impetuous nature.

Though we met while I was still at the pool, I had just been accepted to go on a government sponsored bricklaying course. I loved working with my hands and I had done many stints of work in the building trade. In fact it was on building sites that I usually managed to find work when I was looking for casual holiday jobs as a student. I had ambitions of setting up my own business. The building trade was booming then and it seemed a great idea to get a trade under my belt so that I could then set up on my own after I had gained some experience.

So there I was, heading over to Chepstow each day, leaving around seven when the roads were still quiet, taking a beautiful drive over the Severn Bridge. I loved the challenge of learning a new skill and then racing home in the evening to my new romance. I became good friends with one Welsh lad on the course and I gave him a lift in each day. He was a burly jovial character who never seemed to get put out by anything. He already had some experience of working with a trowel and he used to give me useful tips. I had a flat in a quiet road in the Clifton Wood part of Bristol. It was a cul de sac with houses on just one side of the road. Mary moved in there with me and not long after we were married. Then we had the chance to buy the whole house. It was a beautiful four storey Victorian house in a hilly part of the city that dropped away to the river, not far from the famous Clifton Suspension Bridge. The views from the top floor at the back were stunning. City roofscapes with countryside visible beyond have a particular magic for me. It was in need of much renovation and it became the first of three major house renovation projects we undertook together.

Around this time I came into contact with a group of Buddhists. They were following one of the Tibetan schools of Buddhism. In fact, initially, I met one of them in my capacity as a builder. By this time my course was completed and I had set myself up as a self employed tradesman. I was fascinated by the Tibetan culture which for them seemed to be very much a part of their practice. I spent time with them and went to several of their meetings. Although there was none of the hype and hysteria that had characterised Guru Maharaji's movement, I was still wary of what I saw as a distraction in the emphasis on and interest in Tibetan culture. Still something about them and what they seemed to be experiencing exerted a powerful draw on me.

One of their teachers was a Tibetan llama based at the Lam Rim centre in South Wales. I went to see him a couple of times. He was a delightful man. He radiated a sense of peace and contentment with a beaming smile, as he sat cross legged fingering a Buddhist mala (or rosary). He did not speak English very well but he seemed to understand my sincerity in being a seeker of spiritual truth. To his credit he also understood my reservations and hesitancy over the Tibetan cultural stumbling block, as I saw it. His advice was not to rush anything in the way of following his school of practice. *"Just relax, feel love and try the meditation for yourself before thinking that you have to make a formal commitment."* It was a rather more balanced and sensible approach than I had previously been advised to take.

Though in the end I did not make a commitment to that particular path I learnt some of the meditation techniques they used. In particular I learnt for the first time how to visualise in a meditative way and that is something I use even now in my healing work. Visualising is very powerful and has been used for millennia. Basically the subconscious mind does not know the difference between what we visualise or imagine and what has tangible reality. Indeed it is possible to create our reality with our thoughts. Ancient mystics have said it for ages (the Tibetan practices showed this in a way) and now quantum physicists say much the same thing. I was beginning to see other dimensions opening up within my healing work. At the time I knew nothing of quantum physics. A lot of work has been done and theory developed around the notion of the experimenter influencing the experiment. Despite the same two experiments being conducted under identical conditions, the results can vary depending on the expectations of each experimenter. In other words, our thought and intention has actual power to influence the physical realm. Energy is the more powerful force. In using visualisation and intention in my healing work I can contribute to the effect on my client.

The member of this group whom I had first met became a good friend and some years later we made a pilgrimage together to India. In, the meantime I continued to explore meditation as a basis of my life without feeling the need to be connected with any particular tradition or school of practice.

My building business really took off. It was the perfect time for it. House prices were booming and people were buying in order to sell on after doing some renovations. There was more work than there were builders to do it. I started by doing some landscaping work as well, in which I could use my new skill to build small walls and patios. Gradually as I was offered more straight building work, I concentrated on that. I was able to hone my skills in renovating our house and I taught myself to plaster. I remember my first attempt to plaster a ceiling, where most of the plaster ended up on me or the floor. In the end I got it. Mary did a women's joinery course and with the advice and help of a joiner friend of mine, she rebuilt some of the traditional sash windows. It was a skill she later became very proficient in and put to good use.

The building trade is one of those professions which attract a varied range of people. I met several tradesmen with similar middle class backgrounds to me. A group of them had set up one of the first 'green' building companies and I did some sub contract work for them. One of them was a sculptor by profession and also a gifted stone mason. Rod and his partner became good friends. We employed him to renovate the soft Bath stone, so common in the area, which formed much of the outside of our house. He was a very quiet person, small and wirily built. He worked on his own on our house, spending all day on the scaffolding, making hardly a noise. At the end of the day, covered in white dust, he would bid farewell, looking like a wizened and aged elf.

I worked as a sole trader, using sub contractors when I had a bigger job to do. Working from home without offices or a yard I was a pretty free agent. Sometimes I teamed up with a friend I met who was another bricklayer. Together with a mate of his, we formed a two and one gang – two brickies and a labourer. We worked on large sites doing small contracts, usually on a price basis. It added to the variety of my work and gave me good experience.

I have never built my life round a job, tying myself to one place for the sake of work. I have approached things the other way round. I choose to live where I want to and build an income when I get there. Bristol itself at that time was not as huge as it has become now. It was hardly a pressured place to live, though it was beginning to show signs of the expansion to come. Still, we both fancied living in the country – but where?

The Brecon Beacons in South Wales are beautiful and we explored the area. Mary knew the north of England well as she came from there. We did a wonderful walk on the North Cornish Coastal Path. That was an adventure. We took all we needed in two backpacks, complete with a tent, sleeping bags and food and got a train from Bristol to our starting point. That coast is wild and rugged with steep drops and climbs in and out of every cove.

After a good first day's walk we found a spot to pitch camp. I laid out the tent, which I had been carrying, and then asked Mary if she had the tent poles... we had managed to leave them in Bristol. The spot we had picked was only lightly wooded but luckily there were a couple of bushes that yielded three branches, enough to pitch the tent, and we carried them the rest of the week – in true Boy Scout tradition.

Despite the beauty of Cornwall and the wild call of the Brecon Beacons, we couldn't seem to find what we were after till we took a holiday on the west coast of Scotland. Towards the end of one summer we cleaned out my building van and turned it into a camper for a trip north. I had never been to Scotland though Mary knew St Andrews on the Scottish east coast, having been a student there. The west coast was new territory and it captivated us – empty, wild, windswept with fantastic seascapes, lochs and mountains. It was everything we wanted. It was a big move, not knowing anyone there, but we were confident work would come and we had each other.

Selling the house proved pretty easy. We didn't even need to bother with estate agents. When Rod heard we wanted to sell, he put us in touch with a friend of his who was looking for a Victorian house still in need of renovation (ours was far from finished). We didn't want to be greedy in the way so many people were being in the housing boom, pushing prices sky high. We reckoned up what we needed to clear the mortgage, various debts, something to live on for a few months and the possible cost of a house in Scotland. He agreed. The transaction went smoothly. So with cash in the bank, furniture in storage, my van converted to a camper once more and our two cats for company, we headed north a few months later. We aimed for the mid-Argyll area, found a holiday caravan to rent and set about finding a house. Of course I had no inkling then but my Scottish experience would prove pivotal in my spiritual growth and the development of my healing gift.

Chapter 4: A Step Back in Time

Have you ever seen a cat stalk a cow? The two cats we took to Scotland were city bred so staying in a holiday caravan in mid Argyll was a real culture shock for them. Rabbit (great name for a cat) had never seen a cow and as far as he was concerned they just looked like a large dinner he might catch. It was hilarious to watch him stalk them. On one occasion we had been out exploring for the day and when we got back Rabbit very proudly presented us with a large uncooked salmon. It didn't take long to realise that the owner of the caravan we were staying in, who lived nearby, must have left the back door of her house open. Rabbit had been exploring too. I didn't have the nerve to sneak it back into her kitchen, assuming that was where it had come from. We just hoped she never twigged what had happened.

No commitments, cash in the bank and a whole new place and culture to explore was refreshing after several years of graft building for other people and then coming home to a house which was a partial building site. It seems to be the lot of many builders. Just as the old saying goes that a cobbler's children are always poorly shod, our house in Bristol had been an unfinished building site. At least we had kept the work to the top two floors while living on the two lower floors which had been the original flat. The move north was really invigorating. The Scottish west coast is sparsely populated. The first caravan we rented nestled under a conical hill and apart from our host's cottage there was no one within several miles. Late spring is the time of riotous colours as the azaleas break out in bloom. That coast is kissed by the Gulf Stream and it is very mild, if wet. Hedgerows often consist of wild fuchsia growing thick and high.

There is something about rural Scotland, with its Celtic past, that oozes magic. Of course there is ancient history in England too, but maybe I just never really tuned into it. The Lowlands across the border from England are beautiful but the scenery really changes dramatically further north. The road out of Glasgow winds past lochs both salt and fresh water, along twisty headlands. Glasgow is a bustling modern city and as you leave it there are smart golf clubs and then the Faslane naval base, home to nuclear submarines. Occasionally you could see one wallowing at anchor like a great sinister grey whale. Gradually the roads get narrower and less busy as you pass Loch Lomond on the right, a huge expanse of fresh water reflecting the colours of the sky. On a grey day it has a brooding feel and you might expect to see the Loch Ness monster's cousin pop his head up there.

Gradually the road climbs to cross the narrow pass known as the 'Rest and be Thankful'. Behind lies busy Glasgow and its surrounds and ahead lies the mystical west coast. Burns (small streams), rivers, lochs; everywhere there is water. Just over 'The Rest' there is a beautiful loch to the left below the road. Ahead the hills climb steeply to either side. They form a long deep valley with a lonely road running through the middle. There are only a couple of cottages and the odd bothy, which is a basic shelter, commonly found in Scotland, usually left unlocked and available for anyone to use free of charge. There were seldom sheep visible and no other wildlife. It was a desolate valley. Getting caught here in a winter snow storm can be dangerous as it is high, exposed and the weather really closes in, especially atop 'The Rest' itself.

Already you sensed the ancient power in the land. Some way ahead lies Inveraray, ancestral home to the Duke of Argyll, on the shore of Loch Fyne. As we came round a bend in the road that hugged the shore of the loch, Inveraray was silhouetted ahead against the slowly sinking sun of the late afternoon. In the foreground was the still, glittering water. What a photo opportunity! There was enough room to park the van and then risk life and limb finding the best place on the road to take a shot of the view. But I got a beauty.

From Inveraray on, you begin to feel as if you are slipping back in time. There is new building, of course, but most of the architecture is old. Roofs are of West Highland slate. Granite is used in the main construction and most houses still have old fashioned wooden sliding sash windows. The roads are relatively empty and one can drive fair distances without seeing more than an occasional small cottage. Together with the shaggy brown Highland cattle, a common sight, it all creates a sense of peace and antiquity. Heading on west you reach the town of Lochgilpead. Turn north there and you will come to Oban. To the south lies the Kintyre Peninsula. It has a distinct 'other worldly' feel, enhanced for an Englishman by the thick accent of the west coast natives.

The Kintyre Peninsula is truly a throwback in time. Long and narrow, it sticks out into the Irish Sea and at its head, where it connects to the rest of the mainland, is the fishing town of Tarbert; it is a very narrow spit of land. This helps to create an island-like feel down on the peninsula. Right down south on the Mull of Kintyre you can see Ireland in the distance on a clear day. Winter weather around the Mull itself can be fierce. It is often impossible for fishing boats to sail from the sheltered eastern coast of Kintyre round the Mull out to the open Atlantic if the wind and waves are really strong. Boats still get lost in these seas, as happened during our time in Scotland. We later came to know well some of the fishermen of Carradale. They are a hard drinking, fearless breed; members of a close knit community for whom the dangers of sea fishing are still a daily reality. Their rhythm of life has not changed in many a year. The boats usually dock on a Thursday afternoon. The catch is sold at the quayside and you might be lucky to get some of the cast off fish that are no good for market. The money earned is then portioned out to their wives to cover the week's household expenses. Whatever is left is kept for a long weekend of hard drinking. By the time the boats put back to sea late on Sunday afternoon, most of the crew, though hopefully not the skipper, are still pretty much 'four sheets to the wind'. During that evening the boats sail out to wherever the week's fishing is planned. On Monday morning four days of hard graft start again.

It was in Kintyre that we found the Old Schoolhouse in the tiny village of Saddell, our next home for three years. It had long closed as a school. After that it was rented out as living accommodation but it had been unoccupied for a few years. We snapped it up for a little over £20,000 just in time before neglect began to impact on it. Driving north out of Saddell, the road twists up a steep hill, at the top of which stands the house on the left. As we stood in the front garden, the road curved round the side of the house, with a tall hedge giving us privacy on that side. In the front, at the bottom of the garden, the road dropped away down the hill. From there we looked out over Saddell Glen, containing two farms. There was more garden at the back of the house where we built raised beds for vegetables. Much of the huge hedge round the house was wild fuchsia with delicate, deep red flowers. Great clumps of wild montbretia with rich orange blossom were scattered through the garden. In common with many properties in the area it had a private water supply, which was a tiny spring some way from the house. The water on the west coast is full of peat. Even if you have filters on a private supply, it is quite brown as it comes out of the taps, adding something to a cup of tea.

The house needed some work to get at least one room and a bathroom renovated before we could move in so we stayed a bit further south at Peninver Sands Caravan Park till that was done. Each day for about a month we left the cats in the caravan and headed up the road to work on the house. It was a carefree time and the weather was beautiful. Once I had repaired a roof leak, we set about the inside. We soon started to find out how different country living was to Bristol. Peace and quiet and remote, but in the country the trees have eyes and ears! My white van with my name still advertising my trade as a builder was hardly invisible and we had been spotted.

I was in the back garden when a police car stopped. *"Aye, well I just thought I'd see what you were doing….."* He knew of course, as he would have talked to people in Campbeltown where he was based. But he was the first link in the grapevine and by that evening most of the locals would have known we were Sassenachs, from south of the border, what colour shirt I was wearing and what I had eaten for breakfast. Not so long after that there was a knock on the door. It was an old couple who asked if we were there permanently. They explained that for the years the house had been empty they had visited in the late summer when the bright orange berries were on the beautiful rowan tree in the back garden. They used them to make rowan jelly. Would it be OK if they continued to do that? Of course we were more than happy to oblige, especially as they came from some distance away and it had obviously become something of an annual ritual for them. They came back and in due course we also received some of the home-made jelly.

"And of course you know I am the local builder round here". Billy greeted us with that when we went to a ceilidh one night in the Carradale village hall, which was just a few miles up the road from us. It was a fishing village with strong Viking connections as they had ruled that area for a time in the late eleventh century. There were epic battles on the west coast as Somerled, who was of part-Norse blood, exerted his authority. Though of mixed blood he was resident on the west coast and he pushed out the marauding Vikings and established a settled kingdom that gave rise to his descendants becoming Lords of the Isles. Many people in Carradale had Viking surnames showing their ancestry.

So we had to tread a little warily. I would need to find work but I didn't want to upset local residents. Over time I was asked to do jobs and my work and reputation ensured I was kept very busy for the next three years. I managed to establish a reasonable working relationship with Billy. Anyway there was more than enough work for both of us and as his reputation was not outstanding, the locals were prepared to give me a chance.

Of course I used to give Mary massages and relief for headaches and tension. But otherwise I was not consciously pursuing my healing work at the time, though it was never far away. It was then that I started (almost unconsciously) to experience a healing connection with animals. Our house was surrounded by three farms owned by three brothers, whose father had divided his large farm between them. They all became friends and one of them, Fergus, took me under his wing. *"Come with me and we can fell some old trees for burning for you."* He also taught me to shear sheep, traditionally by hand. No new fangled electric clippers for him. I built my own wooden clipping stool, like Fergus, which was an elongated triangle of wood with legs. I sat astride the narrow end with a sheep on its back in front of me, feet trussed to stop it moving.

The poor beasts found it pretty stressful, especially as they were wild hill sheep used to little other than minimum contact with Fergus for most of the time. I think I spent more time helping them to relax with a gentle touch of my hands than I did clipping. Mind you, Fergus had been at it for fifty-odd years so hardly surprisingly he clipped half a dozen sheep for every one of mine. But I loved it: just the close touch with a much bigger animal than I had been with since my days on the kibbutz – their warmth; the smell of the wool; the snuffle of their breath – all was a way in to animal energy that awoke something in me. I could feel them relaxing as I focussed healing energy on them.

It was hot dusty work that we did at the back of the farmhouse. Many Scots have a notoriously sweet tooth so Fergus' wife Moira produced tea and home-made cakes at intervals. There is a special camaraderie to be shared when you work alongside someone like that. To Fergus and Moira we were slightly strange: from England, unusual attitudes (we were vegetarian, for goodness sake) but they reached out with love and by stepping into their world we were able to establish a precious bond. Of course it also meant that they would have first hand gossip concerning us.

Driving back up from their farm was a challenge. A deeply potholed, very steep track twisted like a switchback up to the road. I had to go at it full speed with my high topped and slightly unwieldy van. When I got to the top I had no option but to drive straight out onto the road, hoping there was no traffic as stopping there would have made a restart near impossible.

I was born under the sign of Pisces and I am a real water person: in it, on it, near it; I am happy. From the upstairs floor of the house we could just glimpse Kilbrannan Sound to the east, looking over Saddell Bay. The bay was a long, sweeping, yellow sandy beach where Paul McCartney had recorded the accompanying video for his hit song, 'Mull of Kintyre'. It was usually empty and gave wonderful views of the Isle of Arran. Swimming when it was warm, scuffing through the sand on cooler days or walking further up the coast, scaling rocks, discovering pools filled with crabs left by the receding tide was bliss. Sadly there was much rubbish swept onto the beach: plastic bottles, old shoes, rope and glass. So many people who use the sea for work or pleasure treat it like a great waste bin, forgetting that their jetsam becomes flotsam which will pollute such pristine beauty.

Somerled had founded a Cistercian Abbey, now ruined, in the depths of Saddell Glen. The ghosts of history were there. It is an ancient landscape with roots going deep. Somehow just being there allowed the energy to seep into my being. Living in such rural seclusion lets one experience the ancient earth energy that is deep within the planet. I have always loved such places and travelled to them on my wanderings but till then I had not lived for any length of time in such a place. As time went by I had to start earning a living again. Business pressures crept in so I was not as aware each day, as I had been at first, of the beauty surrounding me. Yet everywhere I drove to a building job was through fantastic scenery with stunning mountain or sea views. Such a landscape works its magic deep in the soul.

In Bristol light pollution filled the night sky. There was little of that in Kintyre. Stepping out at night in Saddell revealed a star-lit sky with even very faint glimmerings of the Northern Lights at certain times. It was a truly beautiful and peaceful haven. Many people do pursue spiritual enlightenment in remote places, in deserts and mountains. That is not necessary as we can find a connection with the universe no matter where we are, even in the depths of the inner city. Indeed we can be in a beautiful rural idyll and yet be tortured in our souls. But perhaps for the first time in my life I felt that I could have put down very deep roots there. In fact I don't think that is my destiny as I have been moving all my life, before and since then. What I believe happened in Saddell was that the earth energy began to work on me – or I was more open to it. I could not have put it into words then. When I sat on the rocks on Saddell beach something of what I experienced as the little boy lying on the grass came back to me. However, I had said, as a follower of Guru Maharaji, that everything we want is inside of us. I believed that but probably I did not really understand it as I now do. The next few years would teach me that lesson very firmly.

Working with Fergus' sheep, rescuing baby rabbits that had survived the clutches of our cats: such things gave me a greater connection with our animal friends who share the planet with us. But despite this there was also a feeling of disconnection at some level. I still practised meditation but it was outside of a particular tradition. I had no teacher or guide. We did not quite fit into the community. Being in Kintyre really was like going back 200 years in terms of attitudes. We found some kindred spirits in the form of a retired couple. The husband had been a Harley Street psychiatrist. They had escaped from London some years before. But he and his family were seen as eccentric hippies. Although accepted to a point, they were still viewed with suspicion. They had even suffered accusations of witchcraft not long after moving there.

Apparently they had been dancing in the woods at summer solstice not long after their arrival. They had been photographed and on the basis of people seeing the pictures they had been cast as weird and possibly involved in satanic rituals. Certainly this had happened some years before we arrived but attitudes were still pretty backward. The locals were dour Scots indeed! Because of this we thought it best to keep certain aspects of ourselves under wraps. I suppose we often do this to an extent. Now, however, I view things differently. I do not set out to antagonise people and there are times when full disclosure may not be for the best. Nevertheless I believe that personal integrity in the sense of being and speaking one's truth is vital and is fundamental to how I try to live.

A couple of years after moving to Saddell, Mary and I went through some very painful personal difficulties. For a while it seemed that we would separate but in the end we felt we could salvage our marriage if we moved and made a fresh start. After three years in the Old Schoolhouse we moved to mid Argyll, just north of Lochgilphead. It was during the time in mid Argyll that I underwent huge changes – spiritually and emotionally. It was a momentous time.

Chapter 5: Zen; Ten Years Facing a Wall

Ancient standing stones and strange cup and ring marked stones fill Kilmartin Glen. Not far away is Dunadd Hill, with a footprint in a flat stone where the kings of Iron Age Dal Riata once stood to be crowned. There are chambered burial cairns where stepping through the entrance takes you to meet the ghosts of ancient Scotland. From one point near our house the standing stones marched off into the distance in a perfectly straight line – how were they built?

Our cottage at Tayness was tucked into a little glen contained within the old Poltalloch Estate. Bats by the hundreds flitted through the night sky as they poured out of tiny holes under eaves to help keep the population of west coast midges down. Mind you, that was near impossible, and at certain times of day when it was damp or overcast, survival in the garden needed a full midge net covering the head and all trouser and shirt access points completely sealed. You would hardly believe such a tiny insect, hardly as big as a pinhead, could reduce tough forestry workers to near wrecks. The midges were something of a staple of conversation amongst the locals and a topic of amusement to visitors – till they discovered how fierce they were.

We had nearly a couple of acres of land with a burn running down from the hill behind us to form the lower boundary of our property. We had everything from woodland to meadow in which to play. Behind the house the hill rose steeply. The climb wound under dark boughs along the burn that, from a point still higher up, supplied our water. Occasionally there were delectable wild mushrooms to be picked. The low branches forced us to crouch as we climbed, and they created a kind of secret feel to this part. There was almost a sense as if tree spirits might peep out from behind the thick wooden stems.

In late spring the more exposed hillside was a riot of wild rhododendron flowers. They are rampant if not controlled but the pinkish colour they splashed across the slope was beautiful. When I got round to thinning them I discovered the wood was great for burning in our sitting room stove. The rhody (so nicknamed) had not been thinned for years and was a twisted tangled mass that was hard to fight through but it gave us colour, firewood and mulch for our garden. We had plans to set up an organic market garden and obtained funding from the Highland and Island Development Board for a small business venture. One piece of equipment we bought was a large petrol driven shredder/chipper. It could reduce quite thick branches to fine chips that made excellent mulch and ground cover. Starting the business was an excuse for me to get a few big toys, just like a little boy.

Below the cottage was a small section of more cultivated garden and sweeping away past that to the right was a field beyond which we could see the cattle of the Poltalloch Estate. The estate was still well wooded and alongside the track that led up to the house were huge old trees, some a good hundred feet tall if not more. For a decade we nurtured the land and it nurtured us. It was the longest time that we lived together in one place and it was a period of much inner growth and exploration for us both. We began to discover more deeply what we wanted in our lives; what kind of people we really were. When we had met, I was quite immature despite being just over thirty. Mary being eight years younger had perhaps not yet found her feet in life. Growth is not always easy and indeed we reached a point when we realised that our time at Tayness and our time together was over.

Just after moving into the house I went off to a Zen Buddhist monastery in Northumberland for a week's retreat. Before leaving Kintyre we had met a fellow who was a practising Zen Buddhist. Having met the Tibetan group in Bristol I was curious to find out more about Buddhism.

I was looking for more spiritual direction. After being in the ashram in India I imagined that Throssel Hole Priory in Northumberland would be similar in ambience and experience.

Not so; the week I spent there turned me inside out and put me through the wringer. It was a far more disciplined environment. I took a train from Glasgow to Hexham in Northumberland and then a bus out to the Abbey. It was high in the open, windswept hills: a forbidding scene that was extremely harsh in winter. I alighted from the bus having no idea of what lay ahead. Once inside the gate, there was a driveway some quarter of a mile long which wound between conifers initially. As the trees thinned you could see the monastic buildings up the hill with three huge fir trees near them, seen as symbolic of the three tenets of Buddhism: the Buddha, the Dharma and the Sangha. The most striking building was the great Meditation Hall. The Northumberland scenery was not one of soft greenery but rather wind, rocks and sparse high grassland. It was somehow an appropriate setting for a Zen monastery. Zen is a very austere spiritual discipline. There is ritual but it is very different to the more flamboyant ritual of the Tibetan Buddhist practitioners.

It was much more disciplined than the ashram in India and there was a timetable, which though not rigidly imposed, was something that you felt you had to adhere to unless there was very good reason not to. It is part of the Serene Reflection Meditation tradition and the monks (both male and female) are shaven-headed and robed. It is not a silent order though silence is observed quite a lot and especially at breakfast and lunch. In general light conversation is discouraged. Although rooted in a Japanese Buddhist tradition, the residents were mostly English and there was not the same emphasis on a foreign culture that I had found difficult with the Bristol group.

I went to the guest department. The warm and friendly greeting was from an old monk who had a club foot but who was cheerful and seemingly unconcerned by his limited and obviously painful mobility. I was shown to my allotted sleeping space in the large meditation hall. Guests and novice monks slept in this hall. It was a huge room with a high ceiling and a large, life size gold statue of the Buddha on the altar. Down each side were wooden lockers for one's mattress, bedding and clothes. All the monk's possessions fitted into a locker about four feet square and a foot and a half deep. This was certainly going to be a different experience to the ashram in India. There would be no slipping out of the gates to the chai stall. Certainly I was apprehensive but I was also excited at such a new experience.

Something in the discipline appealed to me. Rising at six with bedding hastily put away; a quick wash and then meditation for forty minutes back in the hall; a morning service; a work period; silent breakfast and then a day of work periods interspersed with meditation sittings, meals and services. Lights out was at ten in the evening, when you rolled out your sleeping mat on the floor alongside the other visitors. Males were at one end of the hall and females at the other end, separated by a curtain put up for the night. To someone who has not experienced something like that it might sound like a boring routine, but no worse. In fact it is incredibly confronting. We don't often spend large parts of our day in silence. There was no media distraction such as TV or newspapers. There was no choice as to what you ate or when you did anything, nor to what work were you assigned unless you had a health problem. There was no reading matter other than Buddhist texts.

One reads stories of Zen practitioners who spend many years facing a wall to find their enlightenment. This is what helps give it the impression of being a very severe spiritual practice. One imagines them sitting immobile for ages, years on end; what about eating and sleeping? The image comes from the fact that in Zen one meditates seated just two or three feet from and facing a wall. The eyes are partially closed but downcast towards the point where the wall and the floor meet. One does not focus especially on what is outside, rather on the breath, allowing thoughts to arise and then go without getting drawn into following them. Over time and with persistent practice this forces you to look at yourself; to go within. Things arise as you see aspects of yourself that you are unaware of or usually prefer not to acknowledge. Dealing with these is part of spiritual growth. To become a better more caring person involves looking at oneself. Of course people do this in many ways. Working with mentors, having open and heartfelt discussions with friends or work colleagues, through prayer: all are ways in which we can improve ourselves.

The monastic situation is especially intense in this way. I know monasticism is thought by many to be outmoded in this day and age. Some people view monks as parasites if they are part of an order living on charity. That is a whole debate that I won't get into here, with pros and cons on both sides of the discussion. What I saw was a very sincere group of people, working very hard on their own life journey; a group of people that was very caring and loving to all visitors. They believed that their lives were a service to the sangha (Buddhist community) for whom it was a place of refuge, retreat and spiritual searching.

A couple of days into my visit I was helping in the kitchen with the mammoth task of washing up after a meal for some seventy-odd people. I had been experiencing much inner confrontation and suddenly I broke down in floods of tears for no apparent reason. I was gently escorted to a quiet room and a senior monk was found to talk with me. I was able to pour out what I was going through to someone who listened without the slightest judgement. I don't think I had ever known such an open and loving response to sharing a trauma. I felt a deep healing energy as we spoke, sitting in that quiet little room with a coal fire burning. The energy at the monastery was palpable. You felt it as you walked through the gate at the bottom of the long drive, long before reaching the buildings or talking to any of the residents. There is nothing wrong with enjoying the many things we have in our lives. Unfortunately often they act as a distraction from simply being still and finding a quiet place inside. We get in from work tired and switch on the radio or TV without thinking. This gives us no time or space for quiet contemplation. The monastic setting does not allow that and painful lessons were delivered but they were accompanied by healing if one chose to accept them both.

The huge meditation hall was filled with this energy. It is true of many holy places in many different traditions. I have sensed it in mosques, churches and places of pilgrimage but I had never before felt it to this extent. It was during my time at Tayness that my work as a healer began to develop further and to include healing with animals. The lessons I went through at the monastery were part of this whole process. I went on regular long retreats, three or four times a year for the next decade. My time as a Zen student was profound, as was yet another pilgrimage I would make to India some years hence.

I returned home burning with a new zeal. Before we moved my wife had also been to the monastery for just a couple of days with our friend from Kintyre. She liked the place and the monks but had not been swept away as I had. That was just not her way. Once home I imposed on myself a strict discipline of meditation. I have to admit that it did cause some friction between us but I knew I had to explore this pathway. I will admit now that I was rather insensitive to Mary's viewpoint. I tried quite forcefully to encourage her to join me in meditation. I soon realised that this was not the way to treat someone but even after I stopped doing that I think that she felt some quiet judgement on my part, which I deeply regret.

The spirit of the land where we lived was bruised and neglected. The people who sold us the house had been through a very unpleasant divorce. They had not cared for the land or the house for some time while their relationship was breaking down. We could feel it and we set about loving the land and repairing the house. We had some spare cash from selling the Old Schoolhouse so we began renovation of our third property. I did still need to find work as a builder as we established the market garden project. That was not easy as there were many other self employed tradesmen like me around there. Added to that was the beginning of an economic downturn that got worse in the early nineties. We had moved in 1990.

We set about cultivating the field. We planted an orchard of pears, apples and plums. Mind you, we chose mostly the wrong varieties. Thinking that at those northerly climes we would suffer heavy winters, we reckoned late fruiting trees would be best. The winters are long and wet but mild on the west coast around mid Argyll. We picked trees that blossomed late. With quite a short summer compared to what we had known in Bristol and very different light conditions, most of the fruit did not really get a chance to mature properly. Still, we had some fruit and there was a special feeling in watching little saplings, barely thicker than a finger, mature over a decade into sturdy trees that offered shade to small creatures and helped to create a mini ecosystem in one corner of the field. It also became the burial place for an assortment of creatures that shared our idyllic life there. Various chickens, ducks and other wildlife that died on our land were buried beneath the trees with full Buddhist rites.

Each little part of the property had its own ambience. The woodland was mysterious. The burn and its banks had a serene feeling as the water poured through steep sections overgrown with plants from either bank, and then emerged into quieter, rocky pools at the bottom where the flow of the water slowed down. Sitting in the burgeoning orchard at the top of the field gave sweeping views of the land outside our boundary and of the lower field filled with strip beds packed with potatoes or tall cabbage and sprout plants. Almost everywhere you could glimpse a chicken scratching for grubs.

Henrietta was a rare chicken and she loved a cup of tea. I swear she could smell a mug of tea from some distance away. She would come scooting across the yard to the bench where we often sat for a break. She would hop up on a knee and dip her head in the mug. I used to have a lovely photo of her doing this on Mary's knee. Most people will say that one is indulging in mistaken anthropomorphism in seeing human characteristics in animals. I disagree. All animals have character and 'personality'. Maybe 'animality' might be a better word. Animals show the range of emotions and moods that we do. Most people fail to see that or do not believe it, so they don't see it. I had never before kept fowl. We had chickens and ducks at different times and I began to see in them as much individual character as shown by dogs or cats. We inherited a black chicken with the house who was very bad tempered and I'm sure the vibes she had been living with caused this. Henrietta was quite the opposite, gentle and friendly, and as she neared her end she gave me a great gift. Provided a chicken escapes the fox (in our case usually mink) and is not forced into unnatural egg production she may live past five. Henrietta did so but eventually she began to show signs of age and had some health problems as she became old. She developed a lump on her neck so I took her to the vet. I'm sure the vet thought me quite mad – a chicken in the vet's surgery. *"I'll just wring her neck for you"*, she said.

Not our Henrietta. I took her home and gave her the same hands-on treatment that I had been giving people for some years. She was old and had a tumour so she was not going to recover. However, she did seem to become happier, more comfortable and continued to enjoy sitting in a dust bath in the sun for a few weeks. Then one morning when I went to open the chicken hut I looked at her and I knew her time had come. It was a dry, sunny day so I lifted her off the roost and sat with her on my knee, meditating and focussing energy as best I could. She settled. She was content and she died. She was laid to rest in the orchard. She had given me a rare parting gift, peacefully sharing her last few moments on this earth with me.

With a lot of hard digging we set the market garden project in motion. In reality it was a pipe dream as we had no in depth knowledge of growing vegetables for commercial gain. We set up three large polytunnels, built a fifty foot long fruit cage for a variety of soft fruit and dug great long strip beds for such things as potatoes and the brassica family. I met someone who had mountains of horse manure on his farm that he allowed me to collect in my pickup truck in exchange for doing odd minor jobs around the farm.

It was all great fun and it was very rewarding to see the land blossoming under our guidance. Commercially it was a disaster. I was also trying to find building work to keep us going. There was some, and I worked for some very good clients, but with the economic downturn becoming a recession and not much building work around, we ended up with the market garden going bust. I needed good cash flow. Reluctantly I had to look for a job. I found myself working at the local psychiatric hospital in Lochgilphead, a half hour drive from Tayness. What I saw shook me. I had always had an interest in mental health since doing voluntary work with MIND back in my time in Hemel Hempstead. This was very different. I was working as a nursing assistant, which I could do even though I had no qualification in the field. One reason I took that job was because I believed it was a way I could really help people who were having a rough time in life.

Without doubt it is a tough profession to work in. However well intentioned one is on entry, it can grind you down and of course any institution tends to have its own inertia and debilitating energy. I believe that all the front line nursing staff should have a periodic paid sabbatical. That doesn't happen. So the system gets to people and I saw terrible abuse, both physical and emotional, inflicted on the patients by some staff.

I was assigned to a long term ward where the inmates had been there for as long as thirty-five years in some cases. My prime role was to spend a lot of time with one lovely old gentleman who was deemed to be a 'major management problem'. Oh such 'institution speak'; how I hated it, and I still do. This dear old boy, Malcolm, had been in the hospital over thirty years. He was diagnosed as paranoid schizophrenic though, as he frequently told me, he was now fully cured!

I loved him dearly from the start. How could I not? He was intelligent, had a sense of humour and he was a rascal. I remember once he pilfered my wallet from my jacket, which was hanging in the staff cupboard. He grinned happily and just handed it back when I asked him for it. On my first day I took him for a walk in the grounds and on our return he asked for paper and pencil to write. He loved writing great long, unintelligible missives; it kept him occupied for hours. Suddenly the senior nurse on the ward came rushing angrily out of his office and snatched the paper away from Malcolm. *"He only gets it if he has behaved well."*

What had he done? Well, he had probably wet the bed as usual the night before and he did have some pretty repulsive anal habits but hey, he was a sick old man. In a way these transgressions were the only way he could hit back against a very repressive and punitive regime. I had to tread warily but I continued to give him as much love and attention as I could in a way I thought was right. But by not toeing the line I built up trouble for myself.

Then there was a lady, not as old as Malcolm but she had been in the hospital over fifteen years. She solemnly assured me that she had not had a wink of sleep in those fifteen years. Mind you, when I was on night duty and I looked in on her, she was usually snoring soundly though she often had to be woken and the bed changed as almost uncontrollable incontinence was a constant problem with her. But again things like that were some of the few ways in which the patients could hit back at those staff who mistreated them. Of course there were many caring staff and I do believe that most started out with the best intentions but after a while the system ground them down. Even the charge nurse who had snatched the paper from Malcolm's hands had a good heart beneath the often cruel behaviour.

He was around my age and I think he found it difficult that he was managing me and finding that I did not accept 'the party line' and that I had my own approach to the patients. I have always been my own man. But I remember one time on a quiet evening shift when I played a prank on him. I piled a few things on his desk, including several (unused) urine bottles. He came hurtling out of his office, breathing fire when he discovered them but he did see the funny side. I think it broke the ice a little. Sadly he died, very young, shortly after I left the hospital. I should not cast blame on those I saw behaving in a way I disapproved of. Perhaps then I was not as understanding as I should have been. In hindsight I see more clearly what that sort of environment does to the best intentioned people. After a while Mary too got work at the hospital in the occupational therapy department. Most of the staff she worked with had a more enlightened attitude. In addition they saw each patient for but an hour or two at a time and it was different to the hands-on ward situation. Nevertheless it was hard for us to support each other while both working there.

Thank goodness that at the end of each day I drove back to the tranquillity of our wee glen. I started at the hospital in spring so as I drove home and up the last 150 yard approach to the house I was greeted by a huge, yellow swathe of daffodils - such balm to my soul.

I was at the hospital for three years, which were some of the hardest I have ever experienced in a job. I saw human death for the first time. Statistically it is true that most people die at night when their energy levels are naturally low. As a nursing assistant I was often called on during night shifts to take a new body to the mortuary. A call would come through instructing me to go to the ward where someone had died; usually a geriatric ward. By the time I arrived, together with a second nursing assistant, the body would have been washed, shrouded and labelled. We put it on a trolley and wheeled it through the grounds to the mortuary.

One old man on my ward died with me at his bedside. I was assisting the senior nurse on the ward and we knew that he was near the end. Suddenly I could feel his spirit starting to disconnect from his body. I called the nurse who immediately went into 'action – we have to save him mode'. Now don't get me wrong, of course our job was to try and keep him alive. Yet so often this is done when in reality there is no hope. This will be pretty controversial but I feel that maybe there comes a point where more good can be done by accepting the inevitable; by sitting with the person and holding their hand even if they are unconscious; simply witnessing and truly 'being' with their passing. If one believes that there is nothing after death, the actual act of dying is not significant, though one might still want to ease someone's passing. For me it is an event of much greater significance. Unless someone dies alone, I believe it is a chance to help them move peacefully to another dimension. Desperately trying to hold me here when my time comes is certainly not how I want to be treated.

What is death? There was such a subtle yet huge change in the energy in the room and in his physical body at the moment of his passing. It was like a sigh of relief – he had been very ill and in pain. There was also a sense of supreme peace. Preparing his body to go to the mortuary was a precious and privileged work. Many people say that at and immediately after death there is a palpable feeling of profound peace in the room.

Though it was stressful in the hospital I enjoyed the actual work and the contact with the patients. Sometimes I sat and held the hand of some old lady or gent and I know they felt something of what I was trying to transmit in healing energy. Some even told me so. I worked on several wards over the three years, including intensive care, the admission ward and the alcohol treatment unit. I cared for a potential suicide who eventually achieved his ambition when he hanged himself. I looked after a couple of murderers who were deemed criminally insane. Despite their crimes they were two of the most sensitive people I knew there and I got on very well with both of them. Some people think that someone who is hyper sensitive can be the person to go off the rails most seriously.

I went on regular visits to the monastery during this time and so I was able to share some of what I was going through with senior monks to help me get a perspective and try and see what the deeper spiritual aspects of the experience might be for me. I was troubled by the behaviour I saw from the staff but Buddhists say that everything bad comes from twisted love; there are bad acts but not bad people. I like the notion of twisted love because when you look deeply at that, it throws a different light on the things many people do.

How far do we take that? If we are going to look at people with such a perspective then even the most hideous criminal must be included. Could we view someone like Adolf Hitler in that way? There is a film about the final few days in his bunker in Berlin at the end of the Second World War. He is seen as a monster yet he was also a human being. The film is controversial but it gave me a very different view of him. He did so many appalling things and yet.....he was also capable of gentleness and generosity, especially with children and animals. When we cast such people aside as monsters, which is often said of him, we are putting them in a different bracket to ourselves. We are denying that we all have the potential for doing great harm. I do not say this in the sense that we are inherently flawed and must be saved. I do not believe that. But I have seen some horrible possibilities in me. Fortunately I have not allowed them to take control though I have come closer than I would have liked and I have treated some people very badly.

I was being pulled in many directions. The hospital was tough. Finances were a nightmare. The seeds of the eventual failure of our marriage were already being sown. At times I wondered if I should be living a monastic life. My healing gift was finding more expression, mainly with our animals. My visits to the monastery were usually extremely confronting and painful and a huge emotional drain. Coming back to the cottage was wonderful and I felt great peace there. It may sound as if life was all bad but not at all. There is beauty and joy in everything if we seek it. In all these challenging situations there was also love and beauty. The Phoenix is consumed in the fire before arising again. But there was certainly a lot of fire around just then.

On retreat again at the monastery, I was transported back to the English Civil War. Hiding behind a tree I watched as a man came towards me. Just behind him was a woman. He approached the tree, turned his back and leant against the huge trunk. Carefully, silently I coiled ready to spring out with a knife in my hands. I jumped around the tree, grabbed him from behind and tore his throat out with my knife. The woman screamed, ran towards us and I dropped the body and fled. I could feel the blood on my hands. I could smell his flesh and the sensation of my knife ripping though flesh as if through a lump of cheese.

I awoke, sweating and shaking. So it was just a dream? No; I believe it was a past life experience. Why was it that and why did it happen? Such things can come at any time. There was a quality about it that set it apart from being a dream, imagination or hallucination. I had not had any conversation or read anything about this era. There was nothing I was aware of that would have triggered it. Nothing had occurred that my night dream might just be processing.

The notion of living more than one life on this earthly plane is something many people believe, though just as many do not. The traditional Hindu idea of reincarnation is that we simply shed one body at death and assume another, going through cycles on the earth till we reach an enlightened state when we may choose not to return here. This life is likened to being in a spiritual school from which we will graduate. The Buddhist idea differs a little. They talk about rebirth. In this process we do not return as the same soul. Our consciousness may be likened to being made of strands, rather like the individual strands that make up a thick rope. Some aspects of us may fulfil their karma and not return, while other parts of us do. Part of our being returns. I find it very hard to grasp this concept but for me the basic notion that we may in some way come back here after death is acceptable.

Why should we experience glimpses of a past life? Why did I have that vision? To this day I am not sure. Maybe it was to show me that I had done bad things in my past; just a reminder to keep my ego in check. Being on a spiritual path does not make me a special person. The pursuit of my healing vocation enables me to offer something very special to my fellow beings. I am a channel and I have to remember that I do this work despite all my flaws and imperfections, which are numerous. Perhaps it was to show me that I still have much karma to work though.

What is karma then? It is not a kind of divine punishment, which is the mistaken understanding many westerners have. Karma is simply cause and effect. What goes round comes around. There is a fundamental universal law that whatever we do will bring a corresponding return. We do good actions so we reap good in return. Bad actions bring similar returns. If there is any judgement, it is our own judgement on ourselves, rather than one imposed by an external deity. Our purpose in this life is to learn our lessons and change how we behave. I have also come to see that we have to accept absolutely every single thing that happens. Perhaps I have lived a reasonable life in this present incarnation. Yet still some tough things have happened so maybe I am still paying back for that past murder or other actions. I simply do not know why I had the experience. I have learnt to accept what happens without necessarily trying to understand what is behind it. It has happened. There is a lesson therein, though I may not understand the lesson at the time. By learning to accept all that happens to me, I can often more readily see the lesson. That acceptance also brings peace. We create huge tension by railing against what life has done to us. When we learn to accept, the tension melts away.

I asked to speak to one of the senior monks about what had happened. He allowed me to talk through all I had seen and felt. He did not tell me that it was real or that it was not. That was not his job because that would have planted in my head his understanding, not mine. However, what he did say, and the feeling I had as I shared it with him, left me feeling in no doubt about the nature of the vision. That was probably nearly twenty years ago yet it is as vivid now as if it happened yesterday.

Getting back to the cottage after my monastic retreats was like a holiday, at least emotionally. I think that each time I returned, Mary wondered how I would be, what new ideas would be filling my head. I'm not sure what lessons there were for her in what I was doing and what she saw in my pursuit of my spiritual practice. It was a challenge for her. Perhaps I was there to shake her up, as she was there to help me keep a balanced perspective. Sharing your life with someone is not easy but helping one another to grow is part of that.

Every time I went to Throssel Hole, it seemed that I was confronted with more and harder lessons. Still, it was my choice. By now I had left my job at the hospital. I was nearly fifty years old with considerable life experience yet I did not feel respected or valued for what I could offer. I felt powerless as an unqualified nursing assistant and I could not fit in with the institutional culture in the place. I'd had the offer of some building work so I took the plunge and went back to something I knew. It paid off because a steady flow of work came in and before long I had re-established my business on a very sound footing.

Sharing the lives of the patients in the hospital gave me a real insight into the extent that we choose, on a very subtle level, everything that happens to us. So someone in the grip of paranoid schizophrenia is responsible for their illness? They have chosen to be ill? That sounds pretty cruel and lacking in compassion. Mind you, if I say that then I include myself in it. There are things I do, behaviour patterns I hold on to, beliefs I espouse which no longer serve me. Yet I do not let them go.

Again if it is part of the karmic process, then for sure we have chosen it. I saw so many patients acting out the role to which they had been assigned. Many were admitted to the intake ward in emergency situations. A lot were suffering drug-induced psychosis. Then the hospital machinery was set in motion. They were diagnosed and put into a box; labelled with an illness that had a name and a list of accompanying symptoms and behaviour patterns. A self-fulfilling prophesy was set in motion and before long they were behaving as was expected of their diagnosed illness. Then they were given more of the medication deemed right for that illness. But worse was the way in which they were treated. Everything they did and said was interpreted as if they were the label they had been given. So of course they began to be more schizophrenic or whatever they were supposed to be. An experiment was carried out once with students training as psychiatric nurses. They were each assigned to a psychiatric ward as a patient without the staff knowing that they were in fact students. The staff treated them according to the 'diagnoses' which they had been given. Within a frighteningly short time, each student began to exhibit many of the symptoms and behaviour patterns of their supposed illness. What choice were they making?

There are certainly people who are obviously already in the grip of a severe illness before becoming part of the mental health sausage machine. But even many of these then go on to fulfil the role assigned to them. I witnessed people who were severely ill, in the sense that they had been diagnosed with manic depression or paranoid schizophrenia. Yet if I observed them carefully I could see them playing games and manipulating the staff in a way that suggested they knew full well what they were doing. However, most people would say that someone in the grip of severe mental illness cannot be blamed for anything. Maybe and maybe not…..I now view things differently to the way I did. I believe we must take responsibility for all that we do, even if we feel forced into situations where we act uncharacteristically. I look back on things I have done that I regret. I tell myself that the pressure of my circumstances was my excuse. That is not so. I chose to act in that way.

The next question might be to ask why the patients do not take control and do their best to get out of the system. Unfortunately the chemical straitjacket which is the basis of modern psychiatric care takes people over. There may also be something else at work. There is a story about an old man sitting on the veranda of his house with his dog lying next to him. A neighbour walks past each day and the dog is always whimpering, apparently in pain. One day the neighbour asks the man what is wrong with the dog. "He is lying on a nail."

"So why doesn't he move?" asks the neighbour. "Well," replies the old man, "it is not hurting him enough."

This story makes me think of the lady, Margaret who used to tell me she had not slept a wink during her fifteen years in hospital. Without going into the details of her situation and the family she had 'on the outside', she could have left the hospital with somewhere to go. She chose not to and I really mean 'chose not to'. While on the ward her incontinence was almost continuous – quite literally. It was part of her illness, according to the staff and to her, and it kept her in. However, there were several occasions when I took her for a little outing to a café in town. There was not a hint of incontinence for the whole outing. Yet the moment we stepped back into the ward she flooded the place again.

There is always some payback in every behaviour pattern we engage in. If the payback outweighs the pain we will continue to engage in it. Often we are not aware of the payback. That is why we often say things like *"I don't know why I keep on doing it."* But we do keep on and somewhere there is a good reason. I know I do that.

It had been a long hard few years and when I was offered the chance to visit India on a Buddhist pilgrimage I jumped at the opportunity.

Chapter 6: A Buddhist Pilgrimage

The plane was approaching New Delhi in India. The cabin monitor screen showed the little cartoon plane steadily reducing the mileage to the destination. Then the mileage started to increase. Well, perhaps we were just circling more widely prior to landing. But the distance was increasing quite a lot. Strange, I thought. Then there was an announcement to say that we were diverting to Mumbai, which had changed its name from Bombay three years previously. Our eventual landing in Mumbai added nearly a couple of hours to the flight. Apparently there were air pollution problems over Delhi due to the unseasonable weather causing excessive burning of dung fires. I'm not quite sure why Swissair's navigation systems could not cope but neither could the systems aboard another ten-odd aircraft that were also diverted.

Mumbai was total chaos, with around 4000 extra passengers dumped in the airport in a short space of time. What a scene! There were people just everywhere. It wasn't even worth trying to find a comfortable seat. The passengers from each plane were marshalled into their own area to try and keep them together. Mind you, that didn't work for long as everyone made it their first priority to try and find some comfort. So while the poor exhausted airline representative was trying to keep order, people kept slipping away to 'do their own thing.'

It was January 1998 and having left behind a cold UK winter, I was wearing warm clothing, including heavy, lined walking trousers. It was winter in Mumbai too, but winter in Mumbai is just a trifle warmer than the UK – pretty humid and pushing around thirty centigrade. I had made the mistake of not having a change of clothes in a cabin bag and they would not unload our hold bags. You see, our destination on the ticket was New Delhi. So as far as the authorities were concerned we were not officially in India. Therefore no baggage could be offloaded. Oh the sweet joy of Indian bureaucracy. It is like a great gigantic sleepy dinosaur. It cannot be moved. It has its own unintelligible regulations and that is that.

We had landed in the very early hours of the morning and it took about three hours before any sanity prevailed. I was absolutely exhausted but it was also amusing watching the circus all around. The airline representatives were waving their arms trying to direct their passengers; the passengers who were not flat on their backs were getting hotter under the collar and shouting to no avail; there was nothing in the way of drinks or snacks available and we were all stinking hot.

The problem for the airlines was that finding accommodation in the city for an extra 4000-plus passengers was proving difficult. That is what they had to do. It would be at least ten or twelve hours before flights could be resumed so they were obliged to find us somewhere to rest. I was with two women friends and our plane load was one of the last to be sorted out. Getting out to the buses they arranged was a carefully controlled operation. We thought that once outside the terminal building we might be able find some vendors from whom we could get drinks or a bite to eat as everything in the airport was closed at that late hour. No such luck because as we were not officially in India, it was forbidden to stray from a narrow corridor between the exit doors and the bus.

By then I was so hot and wet with sweat I ceased to even worry about it. We arrived at a smart hotel and I was put in a room with two other male passengers. By that time the whole experience was generating a great camaraderie amongst us all. We didn't know each other but it was fine and we had no inhibitions left. We were hot and sticky and all of us were over-dressed in our heavy European winter gear. We just stripped off, showered and fell naked on the beds to try to snatch a little sleep. Just before I slept I made a phone call home to my wife, courtesy of Swissair. She was out so I left a short message.

It hardly seemed like a couple of hours had passed when we were roused, offered breakfast and told that they would take us back to the plane to resume our flight to Delhi. Well, the experience would make for a good traveller's tale and I wasn't too bothered. We jumped out of the bus at the airport and got aboard. At least back on board there was good air conditioning, which was welcome after another hot bus ride.

Not long till take off. We waited and waited.....it seemed to be taking a long time for the crew to get ready for action. Then they delivered the news. There was a technical fault with the plane. We would have to get off again and wait for repairs. I'm not sure exactly what it was but a part had to be flown out from Switzerland which would cause us a twenty-four hour delay. They say that fact is stranger than fiction. It is probably hard to believe this really happened but it did.

So off we went again. This time Swissair put us in a five star luxury hotel, part of the Oberoi chain. And believe me, five star luxury in India is something special. By then we were all pretty dishevelled and scruffy but the hotel staff greeted us as if we were royalty. My room was on the top floor, at least twenty storeys up, with stunning views over Mumbai. On this second night I was rested enough to appreciate the surroundings and I had a room to myself. I slept sweetly and awoke to the most sumptuous breakfast you could possibly imagine. I was ushered into a large dining room with great picture windows and beautiful ocean views. The spread of food was like a luxury banquet that you see in a movie. There was a complete range of both English and Indian cuisine, breads, tea, coffee and exotic fruit and juices such as mango and guava. The morning was rather more leisurely than the previous day and after a good night's rest I was able to appreciate the view and the food. I knew we would get to New Delhi sometime but I was happily enjoying this luxury, which would not be repeated during the rest of the trip.

Back to the aircraft again, ready for take off......and we did finally. A huge cheer went up from the passengers, to the smiles of the cabin crew, and we were Delhi bound at last. The only letdown in New Delhi was the accommodation. We were travelling budget style and where we stayed was not a patch on the Oberoi but our pilgrimage was beginning at last.

Both my friends were Buddhists, following one of the Tibetan traditions. Janet had invited me to join her and Joan some months before. I had met Janet when I was building in Bristol. She was a client and she was a part of the Tibetan Buddhist group that I got to know. She was just a year older than I was and had led a very interesting life. She was a bustling kind of person, very organised and sometimes a little impatient, but she had a heart of gold and I think she felt towards me like a big sister. Our other companion Joan was a friend of Janet's. She was going through a very challenging time. She had been married for some years but had been very unhappy. What she had realised was that she was lesbian by sexual orientation. 'Coming out' had been very difficult but she was in a relationship with another woman, whom I later met. They were very much in love and made a lovely couple but it was not easy. She felt that certain members of the Buddhist community did not accept her. Janet did not feel that was quite right but anyway she thought that coming on a pilgrimage might help her to accept herself and find the strength to simply be what she was.

We were an amusing trio. Janet was the arch organiser with experience of India and the Buddhist trail. Joan was new to this kind of travel and new to such an exotic country. But though somewhat overawed by many things she coped very well with the flood of new impressions and a potentially frightening event that occurred later in the trip. As for me…..well I could offer male energy when it was helpful though the two of them were no soft touch. I liked wandering off on my own, which is the style in which I have always travelled. I think they felt they needed to keep an eye on me.

The first place we were headed for was Varanasi, which was where Gautama the Buddha had begun his teaching. We had booked a rail ticket back in the UK from Delhi to Varanasi so having missed it due to the delays we negotiated another one. Indian railways are quite splendid. They are incredibly cheap, at least for a westerner. Their booking system is very efficient. You book a ticket for a specific train and they all have names such as the Farkka Express. I still have one of my tickets and across the top is printed 'Happy Journey'! You book the carriage and the seat number. Of course you can reserve train seats here too in the UK but that is optional. In India it is all part of the deal except on the cheapest class. If you are taking an overnight sleeper, the ticket includes some bedding and breakfast too. When you get aboard, everything is as you have booked.

Now efficiency applies to the booking but the timetable is a little different. You arrive at the station for the scheduled time and you wait and you wait. That is where the adventure begins. You see, the advertised platform for your departure is almost certainly not where the train will leave from. Since it is almost guaranteed there will be quite a delay from the supposed departure time, sitting on the platform with hundreds of other passengers, complete with kids, mountains of luggage and probably livestock in cages is guaranteed to be a bit stressful. Nevertheless it is an opportunity to chat with people as they are always interested in any foreigners. Where you come from and what you do for a living are usually the first two questions you have to answer.

It is worth finding and paying a small amount to use one of the waiting rooms, which usually have a charpoy to lie on, which is a basic bed made of woven matting. But the trick is that you still need to keep a lookout for when your train is leaving and from which platform as that frequently changes right up until the last minute. We did this and I was delegated to watch out for the train. So Janet and Joan rested up. I dozed a bit but not too deeply as I had to keep going out to check on platform information. Fortunately New Delhi was a big enough station for much of the information to be in English. That did not apply to some of the smaller stations, as we found out later.

The train pulled in and we battled our way to our sleeper compartment.

With a fifteen hour overnight trip to Varanasi Junction, the few extra rupees for the sleeper were well worth it. It also guaranteed that our fellow travellers would be slightly wealthier Indians, probably better educated and so able to speak English. This proved to be so, which made for an interesting couple of hours before we all bedded down for the night. They were delightful people - a married couple and a single lady. They were fascinated to hear about our journey and our reasons for doing it. The majority of Indians are Hindu although there are quite a lot of Muslims in parts of the country. Hindus in particular are very respectful of Gautama the Buddha although many of them tend to view him as a renegade Hindu and Buddhism as almost being a sub branch of Hinduism.

They also gave us useful tips on how to beat the wiles of the thieves who would prowl the carriages after dark. The first was to put our shoes beside us on the sleeping bunk, or under our pillows. The second was to secure our bags in some way by tying them to something in the compartment so that trying to take them would cause a noise and wake us.

We pulled down the hinged sleeping bunks and with the ladies on the upper tiers, we all bedded down. Going out to the toilet during the night was tricky as you had to pick your way over sleeping bodies sprawled all over the passageway. Come morning we were greeted with hot chai and breakfast. We had slept well. Indian trains chug along steadily at a fairly modest speed and the gentle swaying of the carriages was conducive to a good night's rest. The only thing about the carriages is that the windows are low down and do not stretch the full height of the side of the carriage as we are used to. So you have to bend down to look outside, which creates a slightly enclosed feeling.

Most carriages had two types of toilets – one western and one Indian. The Indian one consists of a hole in the floor with two slightly upraised, foot-sized stands. You stand on these and squat or, if you are a gentleman, you stand upright facing the hole. You can see the tracks rumbling past through the hole. It may sound disconcerting but it is usually a lot cleaner than the western-style one next door. Except for more expensive hotels, the Indian toilet is naturally all you will find, so you soon get used to them.

For some reason we decided to disembark from the train a few stops short of Varanasi Junction. I think it was just a whim and we fancied taking a look at a small place on the way. It really was a small place – a one horse town. Stepping off the train onto a dusty single platform more or less in the middle of the place was rather like the images you see in western movies where the hero gets off the train and is left standing in the middle of nowhere with his bag on the floor, waiting for the bad guys to see him. It felt just like that. The platform was just a strip of concrete in the middle of a street. There didn't appear to be any infrastructure at all. We tried to find somewhere to check in and stay a night. Eventually we came across a real dive. No one anywhere seemed to have more than half a dozen words of English at best so I used my sign language and took over as the 'boss'. It did feel like a situation in which I might have to play the role of protector. I have always felt very safe in India, perhaps because of the old colonial connection. Nevertheless we were well off the beaten track in tourist terms so I wanted to be sure we were not seen as a soft touch.

We reckoned the best thing was to take just one room and stay together. In the end it didn't seem like a very good idea. There was nothing much to see. Food was not easy to find – at least not what we felt was safe enough to eat. Both Janet and Joan were very wary of what they ate, which was probably wise, though I was prepared to chance things. We rested up a bit in the room but after a frustrating afternoon, we decided to check out and continue the journey to Varanasi. Our host was a little put out but he had at least earned a night's lodging money for just a few hours' stay.

Now, how to get to Varanasi? There didn't seem to be any taxis around. The best way was going to be by tuk-tuk, the little three-wheeled scooters with the cab on the back. Some are designed to seat four passengers but three plus three large rucksacks was a squeeze. We found one, did the usual haggling and set the price before leaving. It seemed like it was going to be about an hour's drive. Boy, was that a tough hour. The road was clogged with trucks belching out filthy fumes. With the tuk-tuk being open-sided, we got the lot. Hanging on ourselves and making sure we didn't lose any luggage was tricky. Of course the general rule of the road in India is that 'might is right'. The little fish give way to the big fish. Other than a rickshaw, the tuk-tuk is near the bottom of the pecking order. At times I did wonder if we would get to Varanasi in one piece. Mind you, it was exhilarating at the same time, though I'm not sure the other two felt the same. Being open and nearer to the ground than in a car or bus, there was a real sensation of speed as the driver dodged between trucks, waving and gesticulating at every other driver. You can't help but be amused at Indian driving and hairy though it is, I was never involved in an accident.

As soon as we reached the area around Varanasi the atmosphere changed. It is a wonderful place. Once known as Benares, it is on the banks of the Ganges and is reckoned by many to be the spiritual capital of India. In actual fact we skirted Varanasi itself, heading for Singhpur, as on the outskirts of this little village is Sarnath, the deer park where Buddha gave his first teaching.

Buddha was born into a royal family and, according to legend, a prediction was made that he would become a great spiritual leader. His father was determined that Buddha would be a king and so he sheltered him in the palace and ensured that he saw no common people nor signs of human suffering, illness, old age or death. Buddha was in his twenties when he discovered the reality of human existence

Then he left his father's kingdom and spent many years seeking spiritual enlightenment. During this time, together with five friends he followed many austere practices, as was common among the yogis of his time (and still is to this day). However, he came to believe that the way to enlightenment was not to punish the body so he left the friends in whose company he was following these austerities. They derided him for being a failure but he persisted and found enlightenment sitting under the famous bodhi tree at Bodh Gaya. He then wandered to Sarnath and there his five old friends met him again. At first they were contemptuous of him till he began to teach them what he had experienced and come to see. They understood immediately; they were enlightened and they dedicated themselves to being his followers. Thus the first Buddhist sangha, or community, was founded.

Varanasi is beautiful but it is a big and busy city. Singhpur is small and there is a peace there that is beyond description. We checked into a government-run guest house – cheap, secure and fairly clean. Wandering out into the streets of Singhpur was a revelation for me. In half an hour you can walk around it and out the other side. There are many schools or traditions of Buddhism. It is a religion that spread into Tibet, China, Japan, and through places such as Thailand, Myanmar (once Burma), Sri Lanka and other Asian countries. It adapted to the culture of each country. There are temples in Singhpur connected to most of the major Buddhist traditions. Architecturally this makes for a fascinating and colourful mix as each temple is built in the style of the country which it represents. Within each temple, the altars, decorations and types of iconography also reflect the different traditions. Some of them have accommodation attached as well.

Each of us had come on our personal pilgrimage though we were travelling together. This was now time for us to explore individually in the way that we each wished to. My particular tradition was not represented directly but I found a Japanese temple where I felt at home. I rested up for a day to get over the rigours of the journey and then I followed my personal practice and routine for the time we were there.

I love to rise early and catch the day's first energy. I slipped into that routine, rising quietly and going out into the misty streets at around six. I went into my chosen temple to meditate for a while. Although it was part of a Japanese Buddhist school, it was far more ornate inside than the Zen monastery I went to in the UK. This latter was in the Soto Zen tradition known for its simple, even austere decoration and iconography. The one I went to in Singhpur was much more lavish. I had with me a little folding meditation stool, easily carried in my pack. My knees could not cope with sitting in a lotus position so I preferred a small low stool, about six inches high, on which I sat with my knees folded back under me. It was still, cool and blissfully silent at that hour. The silence externally helped me to find the silence internally.

By the time I left the temple, life was stirring. Though it was a tiny village there were many tourists during the day, though very few stopped overnight. Consequently there were quite a lot of vendors with souvenir and food stalls. The majority slept beneath their stalls so they were stirring sleepily and wandering over to the public water pumps to douse themselves with cold water from head to toe. No matter the poor conditions in which they might be living, Indians are very particular about washing. When they do so at a public pump, they will tie their lungi up tight and get right under the pump or use a bucket. The lungi gets washed as they do.

There were few places to eat in the village and at that hour only a couple were open for breakfast. I love to get to know the local people when I travel and I find the best way is to frequent the same place for a few days. Just a few minutes from my temple was a little café that was just opening at the time I was ready for food. Quite often the proprietor was still getting organised while I sat at one of his tables. When he was ready he would come over with a cheerful grin. He had a young assistant but his job was the general skivvying. He was not up to taking my order. I had tried to learn a few words of Hindi though it is a difficult language. The thing is that generally the locals prefer to try out their English so it was hard to use my few phrases. The menu was not large but a milk coffee (as he called it) and fried eggs were a great start to my day. He got to know what I wanted each morning, which was pretty much the same. I have a lovely photo of him posing proudly in the entrance to his café. I love taking pictures but I am always very discreet when people are in the frame. If I am close up I will ask their permission. I have seldom found many object but it is respectful to be this way.

In the deer park, on the spot where Buddha delivered his first sermon is the huge Dhamek stupa. A stupa simply means a pile. It may be quite small, just a couple of feet in height, and sometimes it houses the relics of a Buddhist saint. The Dhamek stupa is built of brick atop stone reaching up nearly 130 feet and standing over ninety feet in diameter. Approaching as it rears up in the twilight mist of dawn is awe inspiring. I was deeply committed to my practice at that time and the knowledge that Gautama the Buddha had sat at that very place to deliver his first sermon touched me deeply. It is traditional to circumambulate such a large stupa counting the beads of a mala or rosary, maybe reciting a scripture or chanting. This I used to do and on one particular morning I finished counting the beads and stopped just at the same moment as an old man who was doing the same. We were right next to each other and for a moment we locked our gaze and smiled. Then we went our separate ways. I love those moments of two souls meeting.

Little is left in the deer park of the many structures and temples dating back two and a half thousand years, except for ruins. But these ooze history and magic. One early morning as I wandered from the Dhamek stupa deeper into the park I came across a group of Tibetan practitioners sitting in a circle around a tier of candles. Robed and shaven-headed monks sat at the front reciting scriptures with lay disciples around them. Except for the modern dress of the lay people it could have been a scene from antiquity, with mist swirling and just a half light that gave the surrounding ruins a ghost-like quality.

Then I met young Sanjay, or at least first I met his dad. I was strolling on the edge of the village one afternoon when this old man walked past me. He stopped to chat, speaking reasonable English. He invited me to his home where he said that his son would love to meet me. That was enough for me so I followed him along the track, perhaps a ten minute walk into the countryside to a cluster of mud- and brick-built houses making up a little farm. The inner courtyard was about a hundred feet on each side of a square. Around this were buildings that housed both people and livestock, mainly cattle, chickens and a couple of buffalo. Stacked against the walls were great piles of red building bricks. Several shiny-eyed and mischievous little boys of around eight or nine were playing. Although they had of course seen many westerners in the village, I was probably the first who had been to their farm. They were a cross between shy and curious and they were fun.

In one corner of the courtyard was a well and of course the obligatory cows mooched around without restriction. The cow is a sacred beast in India. It cannot be slaughtered nor is it manhandled and it is allowed to roam freely wherever it wishes. They can be found in the middle of busy roads with the traffic desperately weaving a way around them. They will happily wander along railway platforms, anywhere they can access, so here in the yard they were king.

The old man was charming. His English was limited but he had a radiant smile. He insisted that I have hot spiced masala chai. This became a ritual each time I went there. His son, who was around twenty, spoke excellent English and he told me proudly that he was a guide and interpreter for the many tourists who visited. Sanjay was charming and apart from the youngsters, there were two or three other older boys who were around his age.

He insisted on adopting me and he became my self-appointed guide for the few days I had left in Singhpur. He was quite a serious young man and he took his duties as a guide very seriously. Just at that time there were not a lot of visitors to engage his services so he was delighted to escort me around. He neither wanted nor expected any money. He was just glad to have made a friend and to be keeping busy. I suspect too that it gave him some kudos to be showing off his new English friend and to be the main one in the family who could actually talk to me. Mind you, I had fun with all the boys though we could not share actual words.

As I have often found with untravelled and unsophisticated people in places like India, it is very hard to get across to them how we live in the west. They see us all as being super wealthy. Of course in comparison we are. But it is near impossible to explain that our wealth is relative. I tried to explain this to Sanjay. I gave him the example of the trekking sandals that I was wearing, telling him what they cost in rupees. To him this was a fantastic amount of money, especially for a mere pair of sandals which surely did not appear to him to be very special. Yet still he found it impossible to really grasp the concepts I was sharing. We had long discussions and I endeavoured to point out that despite the obvious poverty in India, there are many precious things there that we have lost. The general pace of life is one: even in the city conurbations it is quite different to that in the west. At least it was then.

The other great thing is the sense of family, which is still so strong in Indian culture. To a large extent that has been lost here. Over there, the extended family is very strong and old people are cared for within the embrace of the family. There was no way Sanjay's dad would be in any kind of institution in a few years. They don't exist anyway, but he would live out his days on the farm, sipping masala chai, sitting on a charpoy in the sun. But still so many people there, especially the younger ones, hanker after what they see as our desirable material lifestyle. Mind you, there are downsides. The caste system in India is medieval and very repressive. The place of women is very much one of being second class beings. The birth of a son is celebrated but not that of a daughter. Nevertheless I endeavoured to get him to see the good things he did have, but not with much success.

When I left Singhpur, Sanjay insisted on exchanging addresses. I was a little hesitant at first because often the joy of such a friendship does not survive the reality of thousands of miles of separation and the return to the west for the traveller such as me. We did swap addresses, however, and in fact I felt it right to send him a letter from Scotland. Eventually I received a reply in which he told me that his parents had arranged a marriage for him. I wrote back congratulating him and did get one more letter.

I would happily have stayed much longer in the village. But there were other places we wanted to visit before flying home and Janet was beginning to champ at the bit, as was her wont. So we set about booking a rail ticket from Varanasi to Gaya. Our next pilgrimage destination was actually Bodh Gaya. We needed to get the train to Gaya Junction and then take a short taxi ride on to Bodh Gaya. Compared to Singhpur it was a veritable metropolis. Actually I was quite sad to leave Sanjay and his friends, my host at the café where I took my daily breakfast, and a couple of shopkeepers with whom I had spent time choosing and haggling over two saris for my wife.

There was a sense of peace permeating the whole area. Was it because it was there that the Buddha had set in motion the Wheel of the Dharma (Truth) with that first teaching delivered to his old friends? Was it also because of the energy imprint left by so many thousands, maybe millions, of pilgrims across two millennia? Was it the love I was shown by Sanjay and his family, even by my breakfast host in his own way? All I know was that I left feeling different.

Janet had an extensive Buddhist network. She was a wonderful networker anyway. She had organised some accommodation for us ahead of reaching Bodh Gaya. It was a short train journey to Gaya Junction and there we found a taxi to take us to Bodh Gaya. We were staying at a place about fifteen minutes walk outside of the town – the International Meditation Centre. It was run by a monk of the Theravadan tradition. This tradition is found predominantly in South and Southeast Asia. It is considered to be closest to the original Buddhist tradition of all those now practised. The Centre seemed to be a cross between accommodation and a place where people could spend some time on retreat.

The monk who greeted us wore thick-rimmed spectacles and he had a long, slightly mournful face. The first thing he was very insistent on was that we filled in all the necessary documents as the condition of staying there; more Indian bureaucracy. I must say that this all made him seem quite severe but in fact once this was done he relaxed and made us feel very welcome. He spoke reasonable English and warned us very firmly that we should not walk back from the town to the Centre after dark. We were in the state of Bihar, which was pretty lawless at the best of times. There was also serious political unrest with local elections looming and a European visitor had been attacked after dark just a few days before.

What a contrast there was between Bodh Gaya and Singhpur. It was much more of a tourist destination. A huge temple complex had been built around the famous bodhi tree: the Mahabodhi temple. It was said that the current venerated bodhi tree was a descendant of the one from Gautama's time. Shoots from the original tree had been preserved when it was very old and near to dying off. These were then planted so that the tree's longevity was secured. Standing just behind the main temple building, the tree was huge, with great overhanging branches decorated with prayer flags. I was standing looking at it one day, thinking that it would be nice to have a leaf from the tree as a souvenir. Of course you didn't pluck one and there didn't happen to be one lying on the ground. As I turned I saw an old monk who was watching me. He smiled and silently held out his hand and offered me two leaves. A meeting of minds? What a gift it was. I pressed them. I have one to this day and the other I gave as a gift.

For some reason the temple and the town were much more commercialised than Singhpur and the Deer Park. Around the temple, within the grounds were many shrines, stupas and little quiet corners where you could sit and meditate but it was harder to find the peace and tranquillity I had found in Singhpur. Maybe part of the lesson for me was that the peace we seek is in fact inside us. Still, there were some quiet little spots at the side of the temple with small shrines, out of the way of the main throng of visitors.

The bazaar, the shops and the itinerant vendors were brightly coloured and they were just everywhere you walked. I recall one old Tibetan trader from whom I bought something. He had the most wonderful face etched with lines of laughter and age, a rich warm smile and an assortment of jewellery and rings. It was the kind of image you would find in a history book. I knew he would make a fantastic photo. I stepped back, took out my camera and caught his eye. I held the camera for him to see, asking his permission. He smiled and nodded. The photo is absolutely beautiful.

There was a big Tibetan Buddhist community there and we usually ate at a place run by a Tibetan lady and her little boy. The food was excellent and I believe that at one time they were listed in the Lonely Planet guide. She made wonderful momos, which are dumplings made of dough, filled with meat or vegetables. They are most popularly steamed though they may also be fried or cooked in soup. While we were there, the Dali Llama gave some teaching. Janet and Joan were obviously keen to attend and I did so too. It was all in Tibetan and unfortunately the translation devices didn't work well. Still, it was quite an experience to share the energy in the huge marquee with hundreds of Tibetan devotees.

Their whole way of doing things is quite different to what I had seen at the monastery back in England and to how I imagine would be the case in many different religious traditions. Tibetan style teachings go on for hours and hours. There are no official breaks so the people there simply go about their general business while sitting and listening. They brew tea, eat food and chat away even while the llamas (priests) are talking. Even the Dalai Lama himself is not guaranteed total and silent attention.

The walk from town back to the Centre took me through a small cluster of houses on the outskirts of the town. As normal, life is carried out in public. Men were snoozing on charpoys; kids playing; a little girl was having her hair braided and the lice picked out by her mother; people were eating and I just wandered through all the activity. There was one group of four little girls, aged around nine or ten, and I gestured and asked if I might take a picture. They loved the idea and immediately one of them set about marshalling the others into position and they posed proudly, looking very haughty and composed.

A couple of hours by bus from Bodh Gaya is Vulture Peak. Atop this mountain, Buddha delivered many discourses. We planned to go there. On the morning of the trip, we gathered at a point near the Centre in the chilly early light. Needless to say the buses booked for the trip by a group of pilgrims were late but no matter, it was a chance to get to know people. Quite a few were acquaintances of Janet and Joan, including several Tibetan llamas, a couple of whom were going to England later.

There were also other western devotees. Once we got aboard the buses there was a buzz of anticipation. Mountains have always been places where great sages have gone on retreat. Perhaps because they are remote and symbolically they reach heavenward, it is felt that being in the mountains is conducive to finding spiritual wisdom. Not only did the Buddha deliver many discourses there but his disciples spent time there as well. On the long climb to the top there is a cave beside the path where it is said that the Master delivered two especially important teachings. In this same cave, Sariputta, one of his first disciples, sat and attained enlightenment. A few of us stopped in the cave on the way up and held a small ceremony, lighting candles and meditating. The cave was incredibly still and peaceful. It is said that God speaks to us in the silence of our hearts. For me finding the stillness inside is much helped by being in a still place that is steeped in the wisdom of ages. The energy in such places is strong, deep and all pervading. I have felt it too in the Holy Land in the Middle East. I think any place of pilgrimage holds and magnifies the energy of the many devotees who have trod there and one can feel it in the present day.

The panoramic view from the top over a dry and dusty landscape was quite breathtaking. Once there, the group, consisting mainly of Tibetan practitioners, set about organising things for a ceremony of meditation and blessing. Not being familiar with their particular way of doing things, I let them get on with it while I enjoyed the views. Although at a little over 700 metres the peak is not very high, because of the way it rises up with unhindered views in a full 360 degrees it seems much higher.

Sadly as always in that part of India security was an ongoing concern. With dusk falling as we started to make our way down, we were warned not to stray from the path for fear of dacoits, or bandits. Indeed there were armed guards at the top carrying ancient, British Army-issued Lee Enfield rifles, which probably dated back to the Second World War. In a way it was a valuable lesson. It was, again, the reminder that one may be pursuing a spiritual path but one is not isolated from the world around. Everyone was very vigilant in walking right on the path and not straying. Nothing happened and we reached the buses in the pitch black quite unscathed.

Back in Bodh Gaya we had a couple more days to explore some of the many temples. An especially impressive sight was a huge statue of the Buddha sitting in a full lotus position in meditation. It must be well over fifteen metres high with a long tree lined avenue leading up to it. It is visible from almost everywhere in the town. Janet left two days before Joan and me as she had things to do back in Delhi. She told us later that just as the train was pulling out of the station someone had thrown a brick through the window and she was showered with broken glass but fortunately she was not hurt.

Joan and I caught a taxi to Gaya Junction for our train, which was a mid evening departure. We knew we were in for the usual challenge of making sure we found the right platform. It was made more exciting by the fact that Gaya was a much smaller station than New Delhi and there were virtually no signs in English. We did find a rest room but this time I made more frequent sorties to see which platform our train would be arriving at. The departure time came and passed and still there was no sign of the train.

Even though they are often late, my sixth sense suddenly nudged me and I had the suspicion it was already in the station. I was on the platform where it was supposed to be although the train standing there was definitely not the one we wanted. Then I realised that on the other side of this train was the one we wanted, waiting at a different platform. I shouted to Joan, who came running up. We were both burdened with heavy packs and we had to run up the stairs to a foot bridge over the rail line, then down another set of stairs and onto the platform. I was some way ahead of Joan and running as hard as I could as the train started to pull out. It was just slow enough for me to reach out an arm and be given a helping hand into a carriage. I turned to look and to my horror

Joan was not near enough to the train to jump aboard. It was gaining speed by then and it would have been too dangerous for me to risk jumping off. I still have a vivid vision of Joan waving frantically as she receded behind me.

I was really worried. She had hardly travelled, and never in a country like India. What would happen to her as a lone woman in a fairly small station in the middle of Bihar, which was in quite a state of unrest? One of my fellow passengers assured me she would be fine and I could do nothing but trust his word. At least I was to find something on the journey to distract me. This time we had not booked sleeper coaches. In fact we had the cheapest tickets, which meant that I had to find whatever seat I could. In fact it proved fairly easy and I found myself sitting in a crowded compartment with, amongst others, a young couple with a small baby.

The baby was upset and crying bitterly. Nothing the mother could do would console it or get it to sleep. They were obviously simple peasants and certainly spoke no English. I felt for her and I knew that I could quieten the child – but would she allow me to? I smiled and reached out my arms for the little one. She understood what I meant and to my surprise she handed the baby to me. Even though I was sitting with them it was still an expression of real trust.

I took the little girl, meditated and focused on her as I would with any client who has come for healing. In moments she was asleep. Her mother smiled radiantly and then also curled up and fell asleep. I think she was exhausted. No doubt they too had been waiting for the train for hours. Well I was stuck now. I hardly dared to move for fear of waking the baby and the father seemed happy for me to continue in my role. A few hours later when we stopped at a station there were the usual chai vendors on the platform and the father got me a glass of chai, which was most welcome. By then the mother was awake and she took her baby back and I recovered my numbed arms. I have met so many travellers who have endless tales of difficulties or who say how hard they found it to meet the 'real locals'. I have always found that people respond to natural warmth and friendliness.

When we reached Delhi I booked into a particular YMCA hostel that we had all agreed on before Janet had left. It was around breakfast time but after an exhausting trip I just fell on top of my bed and went out like a light till late morning. When I got up, I walked out onto the balcony attached to the room. This overlooked the downstairs foyer and you wouldn't believe how happy I was when I saw Joan walking in looking quite cheerful, as if her adventure had been nothing out of the ordinary. I rushed down and gave her a hug and she spilled out her story. After missing the train she went and found the duty station master and threw herself on his mercy. He did speak enough English to understand. He insisted she stay in his office, gave her chai and organised to put her on the next Delhi-bound train, which came through near to midnight. I think in the end she had been far less worried by the incident than I was.

So now we had some time in Delhi. Janet had some good friends from England who were travelling in northern India and they were in Delhi for a few days while we were there. They were travelling in more style than us. We went to see them in their hotel and they insisted that we enjoy some of their luxury living. I think their children were a bit nonplussed when we walked through the door travel stained, in need of clean clothes as well as clean bodies and me with a good growth of beard coming on. They knew Janet, of course, but they were seeing her in a rather different light from the smart (and possible slightly fierce) figure they knew. We had piping hot showers with fresh towels, in contrast to the intermittent and lukewarm or cold showers that we had been used to. Afterwards we sprawled around their large room, just soaking in the luxury we had not known since the hotels in Mumbai. We shared some traveller's tales, which entranced the children. Then they took us to eat in the hotel restaurant.

I had an uncle who used to live and work in India. He was there from around 1946 till most English businessmen were replaced by Indians during the 1970s. He had worked for one of the old colonial business conglomerates, Andrew Yule and Co, based in Calcutta. One of his main duties was managing tea estates. Although he later lived in Australia, he made periodic visits to India to see old friends and colleagues. It so happened that he was on one of his visits while we were in Delhi and he and I met for a couple of days. Over the years we had made a habit of meeting, rather like ships that pass in the night, in various foreign places. When I was living on the kibbutz, I had hitch hiked to Tel Aviv to meet him on a similar stop over there.

I always got on very well with him and it was great to have someone show me around who spoke excellent Hindi. Amongst other places he took me to the Delhi Golf Club. Golf clubs around the world have a reputation for often being quite elitist and at the very least pretty smart. Going into the Delhi Golf Club was like stepping back in time to the colonial days.

Back before 1945 – and even when my uncle was living there, though to a lesser extent by then – the ruling elite were largely British. Immaculately dressed and turbaned servants would cater to the whims of this white minority. There were also some educated and high caste Indians who were to a degree part of this minority, but not many. It is interesting to see that now educated and middle class Indians have taken on the role formerly filled by the British. The golf club was a microcosm of this. The members now were almost all Indian. They were generally formally dressed in collar and tie, with any female guests in expensive saris. Most of the patrons were also speaking English rather than Hindi or one of the other Indian languages. It seemed that the ambience of the place demanded a pseudo colonial lifestyle, right down to the language. It was a strange contradiction considering that they had fought so hard for independence in 1947.

Though I was a bit cleaner than before my visit to Janet's friends, my clothes were still not very smart and I felt rather self-conscious going into the hushed and rather reserved atmosphere of the club. I'm not sure anyone working there still knew my uncle but he knew how to 'play the game'. He had a wry sense of humour and it rather amused him to have me there, knowing that some people were probably looking at me somewhat disdainfully – even though nobody would dream of saying anything. Of course tea here was the English variety rather than chai and it was served in fine china along with sweet cakes, for which Indians have a passion. Street vendors and cafes sell many different concoctions dripping with syrup but again here, the cakes were more after the European style of baking.

We visited the Red Fort, a huge walled complex built in the seventeenth century alongside the Yamuna River. So called because the walls are of red stone, it was both a military headquarters and a palace. The sheer scale of all these old structures in India is impressive. Inside most such places there are gardens or great stretches of lawn as well as all the buildings. My uncle was in his element. He knew the history of all the places we saw. He could converse with anyone we met and I was a good audience for him to share his knowledge with. It was amusing to watch him chatting with people as not only was he fluent in Hindi, he had even adopted the typical Indian hand and head gestures.

But all things must pass. We could not avoid our flights home, even though I could have spent twice as long in this marvellous country. We had bought statues of some of the pantheon of Tibetan Buddhist Bodhisattvas and Janet had organised for these to be decorated by a Tibetan painter. They had to be collected. I took a last walk around to get some chai then did my packing. I was pretty loaded with what I had bought along the way: saris for Mary and quite a lot of things for me. The flight left very late, around midnight. After a long final day, sleep came easily on board. We parted company at Heathrow Airport and I caught an onward flight to Glasgow. From Glasgow I took the West Coast Motors coach to Campbeltown, alighting in Lochgilphead. My wife met me there and then it was home to my little glen. In less than twenty-four hours I had exchanged my pilgrimage – all the fascinating interactions with exotic people, the challenging and exciting rail adventures and the colours and smells of India – for the green quiet of a little Scottish glen. It was quite a culture shock. And it was hard to share what I had been through with someone who had never been to such places, but I know that she understood how important it was for me.

So what had the trip meant for me? It was certainly an adventure, and it gave me the buzz I always get from visiting far off lands. But when I went I had approached it as a pilgrimage: a chance to deepen my understanding of the roots of Buddhism; an opportunity to go deeper into my own Zen practice. After such a journey you see things through different eyes, for a while at least. Although our cats and chickens greeted me as if I had never been away, something within me had changed. At the time I was not to know that my commitment to the path of Zen would not be for life. However, I had experienced to a much deeper level the universal energy that I believe is the root of all spiritual traditions. I had also felt the love that transcends petty boundaries, which is the one thing that all men share. I always do experience that when travelling

It might seem to be stretching a point to claim that my experience in India had made an impact on my work as a healer. It was a spiritual pilgrimage with adventures thrown in and my healing is bound up with my inner journey. As I look back on my life and my healing journey I see that it is essentially one and the same. Sharing a precious few hours with the young couple whose baby I comforted; the monk giving me the bodhi tree leaves; meeting Sanjay's family; being nurtured by so many people who passed but briefly through my life: all these things somehow fed into my heart and helped me to feel the universal love that is the energy I channel as a healer.

I have studied many modalities in the field of healing and alternative therapies. Everything has helped to bring me to where I am at present. Yet in a way the most important thing to understand is that love is truly the most powerful force in the universe. Opening up to that and learning how to channel it, rather than getting too sidetracked by wearing a particular 'healing label', something I often see, is what my work is all about. All that happened on the pilgrimage contributed to this.

Already the end of my marriage was looming in the background. Perhaps I was not aware of it consciously but at some level I think I felt it. Life at Tayness resumed but there was something different on a subtle level.

Still there were animals to care for, my building business to pursue and my new training as an alcohol counsellor, which had been arranged before my trip. Summer was round the corner so there was also much to do in the garden in preparation.

In the end I believe that what happens is for the best. But sometimes I wonder if Mary and I missed an opportunity to be more open with each other and to talk about what was simmering below the surface in our relationship. India had stopped me in my tracks and opened me to new depths of experience yet I allowed myself to slip back too easily into old patterns. I became trapped once more in a daily round of tasks and business commitments. With that I slipped into the role that I had played as a husband and builder for many years. I missed something. A new chapter was about to open and within a few short years my life would change beyond all recognition.

Chapter 7: Near Death in a Kolkata Hospital

Autumn 2000 and I'm off to India again. Since my trip a couple of years before, Mary and I had reached a point where we knew that either we sorted something out between us or we parted company. When this happens in a marriage it is never easy. However, I am eternally grateful that what happened between us was not unpleasant and full of bloodshed. I had failed to see how she had felt for some time. Mind you, in any relationship breakdown both parties contribute, except in rare situations. She suggested that we each take time out and go off to do something on our own for while.

At the beginning of the year, she had gone away for a while to immerse herself in the Scottish traditional music scene. She had taken up the fiddle and was proving very good at it as well as finding an important new outlet for her considerable creative talents. In the interim before I went to India I continued to make regular trips to the Zen monastery in Northumberland. I talked to the monks about what was happening. In my heart I knew the writing was on the wall, and one of my concerns was about what would happen to all the animals we shared our lives with. For both of us their welfare was very important. Each of the four was a real little character that we had nurtured through health challenges of their own. We had tried to let them lead a natural and healthy existence, finding a balance between their being pets and also animals with their own instincts. I was beginning to see that they had contributed to my increasing healing work with animals. They too have their own journey. Now that my focus in healing is mainly with animals, I have come to see this much more clearly. They have their karma and we cannot protect any being from their fate, no matter how much we love them. That is actually a misguided love. In the end we found excellent homes for them.

Business was booming, both for me and for Mary. She had established herself, unusually for a woman, as a very good and reliable joiner. She had developed a niche specialising in making traditional sash windows, often in exotic hardwood. Indeed we worked well together as I often fitted the windows she had made. Although working independently, we dovetailed our businesses very neatly. It was a real gift to be working on the west coast of Scotland. The scenic backdrop as I drove to work and at most of my work sites was beautiful. Many of my clients lived in large old houses; one was our local laird in his castle, and I also worked at a beautiful old manse, the name still commonly used for the house in which a church minister lives. The laird's castle, on the Poltalloch estate that enclosed our cottage, was in a breathtaking position, perched on the rocks by the sea, facing west. As you looked out to sea from there you knew that the next landfall was North America. It caught the full force of storms coming in from the Atlantic in winter, which reminded me of the brave fishermen I knew in Kintyre who would be out there braving the elements to bring us food. In better weather, it was a joy to be there. Unfortunately the underlying stress I felt probably detracted from a full appreciation of what was around me.

Loving India as I do, the choice of destination for my excursion was easy. So once more I organised my backpack. I dug out things like my water filtering kit, which is much preferable for a longer journey, rather than imbibing water purification tablets for too long. My digital camera, easily tucked into a waist pouch, was a must. Good sturdy boots were essential, especially as this time I thought I might do some mountain trekking. When I get things ready for a trip like that it never seems as if there is much stuff till it comes time to pack my rucksack. It weighed a lot. I have never managed to travel really light, as some people do. I know my brother and his wife, who are also great lovers of India, have managed to get their travel kit down to little more than a small bag. Ah well, 'vive la difference', as the saying goes.

Mary took me from the cottage to catch the Glasgow-bound coach in Lochgilphead. It is probably as well I had no idea of what lay ahead of me in India. I might have cancelled my ticket then and there. The two and a half hour coach trip to Glasgow follows the most scenic and beautiful route. It was of course this road that we used when we first discovered the area. It hugs the shores of lochs, surrounded at many points by thick forestry. Then there is the steady climb up to the pass, the 'Rest and be Thankful'. Past that the road drops and though the scenery is still beautiful with Loch Lomond to the left, it is less rugged and gradually flattens out as you approach Glasgow. I was curled up in a seat watching the beauty flow past, yet I could not fully appreciate it because I knew that I would not ply the route much more. By then we had put our house on the market. I had decided to go to India some months before but in fact since then we had admitted that we could not go on together. Events were moving ponderously yet without the chance of being reversed. I did not really know what I would do and I hoped that the fun of travelling would help me to see things more clearly.

Still, once I reached Glasgow airport, the travel bug began to bite. I just love airports. They are full of romance and imagination as well as footsore travellers. I often watch people and try to work out where they come from. I enjoy listening to different languages and deciding what they are, as I have a good ear for languages. Sometimes I hear Dutch folk chatting away, assuming that nobody will understand them. This is generally true as few other people speak Dutch. Although mine is pretty rusty now, I smile to myself as I do have an idea of what they are talking about. So I indulged in some people watching. Glasgow was the first step, with a flight to London Heathrow and then on to New Delhi.

The smells and heat of Delhi hit you as you step out of the plane. For many it is overwhelming, especially if it is the first visit. I love it. From the air-conditioned calm of the aircraft, with cabin crew catering to your every need, you step into the madness of Delhi airport. Before you have even collected your luggage you are besieged by taxi drivers and porters. The price the drivers want is extortionate. It is much better to fight your way out to the prepaid taxi office. There you book and pay for a ride to your destination. It is a fair price and it is not subject to change, though you can of course choose to tip the driver.

I had booked in at a mid range hotel. I prefer to start the trip in some degree of comfort even if I later move down to budget accommodation. Then it was time to unpack, don cool clothes and sandals and take a wander on the streets. The only thing is that taking a quiet walk is difficult. As you step out of the hotel every tuk-tuk driver and rickshaw wallah in sight sees you as a meal ticket. They cannot or choose not to accept the fact that you might just want to amble along on foot. Even though you tell them that you just want to take a walk, they follow alongside suggesting places you might want to visit and cheap deals especially for you. Of course they also have a friend who happens to have this amazing souvenir shop; you don't have to buy; just look around sir........it is all a game but sometimes it becomes a little tiring, especially just after a long flight.

It might have been my underlying state of mind as well that caused me to see things in the way I did, but I felt that the vibe in Delhi was just a bit more frenetic and aggressive than when I had been there previously. There was no doubt that it had changed a lot since my much earlier trip back in 1973. I decided to walk into Connaught Place, which is a famous and very large shopping centre. It is built in a big circle with an inner and outer ring, both divided into segments, or blocks. Pretty much anything you want is there, from banks to travel agents, fashion shops to restaurants and everything in between. The problem westerners have with food in India is that our stomachs are just so used to everything here being almost too hygienic that we succumb very easily to the bugs encountered in such countries. The culprit, even in a better quality restaurant, is often the water used for washing salad and fruit. Cooked food is fine and of course it is better to drink bottled water when eating out.

What I really fancied was finding somewhere to have a lassi, which is a blend of yoghurt, water or ice, and spices. I knew that if I made my way to Nirula's I would be safe with their yoghurt and water. Nirula's started in the late seventies and is India's largest fast food chain. But it is not quite like Macdonald's or the like because a lot of their food is very good quality: good fresh salads, great baking, fruit and drinks. I was staying about forty minutes' walk from Connaught Place and I strolled in along Panchkulan Marg, a main thoroughfare that I knew quite well.

Would you believe I saw a face I knew? It was a fellow I had chatted with on my previous trip. Just set back a little from the main drag I was on was a carpet shop selling the most beautiful hand-made rugs and carpets from Kashmir, exquisitely hand woven in beautiful colours. The man I saw, whose name I never knew, was one of the front men, the guys out on the street trying to entice prospective buyers in to the shop. He was a nice fellow and not quite as pushy as some could be. I remembered him well because I had met him at the same spot two years before and he had stuck in my mind because of our conversation. He had family living in Glasgow, though he himself had never left India. With my Scottish connection we had talked before at length. I had been in to see the carpets but I had not bought one. Of course he didn't recognise me and I probably looked different, though he had hardly changed. He came over to me and tried the usual pitch. I said I wasn't really interested but I asked him how his cousin and family were in Glasgow. Well, the look on his face was priceless. He relaxed his sales approach to give me some of their news. We chatted for a bit and then I pushed on to get my lassi.

I hadn't booked any rail tickets before leaving the UK but I had bought an Indrail pass, which proved a real boon. Booking tickets there can be a long drawn out process as you are shunted from one booking office to another. You wait in a long queue, only to find on reaching the kiosk window that it is not the one you want – contrary to what the sign says. Then when you get to the new booth and wait in a long queue, it suddenly shuts for lunch just as you have almost reached the front of that line. The Indrail pass bypasses all that. You pay for the pass upfront, which is not expensive, and you get unlimited travel for a set period. At large stations there are special offices to book at using the pass, and a stack of other things are included that would incur extra charges otherwise.

So with that in my pocket I sat down and started to plan an itinerary. First was a visit to the Taj Mahal, a couple of hours south of Delhi by train. Then I fancied flying into Nepal and doing some trekking. From there I could fly to Kolkata, previously known as Calcutta, maybe take the 'toy train' up to the Darjeeling tea country and perhaps even get to Lumbini, the Buddha's birth place, which is just into southern Nepal. Phew....that sounded quite a lot, and I knew I might get sidetracked somewhere nice and not go on to all the places I had planned. But I enjoyed the planning.

My first stop was Agra to see the Taj Mahal. Everyone knows it as one of the Seven Wonders of the World but you have to see it to really appreciate its beauty. No description can come near it. The white marble from which it is built twinkles in the sun. The scale and fine detail of the carving and inlaid decoration that adorns it inside and out is almost too much to take in. It leaves you in wonder at the dedication, the time and the man hours that it took to create it. The main approach is a great avenue of water, lined on either side with a walkway banded by trees. Even though there were thousands of visitors making movement quite difficult, nothing could detract from its beauty.

What many people do not realise is that close by the main marble mausoleum that is the Taj proper is another similar but smaller structure. The domes of this are white, though the walls are mostly red sandstone. Were it standing alone it would be outstanding in its own right but it is overshadowed by the main building. Yet in a way they complement one another and both are beautiful.

When I arrived in Agra I didn't have anywhere booked to stay so I took a taxi and asked to go to the general area near the Taj. I got out and just took a walk till I found a place I liked the look of. I booked in at a delightful guest house run by a Sikh and his wife. I had really fallen on my feet. They proved to be fascinating people. Unlike many small guesthouses they offered an evening meal, which I was happy to partake of. That became quite a ritual for the few days I was there. After a hot day sightseeing I joined Dalip in the relative cool of their courtyard while his wife was finishing preparation of the food. Dalip had his usual pre-supper appetizer, a glass of whisky. He was a really interesting character. Nearly sixty, he was just old enough to remember something of India pre-independence and of course he had witnessed the huge changes that followed after 1947. We swapped stories as the heat of the day cooled to a pleasant evening warmth. Their house was not very far from the Taj and in quite a busy part of Agra but with a high wall surrounding it; their garden was a peaceful spot. Judging by his girth I thought his wife would be an excellent cook and that proved to be the case. Her home cooking was wonderful.

At some point the conversation with her came round to healing and she told me that both she and her daughter were studying Reiki. We shared some interesting ideas. All energy healing is fundamentally the same in that it is from the same source that energy flows. However, people use different ways to tune in to and channel the energy. After talking with her I was prompted to look at Reiki myself a couple of years later. It is important to keep myself open and moving forward. Working with different practitioners and studying different modalities keeps me open and growing. When I study a new modality or work with another healer, I do not necessarily adopt a whole new way of working. Rather I find that I will often fine tune something I am doing. Sometimes someone else's perspective will prompt me to a better understanding of something I am already doing. Being a healer demands constant growth and a willingness to accept that I am really always in a state of 'beginner's mind', as a Buddhist would say.

I told my hosts about my pilgrimage, which fascinated them. Their reaction was that so common with Indians who see Buddha as a Hindu in disguise, as it were. Nevertheless they recognised my sincerity and were very encouraging of what I was doing. They were very warm and friendly to me and it was nice from my point of view that I was the only guest at the time so they gave me undivided attention. Dalip invited me to his sixtieth birthday celebration, which was happening in a few weeks. I thought that I could probably detour to Agra on my way back to Delhi for my homeward flight, so I accepted. Things turned out rather different as it happens.

The Taj Mahal is beautiful, but equally imposing for me is the ruined palace complex at Fatehpur Sikri. This is about twenty miles from Agra. I caught a taxi there. The approach is especially impressive as it is built on a high rocky ridge, rearing up in front of you as you approach. It was built in the latter part of the sixteenth century as a walled city complex housing palaces, mosques and private buildings. It is made of red sandstone with the most delicate carving adorning all the buildings. It is quite large and has magnificent panoramic views. It is very different to the Taj Mahal, but equally impressive. Mind you, by the time you have spent several hours wandering around, the sheer size and amount of beautiful carving becomes almost overwhelming. The delicacy of the carving makes the stone look almost like lace. I had never seen anything like it. Sadly it was inhabited for only about fifteen years as the water supply was found to be insufficient. Bearing in mind how long it has been abandoned it is in very good order.

Dalip's wife had kindly washed and pressed a lot of my clothing, which was a luxury as I usually washed things out in a hand basin at hostels or hotels I stayed in. I left promising to return for his birthday. I caught the train back to Delhi and had a two night stopover before flying to Kathmandu in Nepal. That gave me the chance to look up some old friends of my uncle's. I did not have a chance to meet them with my uncle on my previous trip but I knew of them and they knew about me.

Uncle John had been Mukta's boss at Andrew Yule. The business was originally founded by Andrew Yule in 1863. During the time of the British Raj the company was a large conglomerate with interests ranging from jute, cotton, coal, tea, engineering, electrical, power and chemicals to insurance, railways, shipping, paper and printing. Mukta and John had worked in the tea side of the company and regular visits to the tea plantations in places like Darjeeling were a pleasant part of the job.

Mukta and his wife took me to the Delhi Golf Club for my second visit there and treated me to a slap up lunch. From all accounts my uncle had been very popular and Mukta, who was about my age, remembered him fondly, always referring to him as 'uncle' John. When they dropped me off at my hotel, they asked me to get in touch again before I flew home. It seemed that everyone I met was so friendly and courteous. Although the latter part of my trip was something of a disaster in one respect, I still continued to experience nothing but kindness and courtesy from all I met.

Nepal was going to be new territory for me to explore. I had heard stories about Tribhuvan International Airport at Kathmandu, and they were a little hairy. It is not the world's most dangerous airport. That privilege belongs to Lukla airport in East Nepal. It's a small domestic airport and videos I have seen of take off and landing there make me feel I would rather access the area by yak. I have to say I had not heard of recent disasters at Tribhuvan but of course travellers' tales are always on the lurid side. India is a big enough country to run jumbo jets on domestic flights and Nepal is counted as domestic, being serviced by Indian Airlines (now called just Indian). Approaching it in a large jumbo with the surrounding mountains forming a steep sided bowl is nerve wracking. It looks as if the pilot is somehow going to have to just drop the aircraft vertically to make it safely. But make it we did.

While I was waiting to board in Delhi I met a lovely young couple. I saw them sitting by their packs and from their appearance I knew they too were travelling budget style like me. Something drew me over to them and we started chatting. Sinead was Irish and her boyfriend Marco was Italian. They had some great stories to share. They had spent time living in Thailand, teaching English for a living, and they loved any chance to explore this wonderful world. It felt as if we had known each other for years. I love it when that happens with new friends.

After landing in Nepal we headed off to different hotels. A couple of times I went to see them where they were staying. We had a lot of fun swapping stories. Both were qualified English language teachers, which enabled them to earn while they travelled so they could prolong their journeys without being so concerned about watching their budget. We promised to keep in touch. I have found that quite often people I meet in these situations do not maintain contact, but Sinead and Marco did. I saw them both back in the UK a year or two later. Then we had only very sporadic contact for some years but more recently Sinead has become a very dear friend as we have rekindled our friendship. Though we live in separate countries we often talk and the bond is such that distance makes no difference. She is now very happily settled with a new partner and has just become the mother to a little girl. I have found that friends in the past have often seen qualities and abilities in me that I do not give myself credit for. It has been like that with Sinead. What I am now doing with my life is a world away from what I was doing when we first met. I have been through many trials and changes since then and she has always believed in me; the essential me, if you like. When people have that faith in me, even if they do not realise it, they give me strength and self belief that is priceless. I have so many friends like that.

Kathmandu has a positively medieval feel to it, at least in the centre of the city where almost all the buildings date back a long way. A lot of the structures are wooden or a mix of wood and brick. Pagoda-style roofs make for a distinctive skyline. Dogs run around looking surprisingly healthy for an eastern country. There is a riot of colour in the painted decoration of the buildings, the colourful clothes, the bright fluttering . prayer flags on temples, flower garlands being sold and the multi coloured vegetables laid out in the markets. Nepal was then still officially a Hindu state though there was a strong Tibetan Buddhist presence. There are several large Buddhist temples in Kathmandu, which I visited. Theses simple Tibetan Buddhists in particular have an amazing capacity to carry out their devotions in the midst of chaos without seeming to be put off by it. They seem to have mastered what I have been talking about for years and am only just getting near. There will be tourists and guides making a noise, children running around, dogs scavenging – and in the middle of this a wizened, swarthy old lady will be sitting quietly, fingering the beads of her mala, totally unconcerned. They really do seem to live like the Buddhist lotus flower, which has its roots in the muddy water yet rises above the water as it blossoms.

For my musical delectation in the hotel, I was serenaded by a Bulgarian fiddle player. He used to stand in the main entrance at all times of day and launch into the most joyous music. He was a guest there and nobody seemed to mind. He was stocky and moustached with an infectious grin. He didn't speak much English but he managed to tell me where he was from.

Of course the other obstacle course you have to navigate in such places whenever you are out is the inevitable flock of little boys that gather around any tourist. Yes they want money, either as a hand-out or in return for acting as your guide, though half a dozen guides might be a few too many. I found them very good natured, more so than in some places, and it was not difficult to divert them. If they agreed to pose for a photo – and the answer was always 'yes' – then I was happy to give them a few rupees.

I made a surprising discovery when I went to book a bus to take me to Pokhara. Next to the shop where I got my ticket there was a tea room and the proprietor was an avid cricket fan. Cricket, of course, is huge in India but I had no idea the Nepalese also followed it. Very few play but quite a lot seem to follow Indian cricket on the radio and I was invited through to the back to listen to a radio commentary on a test match being played in northern India. The common interest created an immediate bond and I went in a couple of times to have tea and listen to the commentary. It really is amazing whom you meet and what you learn when travelling.

Pokhara lies west of Kathmandu and it is a bumpy old bus ride. I was going there because it was one of the best places from which to trek into the mountains. I think the setting for this second largest city in Nepal is possibly the most beautiful I have seen anywhere. It is built beside a huge lake and the surrounding backdrop of the snow covered Annapurna mountain range, containing three of the highest mountains in the world, transported me to another place.

Before I went out to the mountains I hired a boat and paddled across the lake to climb a small peak to a Buddhist shrine where I meditated for a while. It was a real bird's eye view from the top down to the city below on the other side of the lake. I stayed as long as I could but with dusk falling I scrambled back down. I knew that with dusk and the water to cross, the mosquitoes would soon be out and keen to feast on tourist flesh. I took the boat back, popped back to my hotel to get some mosquito repellent and then went to eat at a place by the lake. The water was still as glass with a clear starry sky though not much moon. But at those altitudes the sky is so much clearer that even the starlight is brighter. You hardly need the moon to see things.

I joined a small trekking party; just me and a German couple with a porter for each of us and a guide. We headed off towards the Dhaulagiri mountain range. Dhaulagiri itself is 8000 metres high; that is over 26,000 feet. We certainly weren't going to climb that, which is strictly for mountaineers, but we still had some steep trekking to do. The clarity of the light in the mountains makes everything seem very close and it can give a slightly false perspective. You can be looking at a huge sheer wall of ice-covered mountain, which appears quite close and deceptive in seeming not as high as it is. Then the guide calmly says that it is twenty miles away and 7000 metres high.

Perhaps the German gentleman with us was going through some personal challenges but I have never met such a miserable and argumentative fellow. He picked fault or argued with everything I said. At least his wife was a cheery soul, as were the porters and our guide. In a party of seven I managed to put reasonable space between him and me most of the time. Our guide spoke fluent English and the porters had a good command of English too. One of them, who was only about eighteen, had a very mature and surprisingly worldly philosophy of life, despite never having been out of the country and having very little formal education. He and I spent long hours talking, both while walking and late into the evening. He had a fundamental belief, which I shared, that all men are good at heart and that we do bad things because we are under pressure of one sort or another. There are bad acts but not bad people. He yearned to travel the world but of course his challenge was earning the money to do that on the very low wages earned as a porter. Nepal is one of the poorest countries in the world. However, I had the feeling that one day he would fulfil his ambition, simply because he so strongly wished to do so and because he had such a good heart.

One time we stopped for lunch at a trailside lodge. It took a while to prepare our food as most times the meal was made from scratch once you had placed an order. Food was seldom kept simmering in a pot. There was an exhausted-looking dog lying by the trail. It seemed not to have an owner though it was not feral. My young friend insisted on helping it by giving it water and some of the food he was carrying as snacks. I joined him and helped with a little healing. Over the course of our long lunch break the dog revived well and when we set off it followed us for the rest of that day and a good part of the next day too. Few people in poor countries care for stray animals with such compassion. They are not necessarily unkind but usually indifferent. I was very impressed to watch him with the animal.

Before reaching higher altitudes there are carpets of wild flowers of every colour. The rivers and streams are all fast flowing and often fierce as they leap over rocks and boulders. The only way to cross them is on rickety rope bridges. These consist of two heavy ropes about shoulder width apart with cross planks fixed between them. Two further ropes above act as handrails. They sway wildly and then when you are half way across you discover a couple of the planks have rotted away, which adds to the adventure. One bridge we aimed for had been swept away in a winter storm so we had to go further upstream to find a crossing point.

The higher you go the more the trees thin out and often the mountain sides are terraced for growing vegetables. There are masses of chickens, and goats with long floppy ears. There are lots of lodges along the trails for trekkers. It has become quite commercialised but still it is tough terrain through which to take supplies. Donkey trains are the only way to transport things. As a result most of the lodges have their own gardens for growing what food they can and of course they can get extra supplies from surrounding hamlets. We passed or were passed by many a donkey train going up fully laden or heading down the mountains for fresh supplies.

We were very fortunate with the weather and the days were warm but at night the temperature dropped rapidly. If we wanted to get a shower at our night's lodge, assuming that was even possible, it was wise to get it quickly as it was likely to be lukewarm at best so trying to warm up after it once the temperature began to plunge was not so easy. Even if there was some tepid water, there was often only enough for one shower. So if you were not first in, you had cold water; better not to bother.

At most of the lodges the guests sat around the big tables, which had thick rugs or blankets thrown over them. Under the table would be a wood brazier burning steadily. With legs tucked under the rugs you could keep your lower half warm but you needed a good heavy jacket to stop your back freezing. Then you hoped that your meal would be brought to you to save moving out into the cold. One of the coldest lodges we stopped at was pretty high up and it had the luxury of a stove in the middle of the dining room. The stove was a big old fifty gallon oil drum with a metal chimney coming out of the top, and it threw out a good heat. But bearing in mind that we were well above the tree line by now, even the firewood had to be brought by donkey so it was little wonder that the stoves were not kept burning all the time. After leaving the huddle of guests around the stove I went to my room and had one of the coldest nights I have ever suffered, with paper-thin walls that made little barrier to the biting cold coming in from the freezing night. I had hired a sleeping bag for the trip but it had seen better days and was getting a bit thin on its filling.

Fortunately it was a short night as we were roused at around four in order to climb a nearby peak to catch the dawn. We were told it was well worth the effort and indeed it was. We left in the dark with head torches to light the way. As the dawn came up the magic of the mountains was gradually revealed. At first the light caught just the icy peaks, which seemed to be floating on a sea of dark mist. They glinted orange and slowly the light revealed their lower frozen slopes. From the top we had a full three hundred and sixty degree panorama as the full light exposed the lower slopes, although the deeper valleys were still shrouded in dark shadow. I have never been a mountaineer but I can fully understand the appeal. Mountains are such a powerful reminder of nature's majesty and our small place in the scheme of things. There were quite a lot of people up there but most were silent, in awe of what we saw. Fortunately there was little wind but the chill was still biting so by the time we got back to the lodge a piping hot breakfast of porridge and coffee went down a treat.

We were in the mountains for six days and I gave myself just a day back in Pokhara before getting a bus to Kathmandu. I planned to take a flight back to India, to Kolkata. Back in Kathmandu I checked into the same place I had stayed before. I felt awful when I arrived; I collapsed on the bed without washing or undressing and slept heavily. I thought it was the exertion of the trek and the lack of really nutritious food at the lodges and didn't think too much about it at the time. The next day I booked a flight to Kolkata for a couple of days' time and then moved to another hotel on the edge of the city near a Buddhist area I wanted to explore. In fact I didn't explore much as I was beginning to feel quite ill. I felt drained of energy and very cold despite warm clothing. I had little appetite and not eating well is always going to exacerbate any illness.

On the morning of my flight I woke with a splitting headache. I had suffered severe migraine since my teens and I thought that was the trouble. I had the usual symptoms to go with it, such as nausea, dizziness and vomiting. I had quite a job packing my rucksack and getting a taxi to the airport. After I had checked in I found a seat and slumped miserably for the wait till my flight. I was almost unconscious and to this day I don't know how I managed to board the plane and last the journey. Arriving in Kolkata I felt like a zombie. I staggered out to a taxi and just asked to be taken to a hotel that I had chosen from the 'Rough Guide to India'. That was my trusty guide. Travelling in those days we used an actual book whereas now I think most travellers use their smart phones to find what they want online.

I don't know what they must have thought of me at the hotel reception desk. I was unshaven, unkempt, hardly able to stand and semi coherent. Of course I was pretty sick but being in the grip of something, my brain was hardly functioning and I didn't realise how ill I was. I had never experienced anything like it in many years of travelling in often rough conditions. I still kept thinking that some food and rest would sort me out. I couldn't leave my room. I had no energy for even basic washing. I just shivered under a pile of blankets. Despite the muggy heat of Kolkata I was freezing and used every blanket I could find in a vain attempt to keep warm. I used room service to order food but I barely ate what they brought me. After about two days some little voice in my head fought through the fog of pain and misery and said 'You are very sick.' I managed to get down to reception, keeping myself upright by hanging on to the walls as I went. All I could say was *"Get me a doctor."* Then I staggered back to my room.

I had no real concept of time but eventually there was a knock on the door and a doctor walked in. He spoke good English and immediately I felt I was in good hands. I had been lying there feeling like I was dying and apparently I was quite close to that. The doctor said I had certainly picked up a serious bug in Nepal. He was rather critical of Nepali conditions. I daresay he had seen the effects on travellers before. Hygiene there is poor and of course at altitude, where I was trekking, the water boils at a temperature below one hundred degrees centigrade so all manner of bugs survive to be consumed in food and drink. He said he would try to treat me in my room with medication but as a precaution he would provisionally book a hospital bed for me. Quite obviously I was a sick little bunny.

He did his best for a while. It was probably just one or two days. I'm not sure as I was floating in and out of consciousness with no idea of time, where I was or anything else. In the end he came in, took a look at me and told me he would take me to hospital. He ordered a taxi and helped me downstairs, one arm supporting me and carrying my pack in his other arm. On the way we had to stop at a cash point so I could use my credit card to draw money. I had to pay the taxi and I would need money initially for the hospital before my travel insurance could be activated.

Many people I have told this story to have reacted in horror at the thought of being incarcerated in a Kolkata hospital. It could not have been better. English is widely spoken in India but of course most people out of a huge population still have little or no command of the language. My doctor spoke English fluently and he dealt with the reception staff, who were gentle and compassionate but spoke little English. I was taken to a private room and put to bed. It was clean, comfortable, air conditioned and I fell into a deep sleep.

I woke to find the doctor sitting by my bed. Really I could not have asked for a better person to be dealing with me. He had trained at a London hospital, which gave me great confidence. He was also charming and chatted very warmly. I was very touched when he said that as I was a guest in his country it was his duty to get me well before I went home. He was also somewhat scathing about general hygiene conditions in Nepal. Obviously they had to perform tests to find out what I was suffering from. There was also the business of my travel insurance. The way that works is that normally you have to pay the costs while you are in the country and then make a claim when you get home. I had limited funds and not a very large limit on my credit card. Somehow he managed to organise it so that the insurance company would make payment direct to the hospital while I was still there. That was a life saver. There were a few hiccups as the hospital finance department would send me a bill to my room and say that treatment would not continue till it had been paid. That gave me a bit of a shock the first time I received this but my consultant just took charge, put the office staff in their place till payment was sent and carried on with my care.

Later in the day my doctor came back to tell me that the various tests had not revealed exactly what I was suffering from, though my red blood cell count was seriously low. There are just so many unpleasant things that can get into your system in that part of the world. But I guess he had enough experience to prescribe a cocktail of drugs that would be something of a catch-all. He also told me that in view of how ill I was he was arranging to call in two personal nurses who would be with me twenty-four hours a day – one for the day and another for the night. I was deeply affected by his concern and the whole way everyone was treating me.

The matron was quite fierce in that typical matronly way, but she had a twinkle in her eye. Even the fellow who came in to mop the floor and clean my bathroom was lovely. He spoke just enough English to say *"hello", "how are you?"* but no more. But he always had a beaming smile and acted as if my room was the most important one he had to clean.

My two nurses were a delight. The one who did night shift was tall, slim and quite shy, probably because she had only very limited English although that hardly mattered. The other one could chat a bit more. She was quite tiny but bounced around my room and despite her size had no trouble in supporting me as I began to move around a bit. She loved to tell me about her family, with whom she still lived. I guess she was little more than twenty years old. Initially I was confined to bed with drips and all sorts plugged into me. For a few days I was pretty comatose and spent most of the time asleep. As I recovered slowly I tried to sit up in bed when I awoke in the morning and meditate for a short while. I explained to my day nurse that I was a Buddhist so she said that she would not disturb me for a little time when she first came on duty so that I could practise as I wished.

Till I began to regain some strength I did little but sleep. I could not even take much food, though they did all they could to prepare things that I might find more to my western taste. I managed to make a call to my wife and she set about informing family and friends for me. For the first little while that I was there, it felt that I was teetering on the brink of a dark, deep abyss. I could so easily have slipped over the edge and that would have been it. Yes, I think I was probably looking death in the face yet I felt no fear; rather a kind of resignation. At the same time I knew I would not allow myself to go. It seems that my life experiences are often quite dramatic. Maybe that is just my lot in life. I daresay some folk would say I am a bit of a drama queen! Maybe it is also part of my ongoing apprenticeship as a healer. You can only feel empathy for others if you have been through hard times yourself. Of course there is no need to have experienced everything that each person brings to me, but I would find it hard to feel for people if my life had been a bed of roses.

While I was going through this, on the other side of the world Mary was activating a network on my behalf. I started to get phone calls. My parents called, of course. Then my oldest friend from college days, Hugh rang through. It was very late at night and his first question was *"I hope this isn't too late – what time is it?"* I didn't mind at all. It was such a blessing to hear friendly voices of loved ones wanting to find out how I was.

Then one day in walked this Indian gentleman. *"You don't know me but I used to work with your uncle John. My name is Bunny."* Well that was his nickname, but in reality he was Subrata. My parents had been in touch with my uncle, who was now living in Cyprus. Having spent his working life in Kolkata he still had contacts there. He had phoned Bunny and asked him to visit me. Bunny came several times and always brought a little gift and a cheery smile. He also regaled me with tales of Uncle John, as he always called him. Just as my uncle's friends back in Delhi had told me, John had been very popular and well thought of in the company. He invited me to visit him when I was discharged but unfortunately his wife became ill and the visit had to be cancelled.

It was quite a special experience. Would I have chosen to be so ill and spend time in the hospital? Of course not, but whatever happens to us gives us two choices. We accept it and try to take whatever positive things we can from it, or we kick against it, cursing and wishing it had not happened, which is futile. Just before I was discharged I left my room for a short walk and met another European who was a patient like me. He was critical of all the staff, moaning about everything but I said nothing. I knew he wouldn't want to hear anything positive. By accepting what had occurred, by being grateful to everyone for what they gave me and by reciprocating the love they showed me, the whole experience became something very beautiful. It might sound strange but once I began to recover I actually enjoyed my time there. It was a profound experience of the healing, loving energy that is all around us. Everyone had that within them: my two nurses; the cleaner; the matron; the doctor. Anyone can channel it, often subconsciously. I channel that in my work but it is there all the time. Without it we would not be alive. It is our source and our life. I was experiencing it directly and very strongly.

As I neared a point when my discharge was imminent, the doctor who had attended me in the hotel came in a couple of times. It seemed that when I left the hospital he would resume some responsibility for me. He was most insistent that I should not head back to Delhi too soon. Of course I would have to cut short my time in India and try to get a much earlier flight back to the UK. However, he was concerned that I did not leave his care too soon in case I relapsed. So he took me to a hotel and suggested that I stay there for at least three or four days, continuing with the medication I had been given. When he felt I was OK he pulled a few strings with my travel insurance company and arranged a flight back to Delhi for me, which they paid for directly. He told them that I was not up to a twenty-four hour train journey. I was certainly being well cared for.

Back in Delhi it was time to forgo budget travel and I found a good hotel; expense be damned. It was worth it too, from the point of view of email and phone access. Rather than having to find an internet café, I could do all I wanted in the hotel. I emailed Dalip in Agra to say I could not make his birthday celebration. I could email home. I had calls to make, including trying to change my flight. That proved easy, and I had only three days there before heading home. It was just as well because I had little energy or enthusiasm to do much. I took a couple of short walks but otherwise stayed in the hotel, ate there and just rested. I looked like a skeleton and I needed to fatten myself up.

The flight to London and then on to Glasgow was uneventful. Mary met me off the Glasgow bus in Lochgilpead and half an hour later I was home at Tayness cottage. It felt surreal to be home after my recent experience. What had happened had been so all-consuming that I found it difficult to adjust to being in Scotland. On some emotional level I was still in India. Being so ill and possibly near death seemed to heighten my sense of being alive, once recovery began. On some level Tayness just did not seem very real. I was still in another world.

During my absence a buyer for the house had made a firm offer, which Mary had accepted, so it would not be long before Tayness would no longer be my home. With that my life would change radically. Everything that I knew and had put together over our twenty years together was going. My business, a beautiful home, our animals and a whole way of life would all disappear. Yet somehow the experience I had just been through cast it in a very different light. It certainly would prove to be one of the toughest times of my life. To rebuild a life at the age of fifty-three was not easy, though it happens to lots of people. Yet right at that moment it seemed unreal. I was very much in the present moment, focused on full recovery. Looking death in the face and yet experiencing so much love from so many people who hardly knew me somehow transcended the harsh reality that awaited me, for a while at least. Christmas was coming but it would not be a particularly joyous time, and I was still very weak. I had some unfinished building contracts but I was quite unable to do anything for a while. Mary cared for me very well but by then we were living separate lives. Emotionally we had moved onto different tracks. She was developing a life of her own, which was good. Whereas I had decided to leave Scotland when the house went, she wanted to stay in the area.

I spent most of my time sitting by the fire and getting back into some nutritious food. Our four cats were good company. Animals always sense what is happening and just offer the same unconditional love to everyone. The west coast of Scotland, at least till you get much further north, is seldom very cold in winter but the days are short. Getting up quite late, watching the short day drift by sitting near the fire gave me the chance to look back over the time we had been together, and especially our years in Scotland.

I have found that physical illness often has the effect of putting me in an introspective state of mind. It helps me to see things from a detached view point. Having just been through such a trauma I was viewing life around me almost as a different person. Mary's business was thriving and she was kept really busy during the day in her workshop at home. Sometimes I wandered out into the yard to take her a cup of tea. We had built a life there for eleven years. We each had a successful business. We were part of the local community. We both worked as voluntary alcohol counsellors. Hour upon hour of loving work had been poured into the land and it was now very productive in edible produce and also in beautiful, quite mature trees that we had planted and nurtured. Chickens scratched in the yard and our cats prowled, undisturbed by traffic or neighbours as we lived well off the beaten track.

It was idyllic and I had often said that I could not see myself living anywhere else; that this wee glen would be our home for many years. Yet in just a few months, it would all become memories. Somehow it would not quite sink in. I had talked about things I wanted to go on and explore but there was nothing right then that really grabbed me. Some years were still to pass before I would grow enough to dedicate myself to the healing gift that was still gestating within. It might seem a long time considering that it was now nearly thirty years since I had first discovered it. But timing is everything. The nature of such a gift, so I believe, is not a thing to be rushed, to be treated like a conventional skill or profession. To be a truly empty channel and thus a powerful tool for universal energy to use takes a life of dedication.

That does not mean we have to become enlightened souls to do such work. I am a mighty long way from being anywhere near that. But there was still more to go through and experiences I would need before reaching a point where I understood what my passion and life purpose truly was; that other things I do are just diversions. Many more adventures awaited.

Chapter 8: The Magic of the Alpujarras

Christmas passed. A new life would begin in April. Time was catching up with me and I realised that I would only be able to complete a few small building works. I was recovering well but I could not manage anything requiring major exertion so I started to move into 'wind down mode'. After twenty years of building I had a lot of tools and equipment to sell off. I advertised among the other tradesmen I knew. I watched as a succession of them drove up to the cottage and took things away. It was rather like watching vultures picking over a corpse. Great bargains for them, but I was left feeling a little strange. To someone who has never been involved in the kind of work I did, it might seem odd. So you sell off a load of tools, so what? Some of the equipment I had dated back to when I first started. I had seen old joiners, real craftsmen, wax lyrical about beautiful old tools that they had inherited from their fathers. I had nothing quite like that but still almost every item I had could tell a story and I had always taken great pride in keeping things in good order. My old life was being slowly dismantled before my eyes but at least there were a lot of happy bargain hunters making off with new 'toys'.

We managed to re-home the cats and chickens with people who would look after them well. I made a round of farewells. I had no idea when I would see the west coast again so there were some sad partings. As I was heading off to who knew where, we agreed that Mary would take whatever she wanted from the house. I wanted nothing. I took just my personal possessions and no more than would go into my new estate car. It was a large Ford Mondeo and it took quite a lot inside and on the roof rack, and I had a bike rack on the back. I felt like a snail with my house on my back. Of course it was a painful process, but it was amicable. We had been together twenty years. We had grown apart and it was for the best, but why should we fight? So many people do – and if there has been cruel infidelity then it is understandable. We had been through a lot and there had been many good times. I had grown as a result of sharing our lives. We made a simple even division of any money and I left Tayness. I have never been back.

My first port of call was with a close friend, Sue, who lived not far away on the side of a sea loch some way south of Tayness. She was someone whom I had introduced to Zen practice. It was the perfect place to spend some time adjusting. We paddled on the loch in an open canoe. She had taken one of our cats so I had him for company for a while. If I walked some way from her house there were wonderful views looking out to the western Atlantic and some of the many islands that dot that coast. Sparsely populated with people, there was an abundance of bird life and seals. If you were out on the open water there were sometimes porpoises to be seen. If you were lucky you might even spot a whale or a basking shark. The algae covering the rocks were brightly coloured, often yellow. The radiant colour was a sign of the relative lack of pollution on that coast. In more polluted areas algae will look more lifeless. Great masses of seaweed drifted in the gentle currents. It is a wonderful fertilizer for the garden and I had often collected trailer-loads of it for the cottage.

Sue has now moved to the Isle of Wight with her partner. We don't see much of each other but they are both dear friends and when we do catch up, it is as if no time has passed; a sign of a true friendship. I was planning some time in Spain later in the summer but meantime I was in a kind of drifting mode. My old friend Hugh had invited me to spend as much time as I wanted with him and his partner in North Wales. Before I headed down there I went over to Edinburgh to stay with another friend for a few days. I was very blessed in that so many people rallied round and offered me space to stay. I was the only one who could sort myself out but it was good to be able to share my feelings and get a bit of a lift from people who knew me. Looking back, I realise that I was probably not very good company for a while but I really appreciate the fact that my friends tolerated me. But then good friends are those who are there in good times and in bad.

In Edinburgh I had a chance meeting with an Israeli woman who was there for a few weeks. Nagida lived on a small settlement in the Negev Desert just about an hour's drive north of Eilat, right down on the Red Sea at the southernmost point of Israel. She told me about a fascinating project that she and her husband, Gidon, were undertaking, which was to build a large, traditional adobe house. An adobe house is a mud-built house. They were doing absolutely everything right from scratch, including making and baking the bricks in the sun. I was intrigued. They had one or two volunteers (along the lines of WWOOFers) to help and she invited me to go out there. WWOOFers are people who volunteer to help out on organic/green type farms or projects around the world. It was too good a chance to miss so I drove down to Wales to stay with Hugh and booked a flight for a couple of weeks hence.

I arrived at Gatwick Airport to board a flight with the Israeli airline, El Al. I was dressed pretty casually and I was carrying a small pack. Of course Middle Eastern tension has been simmering for years and there had been yet another incident just prior to my going. Security on the airline was very tight. I guess a single man, looking none too respectable aroused possible suspicion. *"Where are you going? Why? Who do you know and how long have known them?"*

Well, my replies were rather vague. *"I just met a woman in Scotland and she invited me to go there. I hardly know her."* I knew her first name but not her surname. Semi automatic guns were loosened a little from their shoulder harnesses and I was requested to step into a side room. There I was strip searched and my bags were tipped out. Luckily I had a phone number so I gave this to the security guards. They phoned Israel immediately. By chance Gidon answered the phone. He was able to confirm that I was not a terrorist so I boarded the plane. There was a brief stop in Tel Aviv, where I boarded a tiny aircraft for the onward leg to Eilat. It was the tiniest thing I have ever flown in. You almost thought it might have a wind up engine, powered by a rubber band. It skimmed over the desert at minimum altitude, which gave an incredible view of the landscape; so close that you could spot very small details and even people appeared almost normal size.

Gidon collected me at the airport. This was July and temperatures were fierce. Eilat was around forty centigrade (over one hundred Fahrenheit) and heading north into the desert saw the thermometer going even higher. I was excited. I love the heat and this was different to previous desert conditions I had experienced. Rather than sand, it was rock, at least where the settlement was. It felt almost like a lunar landscape and as you walked on the rock, particular in heavy boots, it gave off a ringing sound. There was a mix of houses at the settlement. I guess there were thirty or more and many were fully built while others were still under construction. Gidon and Nagida's place was in the early stage of construction. They stayed in a small caravan and there were some basic, wooden-built rooms for the few volunteers. Just then it was me and a Czech. We had a composting toilet and we showered outside. Water seemed to be no problem and it was piped in to the settlement from a source outside.

We started work just before six while it was still cool. Once the sun came up, the temperature soared and the work rate slowed though we kept going till lunchtime. After eating we just flopped around in the shade and then usually did some more work for a couple of hours in the early evening. Often I walked out into the desert after supper. I had never felt that kind of desert energy before. It felt ancient, deep and beyond the pettiness of man, especially all the tension in the region. Where the skies are so clear and free of pollution, whether dust or light pollution, the stars burn with an intensity we never see here. The rock underfoot was still hot from the day and shoes were needed but the air gradually cooled so that from midnight till the early hours it was pleasant. Gidon and Nagida had a dog that befriended me and frequently came with me. He would snuffle around in the rocks, unearthing little creatures. I had the feeling he thought he needed to keep an eye on me.

The landscape was a mix of solid multi-coloured stone and a light coloured stone that looked almost like honeycomb. The amount of plants in such a desert surprised me. I had expected there to be virtually no vegetation but there is enough moisture in the air and it precipitates at night so tiny plants tenaciously get a hold in all sorts of little crevices.

The hard work in the broiling sun was just the therapy I needed. The bricks were made from a mix of straw, goat dung, a local earth/clay mix and water. There was a great pit that everything was thrown into and we mixed it by trampling it barefoot. I really enjoyed that, imagining myself as an ancient builder in biblical times. Then it was cast in moulds and put in the sun to dry. There were three sizes of bricks and the smallest were ready to use in about three days, though the biggest ones took a couple of weeks to be firm enough. The mortar used to lay them was almost the same mix but without the straw. Finally a render coat, the same as the mortar, would be applied to the outside.

My Czech friend was an experienced builder so between the two of us we made good progress. He was as strong as an ox and he worked like a Trojan. He too was getting over some personal difficulties. He did not elaborate much but I know that he valued being able to lose himself in hard work. It helped him to keep away from alcohol, which was a weakness of his. Stripped to the waist and with a blue bandana around his head, he worked at a punishing pace despite the heat.

There is a strong sense of ritual in Israeli society. I think that applies to most Jews worldwide. The evening meal, especially on the Sabbath, was an important time to be together even if we had been scattered during the day. Conditions were basic, with long low tables around which we squatted. We had to make sure the dog and the cats kept away from the food while it was being laid out. The white adult cat was a superb snake catcher, which was one reason why she was there. Around her swarmed a brood of kittens. Gidon and Nagida often had visitors at the weekend so there was a great buzz for the Sabbath meal.

An adobe building is very cool by the nature of the material. Combined with careful design, utilising internal courtyard space and shade, and encouraging air flow over water in pools, it is possible to build a house where the inside temperature can be at least fifteen degrees cooler than the outside, with no air conditioning system used. Gidon and Nagida were building the place not only for their own use but as an example of good eco-building in that climate. They also planned to run workshops there so that people could learn about adobe construction.

While I was there I made one trip to Eilat for a day to swim in the Red Sea. I snorkelled to look at the multi-coloured fish and spent time watching some semi wild dolphins. Otherwise I was happy to stay in the desert and soak up the ancient energy. Then one day, a young fellow turned up to stay for a week. He was an Israeli. He spoke good English, as indeed most of them do. It turned out that he had been born and brought up on a kibbutz. After my time on the kibbutz as a youngster I was interested to find out how they might have changed over the years. As we talked, the most amazing coincidence unfolded. I asked him which one he had been on. The name of it was 'Ginegar'. It was where I had been. But there was more. He told me about his mother. As I pieced the puzzle together, with her approximate age, a description of her and of the work she did there, it turned out that we had worked together long before this young lad Yair was born. Her job had been milking the dairy herd, which was where I had spent most of my time working. It created an immediate bond between us.

Something else that began to grow more was my healing work. My Czech companion suffered a lot of tension and I used to massage his shoulders and neck. I also did more direct hands-on work with Gidon, and some with Yair. As I always find when I share this gift, the energy flows in a circle and I too benefit from the flow of energy coming through me. I guess I needed it too.

Yair had brought a didgeridoo with him and he taught me how to use it. The really difficult part is the circular breathing. The sound of the didgeridoo is made by exhaling through it. Now if you have ever listened to any 'didge' music, as it is often called, the sound is continuous. There is no break for an in breath. You have to learn a technique called circular breathing, whereby you inhale through the nose while continuing to exhale through the mouth. It sounds impossible but it is not, though I never mastered it. I could get quite a good sound but I never got past being a novice. Later when I lived in Exeter I joined a didge club. I find the sound quite beguiling and hearing an expert play is entrancing. When I left they gave me a 'didge' as a parting gift. It was nearly five feet long and caused further hassle at the airport security though I managed to get it home. I used to take it to the didge club but so many of the guys there were so good that I didn't dare to have a go myself.

I loved the month I was in the desert. Interesting people dropping in; good, basic but plentiful food; a stunning setting; hard work and exercise; the magic of the desert energy washing my soul took me far away from the grey sadness I had carried when I left Scotland. Finally Gidon took me to Eilat, complete with didgeridoo and a load of desert rocks, to catch my flight home. I have always had a connection with stone and rock. I could really feel the embodied desert energy in the pieces of stone I took with me, and I still have them.

Back to the UK and back to North Wales. My time with my old friend and his partner introduced me to a lot of new things. For many years they had followed an American Indian Shamanic path. Hearing them talk about what they did and the aim of shamanism showed, as I have always believed, that at heart all the spiritual traditions of the world are seeking the same thing. When I hear people claim exclusive spiritual gains to be had from their particular belief, I feel they are usually missing the essence of the teachings behind their discipline. I believe that we are all on a journey. There are many paths to the top of the mountain. As long as you reach the top, it does not matter which road you travel. In addition spirituality is not something that is found only in monasteries, scriptures, chanting and esoteric rites. It is a mindset that guides our actions and our daily living. I have met deeply spiritual people who have no particular belief system, nor do they follow any special creed.

In Shamanism there is a lot of significance placed on animals and their role as our teachers, which I have come to understand as well. Hugh and his partner shared their home with several cats and members of what might generally be called the parrot family. I had never been in such close contact with birds, particularly ones that shared the house, flying free and being equal members of the household. I began to see their individuality and Hugh was absolutely adamant that their speaking was not simply the mindless repetition of sounds that most people think it is. They understood what they were saying and grasped what was said to them. I began to see what he was telling me. I could also see over the time I was there how the birds began to view me very much as an individual and as a temporary member of the tribe. I'm not sure if they granted me the same respect as they gave Hugh and Maggie but they tolerated me. In fact there was a little one that shared my bedroom. He had come to them from an abusive situation and he needed a lot of nurturing. Small though he was, he could be fierce. Once I put my finger through the bars of the cage and he took a good chunk out of it.

It was a wonderful place to be. I wandered the extensive grounds, which were managed but not manicured. It was mostly woodland, with lots of little clearings that offered open spaces to bathe in the sunlight. In one clearing they had built a stone circle, which I found was a good place to meditate. Something strange happened to me in connection with a little wild animal, a mouse. My hosts had been telling me about animal guides. In Shamanism it is believed that we all have animal guides. Maybe not always a particular animal, though that may be the case, but a particular species may be our guide. Our guardian animal may also change. They took me through a guided meditation to see if I could contact or find my guide. It seemed that the mouse was an important totem for me at that time. Such a little creature: not a great lion or bear, a wolf or a tiger; just a tiny mouse. But the size or apparent strength of an animal has no bearing on its power as a guide.

There are many things that the mouse can teach in Shamanism. It is a shy quiet animal, as I am. It teaches us to examine life's lessons and it helps us to find focus. It helps us to look closely at things; perhaps to become more discerning – and that is something I am slowly becoming

MY HEALING JOURNEY

better at. I have not gone deeper into Shamanism and that may not still be my guide. I don't know – but something very interesting happened the next day.

The next evening I saw that one of their cats had cornered a little mouse in the kitchen. I managed to rescue it and take it outside. I held out my hand and opened it so the mouse could jump free. It didn't move. Thinking it was too scared to move I prepared to tip it gently out of my hand. Suddenly it ran up my arm, across my shoulder and on to the top of my head where it sat motionless for several minutes with me frozen still. Eventually I lifted it off my head and placed it on the ground. What did that mean? Well, I didn't have any deep insights and one could easily discount it, though for a little wild animal to behave like that is unusual to say the least. It happened, and maybe it was simply part of my growing and deepening connection with the animal kingdom.

The unexpected trip to Israel had been both enjoyable and therapeutic. However, it had been my intention on leaving Scotland to spend some time in Spain. I felt a calling to explore my Spanish heritage. My Spanish grandmother was a distant figure, having died when I was only thirteen, although I remembered her as a passionate and fiery person. Though my father had adopted England as his home and had married into an archetypal, middle class English family, the Spanish side of him was always very strong. I decided to set off on that exploration and I booked a ferry ticket. I took the Portsmouth to Santander boat, which is an overnight trip. My eventual destination was the south of Spain. This proved to be the start of a hugely significant period in my life. I was heading to a place called Cortijo Romero, just outside Orgiva in the Alpujarras, which are the southern foothills of the Sierra Nevada Mountains of Andalucia. Cortijo Romero is a holiday retreat centre with a difference. Each week has a different theme: yoga, drumming, creative dance and so on. You share the week with up to about twenty other guests. There are a number of classes or sessions in the day and the rest of the time you eat, swim in the pool, soak in the sun, meet new friends and experience the very special ambience and magic of the Alpujarras.

If you drive steadily down through the country, you can get from Santander right down to the Costa del Sol, looking over to the African coast, in a couple of days. I had allowed nearly a week so I could meander gently and explore. Sometimes I found a 'hostal' to stay in. Other times I pitched my tent. One night in the tent was spent by a secluded lake. I was looking for somewhere to pitch my tent one evening. Driving through a wooded area I chanced on a small track leading off from the road into the woods. I drove down it and suddenly came upon a beautiful and deserted lake. I parked up, pitched my tent then stripped off and plunged into the clear water. Supper was eggs cooked over an open fire; eggs never tasted so good after that. The route through central Spain easily evades the tourist centres. These are mainly on the coast or around the bigger inland cities. I skirted Madrid and stopped either at villages or roadside bars, which were plentiful. Being a vegetarian, as I was then, is a challenge in Spain. They do have quite a lot of traditional recipes based on a variety of legumes but mostly they are big meat or fish eaters. Trying to get my requirements through to the owner of a little bar in a remote village, with a poor command of Spanish, was quite difficult. I remember in particular one incredulous fellow who kept asking if I had ever eaten meat. It was all too much for him. More often than not I made do with salad and bread, possibly with eggs or cheese.

As you get further south the centre of the country has acre after acre of commercial olive groves. They seem to stretch for miles. Commercially grown olives are generally quite small hybrid trees, quick growing and quick to crop. Unlike the old varieties that grow into tall handsome trees, they don't offer much shade. One day I stopped to eat at midday in the middle of one of these huge expanses of olives. The air conditioning in the car was good but once I stopped, the heat really took its toll. Midday in the hot dusty interior of Spain saps one's energy.

Orgiva is a market town in a valley. Behind tower the majestic peaks of the Sierra Nevada. In winter they are snow capped and very cold high up. Sometimes even in summer, there may be tiny pockets of snow that survive, sheltered from the sun in a dip in the rock. It has long been an area hard to penetrate. Many of the villages have only had dirt track access even till quite recently. During the Spanish Civil War and the time of Franco, people would disappear into the depths of the Alpujarras to escape persecution. It is the sort of place that gives rise to romantic tales of daring deeds and massacres. Near where I later lived there is a place called the 'El Barranco de la Sangre': 'The Valley of Blood' – so named because of Civil War butchery that took place there.

During my second week at Cortijo Romero (which means the Rosemary Farm), I was offered an introduction to Tai Chi. This was something I had long thought to find out about but being secluded on the west coast of Scotland had not given me the chance. I was very taken with the gentle flowing movements and the sense of calm they brought about. Later when I returned to the UK, I found a teacher and dedicated myself to this ancient tradition. Although I did not fully realise it while at Cortijo Romero, it is in fact a way of working with universal energy. One might almost call it a 'moving meditation'. For some years it formed part of my inner work.

On one day of the week during the holiday there is a bus trip up to the mountains. We visited three very picturesque villages, the white villages of Pampaneira, Bubion and Capileira. In fact most of the mountain villages have predominantly white painted cottages. As the road snakes tortuously up the steep climb there is a point where these three villages are visible together, one above the other. Barely three kilometres separates them as the crow flies, though it is more by the road, which winds in great bends to accommodate the sharply increasing altitude. Capileira is a kilometre above Orgiva in vertical height. That is a lot in quite a short distance if you were to go directly. By road it takes around an hour.

I was drawn to these villages. Many tourists are because they are so picturesque and there is a thriving tourist trade in these three villages. I wanted to explore my heritage. My paternal grandmother was Spanish and my father was born in Madrid. I hardly spoke the language and the few visits I had made to the country had been to the island of Mallorca.

So how could I spend some time exploring these mountains? Well, an English lady who worked at Cortijo Romero owned a cottage in Bubion. So when my two weeks at the retreat centre finished I spent a couple of weeks at Jenny's cottage on a bed and breakfast basis. It was great. Those mountains are big, being home to the highest peak on mainland Spain: Mulhacen at nearly 3500 metres. The river Poqueira tumbles and races through the Poqueira valley, on the steep sides of which hang these three white villages. And I do mean hang, as the houses perch on the steep slopes. The entrance to a little house might be off the street at the front, yet the balcony at the back might be one or even two levels above the ground. Some of the houses have a street level entrance but the rooms at the back might disappear into the rock of the slope behind. The electricity for the villages is supplied by hydro power from the river, which even in summer continues to run fiercely.

Although there are years of water shortages the old Moorish irrigation system never seems to run dry. Over 1000 years ago they built a complex system of channels throughout the mountains. These take the water of innumerable springs and channel it throughout the area for the benefit of anyone with land or a garden. They also provide water at little public drinking troughs. The water flows continuously in the channels, which may be half a metre wide and the same depth, or smaller where they sub-divide. Each village has a water bailiff who allots you a specific time of the day, maybe an hour two, during which time you are allowed to open a small sluice gate and irrigate your land. If you are out of favour with the bailiff, you might be given two hours in the middle of the night. It is absolutely forbidden to open the gate at any other than your allotted time.

It was a hot time of year to do much serious mountain walking but I explored down by the river and skinny dipped in the biting water. The source of the river is way up in the springs and snows that are at least 2500 metres high so even in summer the water is cold. I decided then that I would come back for three months over the winter. Jenny said she would be happy to rent me her cottage for that time. I had made some contacts in Bubion so I would be coming back to new friends. I had discovered one bar that I liked to frequent. The owner was a small man, always bustling with energy and constantly trying new things to draw the customers in. If the place was heaving with people he would greet me with: *"Oh is terrible, so many people. I am exhausted."* When I was there for the winter, the greeting was more likely to be *"Oh is so quiet. Where is everyone?"* He was great company and he had a wicked sense of humour. Although he had been born in the village, he had lived away in the cities so he had a much broader view of life than many of the villagers. Unfortunately, as he spoke very good English, I was lazy in practising my Spanish. My father had not taught me the language though I did have some private lessons at school. In effect I was only just starting to learn.

After this short spell in Bubion I drove up through Spain to catch the ferry over to Mallorca, where my youngest brother had been living with his family for many years. I planned to spend some time with him and some time on an organic 'finca', or smallholding. It's always good to spend time with my brother and his wife. They are both very easy going and relaxed and they have established a good lifestyle living in a lovely house with a large garden just outside the village of Valldemosa. They keep chickens and grow quite a lot of vegetables. I stayed just a short time before moving on to the organic finca. That proved disappointing. There wasn't a lot to do and I didn't really get on with the English woman who ran it. The best thing to come out of it was meeting her donkey. Donkeys are still used in Spain as rural beasts of burden. Despite the image people have of them being stupid and stubborn, they are very intelligent and mischievous. They certainly won't do something they don't want to do, but that is fair enough. He was quite a character, still young, and he had a habit of sneaking up behind and nipping you in the backside. It was never really painful, just playful. I was quite relieved when it came time to drive over to Santander for my return trip to the UK. I went back to North Wales to stay with my friends and prepared for going back to the Alpujarras for the winter.

Many people assume that Spain is hot all the time. Not so. The winters in the north often bring heavy snow. Where I spent December, January and February in Bubion was just a little higher than Ben Nevis in

Scotland. It was very cold. Unfortunately many Spaniards also seem to deny the winter cold, or maybe the houses there were built by much tougher folk long ago. They have great thick walls and they all have beautiful open fires. Lovely though these fires are, they are not very efficient. Once they go out overnight, the temperature drops rapidly. The house I was staying in had quite a cheap wood burning stove that didn't work very well. I seemed to burn through large amounts of the oak and olive that made up my deliveries of fire wood so I spent a lot of time in my favourite bar where Paco was bemoaning the relatively light winter trade. It was charming inside. There was a cosy, small bar behind which was the kitchen area. It was just a work surface and stove in full view and I'm sure it would not pass all the health and safety requirements imposed here. Quite likely it broke all the Spanish regulations too, but they have a much more laid back attitude to rules, especially in a small village. They just ignore them.

Paco had a young Englishman, Mickey, acting as his chef. Well, that is a grand word. Mickey was his cook but he was pretty good. With the food prepared behind the bar, Paco had to come through or under the bar to deliver it. It was amusing to watch. There was a lift-up hatch but rather than put the plates on the bar, lift the hatch to get through and then pick up the plates, he used to duck under the hatch carrying a plate in each hand. I never saw him drop one but I expected him to each time he did it.

The two were in complete contrast. Paco was a really small man, swarthy, chain-smoking and full of bounce. Mickey was tall with a long blonde ponytail and fairly quiet with a dry manner and sense of humour. There was a constant banter, which sometimes got a bit heated. Still, they got on pretty well and as I got to know Mickey I discovered he was an aspiring writer. People always surprise me with their oft hidden talents. Though I got on well with Paco and loved spending evenings in the warmth and conviviality of the bar, I was not one of his best customers. I don't eat late in the evening, Spanish style, so I had generally had some food before going there for coffee. I paid to use his internet facilities but otherwise I didn't really boost his profits much.

Paco was always coming up with new ideas to draw customers in. He started to have musical nights, getting local groups in, and they did prove popular. It was fortunate that the bar had been in the family so there was no mortgage to pay. There were other running costs of course, but in the villages they are not too bad. Many of the little shops and bars are a hobby as much as being very lucrative businesses.

Then I met Sofia selling crystals by the roadside and I discovered a whole new area of healing. Sofia was from Catalonia. She had a regular pitch on the mountain road that ran east from where I was staying and threaded its way through the upper levels of the Alpujarras. If you followed it far enough you could get to Almeria in the eastern desert area of southern Spain.

I knew very little about crystals and semi precious stones. I had read something of the properties attributed to them in old mythology. I was aware that they were part of many New Age beliefs but I had never looked into them. At first I was struck by their beauty and the radiance of the colours. I was also amazed by the sheer range of stones available and Sofia had a vast range of crystals. She had a beaten up old van that she parked up near a roadside 'fuente', or spring. It was a popular stopping point and the water was full of minerals, quite rusty in colour and strong tasting. Many people stopped to fill containers with it and I must say it tasted very good. She pitched her stall under an oak that gave good shade from the sun. There was also a good picnic area behind her so she had picked her spot well. She was not of gypsy stock but she fitted the stereotypical image of the gypsy: small, thin, hair tied back, earrings and crystal jewellery.

It turned out that she too was a healer and she used crystals in her work. Of course I shared what I did. I must admit that at first I was sceptical about the crystals as I thought them a bit of a 'New Age thing'. But one could hardly describe most of her mainly Spanish customers as New Age types. I discovered that many quite ordinary people there are aware of the healing properties of stones, and she had an endless stream of buyers. This small, wiry woman sitting under a tree by a dusty Spanish mountain road, with a table of beautiful, multi-coloured crystals, presented an image from years gone by. It would hardly have been a surprise to see a donkey tethered instead of her old van.

I spent a lot of time sitting and chatting with her. At one point she gave me a piece of Blue Tourmaline, so dark it looked almost black, and suggested I put it under my pillow at night. *"Just observe and be aware of any feelings you might have,"* she said. I was happy to do that. With the tourmaline under my pillow for several nights I experienced vivid dreams, which does not often happen. At least if I dream, I seldom remember. It felt as if something was rising to the surface to be melted away. I woke each morning feeling calm and peaceful. I talked to Sofia about this and she confirmed that on the emotional level, this crystal can help to dissolve blocked feelings and help one through sadness.

This was all new to me. Apparently crystals work on our whole being – physical, emotional and spiritual. It was a lot to take in, but I had no reason to doubt what she was telling me. I continued to buy stones from her, usually selecting what attracted me, because of either its colour or its shape. Sofia said that picking stones intuitively like that was the best way. It is the case that certain crystals are reputed to be good for particular conditions, but following the intuition is always best. That applies to all energy healing, no matter what 'tool' one works with to channel the energy.

Meanwhile Sofia encouraged me to offer my skills to some of the people who stopped at her stall when I was with her. Some of her customers would talk to her about some ailment they were suffering and she would introduce me and ask if they would like me to do something. I would ask them to sit in a chair under the tree and lay my hands where it felt right. Because my Spanish was still not very good at that time I was forced to really depend on my gut instinct. That of course is how I had always operated. But now I was not able to get much feedback from my clients while I was working. Once they had told Sofia what the problem was and they had given themselves into my hands, I worked with no spoken communication. I liked that. It forced me to trust completely what I felt guided to do; where to place my hands. They all felt the energy being channelled and felt benefit where immediate relief was likely, such as for minor aches and pains.

I did some work with Sofia herself. She came to the house where I was staying. I didn't have a treatment couch with me but I put a couple of blankets on the big dining table and she stretched out on that. Mostly I used the instinctive hands-on techniques that I had always employed. However, I did try some crystals as well from the small collection I was building. What she was in need of was support with certain emotional issues, and she did indeed find the sessions very powerful and helpful. This proved to be the start of an exploration of the use of gems in healing, which I have pursued ever since.

This was a much better time of year to be walking in the mountains in terms of the heat. In fact, on the high peaks one had to be careful of the danger of winter weather closing in. People die in the high Sierra Nevada. They make the mistake of assuming that mountain conditions in Spain cannot possibly be as bad as those in the high Alps or the Cairngorms or Highlands of Scotland. One moment you can be climbing high up on Veleta or Mulhacen with stunning views towards the coast of Morocco, in clear sun. The next moment with a sudden change in the wind direction cold damp mists roll in and visibility drops to near zero. You become disoriented and the temperature starts to fall. Climbers died while I was there.

I climbed Mulhacen, the highest peak, in December and I experienced something of the weather closing in. It was when I was on the way down. The mist rolled in frighteningly quickly. I could see barely twenty metres ahead and it got very cold. Luckily the visibility was just enough to allow me to see and stay on the track so I was fine.

Still, it was a great feeling to have made the top. On the peak you can clamber up onto a flat-topped rock that affords a wonderful 360 degree view, taking in Morocco far to the south with a glimpse of a band of the Mediterranean; the other two major peaks, Veleta and Alcazaba, to east and west; and a view to the north of the very steep slope which falls away to then flatten out into a very dry and dusty landscape. There are often eagles floating high on the thermals and sturdy mountain goats adding to the scene. There is a deep stillness in high mountains. Literally and figuratively you are above the bustle of life. The high peaks always induce in me a profound sense of union with the source of our being.

Across the other side of the Poqueira Valley from where I was staying was the Tibetan Buddhist Retreat of Ose Ling. It was founded in 1980 at a remote spot at a similar altitude to my village but way over on the other side of the Poqueira River. To reach it, you drive up into the mountains as if going to where I was staying. Then, rather than carrying on up the main road there is a turning to the left up what immediately becomes a small, steep climb. Finally you turn right off this road onto a rough track that arrives at the retreat centre. It is perched right on the edge of a huge steep drop. The buildings are back in the lee of a natural bowl but the edge of the grounds goes up to the cliff edge, from which you can look across to the three white villages. There are courses, individual retreats and teaching available. It is also possible, or it was, to simply drop in and spend a little time sitting and meditating in a room that is set aside for that purpose. I made a couple of visits, once by car and the other time I climbed down to the river from Bubion and then up the other side, to emerge near the centre. It was hard going, taking several hours, but it was a great way to do it.

During this short winter period I took some Spanish lessons so gradually I became better able to converse with more people. Unfortunately it is a difficult place in which to learn Spanish because what they speak in Andalucia, especially in the mountains, is a strong dialect with rules of pronunciation unique to the area. In addition several people I spent time with were a mix of German and English or the people like Paco, who preferred to speak English to me.

I found it very difficult to leave the Alpujarras at the end of February but I had only booked Jenny's cottage for three months and she had people coming to rent it. I had made good friends, opened up to new ideas and been entranced by the magic of the mountains. I felt sure I would return at some point but for now, a year after leaving Scotland, I felt ready to return to the UK and start to explore a way forward with my life there. So, reluctantly, I loaded the car and set off on yet another drive through Spain. I was becoming familiar with the route and it was fun to pass places I recognised and to stop to eat at bars I knew. This was the fourth time I had made the journey either going north or south.

A couple of years after this I returned to Spain to live for five years. Initially I returned to the Alpujarras and I was able to pick up the threads of the exploration which I had begun over this winter time. It is a magical area. It is a magnet for people who are looking for something different: the hippies and New Age travellers who inhabit the tepee village of Beneficio; wealthier people who buy a cottage to escape their pressured, northern European rat race existence; people setting up yoga centres and eco friendly holiday retreats; folk passing through who are seduced for a while by the mystical energy that suffuses the mountains and hidden valleys; and Spaniards escaping from the cities in the north. The range of nationalities you meet and the languages you hear are a constant source of amazement. But in the meantime the UK would bring more adventures.

Chapter 9: Falling Off a Ladder

Back in the UK I spent some time with my parents. They wanted to see how I was and of course my father was keen to know how I had enjoyed my Spanish winter. He was pleased that I was beginning to learn the language. I discovered a crystal shop in Berkhamsted, where I had been at school, just a short distance from where my parents lived. I went in to browse the crystals and I saw an advertisement for Reiki training. Having come across Reiki when I was in India I decided to look into that further.

I did not fully embrace it as the way in which I wanted to move forward in my healing work. I believe that there is one source of healing energy and as we are all unique, it is likely that we will each have our own way of becoming a channel for it. Nevertheless it took me another step along my path. Being in the company of like-minded people is so important and my Reiki teacher was a delightful person and a practised healer. Sometimes that helps us to learn; simply sharing the energy lifts us to a new level of understanding. When I was working with her I discovered that I have a particular connection with Lapis Lazuli. This is a predominantly blue stone, sometimes having inclusions of Pyrite, or Fool's Gold. Many healers who work with stones have a particular affinity for one or two in particular. Lapis Lazuli is important in certain Buddhist healing traditions so perhaps that is why I was drawn to it initially. Whatever the reason it has become a crystal that I use a lot and when I was in that shop I bought a beautiful Lapis pendulum, which I use for dowsing.

For some reason Exeter beckoned. I had never been there and I knew nothing about the area. I went for a visit and quickly found a house to rent so it seemed a good move. I guess it was another of my 'spur of the moment' decisions to move. Finding work also proved quite easy though it was physically very heavy, which aggravated the cumulative damage I had done to my back over many years of building. I realised that I had to do something about my back and I found an extremely good osteopath. Actually though he advertised himself as that, he was really something more. He too was an energy worker and also a very good listener. It took quite some time to sort out the serious damage to my spine and though I have a little residual damage to my right shoulder I have a lot to thank him for. We spent a lot of time talking over some six months of treatment and he encouraged me on my own healing exploration. I think the chatting was as important as the work he did on my back.

In Exeter I met a young crystal healer who, in appearance, really did fit the New Age image; all beads, bangles and clothes to match. But she was wonderful and full of energy and enthusiasm for her work. She and a friend ran a basic course in working with crystals one evening a week for several weeks. Sofia in Spain had got me started but these two helped me to explore crystals in a more structured way. Working with stones in healing is a case of using them as an extension of oneself; as another channel.

Certain crystals are believed to be good for particular ailments. For instance, amethyst may ease headaches and tension and yet with a particular client I may be guided intuitively to use a piece of turquoise for their headache. Always in my healing I will allow my intuition to tell me where to place my hands and which part of the body needs particular attention, and if I employ crystals in my work I use them in the same way. I really enjoyed their course. They were full of enthusiasm as well as being very dedicated and they encouraged the group to have fun as well. That is always a great way to learn. Usually after healing, a practitioner needs to ground himself. There are different ways to do this and it is also good to do it before working. They had a theory that having some chocolate was a good way to 'come down' after giving healing.

That was certainly well received and there may be something in it. They used a room above a crystal shop in Exeter for the course, which was a wonderful reason to go in the next day and treat myself to more beautiful stones

Part of the work with crystals may involve the colour of the stone you are working with. Colours have an effect. I remember years ago when I spent a brief period in the Life Insurance industry, my manager said that wearing a blue tie helped evoke trust. It is a colour that can cause the body to produce calming chemicals. All colours trigger bodily reactions in fact. With this growing awareness of the power of colour I decided to do a short colour healing course which had a particular focus on working with animals. Of course I had started to heal animals in Scotland but this was the first time I had spent time with another healer whose work was specifically with animals.

The general principles behind her use of colour tied in with what I had been learning on the crystal course. During the course we spent time at an animal sanctuary near Exeter. The two creatures I worked with there were an owl and a donkey. That was undoubtedly the first time that an animal spoke to me very clearly. The donkey shared its feelings. People often ask me how an animal talks to me. Does it speak in words? Usually it tells me things in images and pictures, often with feelings, though sometimes I will have a word pop into my head. Animal communication is definitely something people find hard to grasp, or even to believe. All I can say is that it forms a vital part of my healing with animals now. Very simply, the donkey shared with me that it was well cared for, which was good. However, it felt exposed and sad that it was the object of constant observation. Where it spent the day offered no little corner for privacy so it was always on view. Donkeys usually live to a good age, far longer than horses in general. It was already nearly forty and had been in the sanctuary a long time so maybe it would not have had too much longer to live, but how sad it was. I felt the sadness looking at him before I even went up and 'talked' with him. The way he communicated was somehow to put the words into my head. It was as if he had spoken, but silently.

I had begun to see animal emotions in Scotland but that was the first time that I experienced their emotions as strongly as that. A lot of people say that attributing emotions to animals is anthropomorphism and not real. In fact there is increasing evidence showing that they do have emotions. Animals in zoos can be seen acting almost psychotically; behaviour that is caused by their incarceration. Animals react differently to different people, showing quite varied reactions and feelings of like or dislike. Of course many people know this with their pets.

I had been forced to give up the job I had found when I first moved to Exeter due to my back so I set about exploring the growing world of IT. Apart from using computers for email, they were an alien world to me. Still, it was the way the world was going, so I decided to do a course. I learnt enough to find some work with Exeter City Council but I really never got to grips with the more complex aspects of IT skills. To be honest I never felt 'at home' doing the course. It was like forcing a square peg into a round hole and I couldn't be bothered to complete it. Doing something just for the money may be necessary for a short while but it is never fulfilling for me for long.

I still practised meditation daily using the technique that I had learnt during my Zen days but I felt a growing separation from the rituals and dogma of Zen Buddhism. One of the monks from Throssel Hole was based in Exeter to support the sangha there. We met a few times but increasingly it seemed less relevant to me. Possibly as a result of meeting and sharing ideas with such a range of people in the preceding couple of years, I was beginning to question the need to be part of a particular group to be able to experience and be one with the universal energy. This is a subject that often arouses strong passions. Do we need the discipline of a particular creed, sect or group? Quite obviously many people do. If we are not part of such a group are we not able to become one with whatever power there might be? Of course one cannot necessarily judge a belief system by the frailties exhibited by its followers. We are all trying the best we can and presumably people follow a spiritual path because they feel they want to better themselves. Yet I have witnessed first hand much corruption in groups of which I have been a part, and also second hand in churches and other organisations around the world. Often this has been at the hands of people supposedly well advanced in terms of enlightenment or spiritual growth. There is an old saying that 'you shouldn't throw the baby out with the bath water' but even so, I was at a point where I was seriously questioning the need for a particular spiritual framework.

After my brief introduction to Tai Chi at Cortijo Romero I had been to a class while I was in Mallorca seeing my brother. It was another look at something that was arousing my interest. I found a class in Exeter and as is usually the case with most Tai Chi teachers, a first taster class was offered at no charge and no obligation. Immediately I liked what I felt at the class and as I discovered over time, Tai Chi is all about energy and feeling. It is a very pure and direct way of working with energy. Chi is a Chinese word that means 'life force'. It is also called Qi and Prana in Sanskrit.

Larry was an outstanding teacher and very dedicated to his study of this energy work, which is how I describe it. He had worked with many teachers before finding the master who he felt could help him develop most deeply. Although very practised and adept, if that is the right word, he was also very humble. Having spent so many years practising seated meditation this was completely new for me. There are different 'forms' or sequences of movement in Tai Chi which take quite a bit of space. Practising at home began to get difficult as I learnt more of the form and I needed more space to move. I kept pushing furniture out of the way to find more room and then I had to change direction yet again to try to keep the correct sequence flowing. I guess because of the type of person he was, he had attracted an excellent group of students. They took the practice seriously but they were light hearted as well. They were helpful; more experienced students were always keen to help the less experienced. During the summer break I went round to the house of one of Larry's more senior students to work with him. There was a particular section of the form which I could not seem to master and I was determined to make progress before starting classes again. With infinite patience he guided me as we kept repeating what he had long mastered.

Some seated meditation does form a part of Tai Chi but I found that the movement of the form helped me to feel my Chi energy in a way I had not done before.

Then I discovered that an old college friend, James, was living not far from me, a little south of Exeter. He was in the early stages of setting up a charitable social enterprise company on a fifty acre piece of land. It was a beautiful spot with woodland, a small lake and rolling grassland. He ran courses there to explore sustainable living and responsible social awareness. It was at an embryonic stage though it has now become well established and has a worldwide reach. At that time there was just James and one other fellow living there on a permanent basis, though others would come for weekends or a few weeks at a time. I was invited to stay with them for a while.

James was not only an old college friend but of course he had been the one who introduced me to Middleton Place. My friend Hugh in North Wales was also a part of that circle. Both of them had spent a lot of time together after leaving college, whereas I had lost touch with them for some years. James too was basing his life and mission on the principles that he had learnt from the Shamanic teachings. Indeed at that time he still worked with an American Indian teacher. Whether he still does, I don't know but I imagine so, or at least those teachings still inspire his life.

The foundation of Shamanism is our connection to the natural world around us. We are not simply living on the planet to plunder what we can for our use. We are an integral part of all of nature; of all creation; beasts, birds and the land itself. I had long felt this even though I might have described things in different language. All I experienced in Scotland nurtured this belief. Buddhists see all beings as equal. The mountains of southern Spain evoked this in me. Going to live at this small commune was a very expansive experience. Compared to the tiny garden I had just left with my previous house, this huge stretch of land was a wonderful back yard in which to play.

Strangely enough when I first left Scotland I had considered living in some kind of communal setting. I thought it might be a good way to live in terms of sustainability. Well maybe that is just not quite what I am suited to, or maybe it was due to a degree of personality clash, but it wasn't what I felt was going to be right for the long term. Certainly people did spend several months at the place without a view to it being permanent so there was no expectation in that regard. But what a place it was to spend some time. The woodland was dense and full of ancient trees. Around the house were grassy banks and a flower garden. Just beyond that the lawn stretched out towards a lake. This area was bounded by hedging beyond which the open meadow rolled up a great slope with a huge stone circle in the middle that had been built in the Shamanic tradition. When you reached the top of the hill, there was a wonderful view down and to the south, way beyond the grounds. The lake, quite near the house, added a touch of mystery as water usually does for me. On the far shore the woodland dropped close to the water, casting long shadows even during the middle of the day. This thick woodland spread up the hill forming the boundary of the open meadow.

I had all the space I could want to practise Tai Chi without having to move furniture around. The main house was a large, rambling, traditionally thatched building with huge rooms. One upstairs looked out towards the lake. If it was cold I could work inside. If it was warmer I could practise on the balcony leading off this room or anywhere outside.

There were many meals shared around a fire outside. One was held at New Year's Eve. It was dry and not too cold. There were wisps of cloud but largely the stars were clear to be seen. James lit the ceremonial fire and we shared stories till the early hours. Further down the slope the stone circle was a haunting presence that seemed through each of the tall stones to reach deep into the heart of the earth and then to call to anyone who would listen to connect with mother earth. The circle was visible from anywhere in the main field. Though hidden from view if you were in the woodland or near the lake, it reasserted itself as soon as it came into view. It was a vortex of energy that could not be ignored.

I was exploring how to integrate crystals with my energy work and the third chap in the house, Matthew was a very willing subject. He was very receptive to energy work and always gave me helpful feedback as to what he felt when I used particular stones. Some of the other visitors were also happy to receive treatment. Healing is not exactly a skill that you hone quite as you would a sport or a trade. Yet the more you do it, the more strongly the energy seems to flow; the more your intuition develops and you gain insights into how you should work. A lot of it has to do with trust. There is nothing in healing that you can get hold of. Because I am simply a channel, it works only when I am empty and I have let go of trying to do anything. Yet at the same time I have to do something. I have to decide where to place my hands or which stone to use. Although that is guided by intuition it helped in earlier years if a client gave feedback. It built confidence in being able simply to trust the energy. That, ultimately, is all I can do. As time has passed I have come to trust much more deeply and I don't need someone to tell me what they are experiencing while I am working. Sometimes they do. Even when it may appear as if not a lot is happening during a treatment, almost always the client tells me afterwards how much they felt and of course it continues to work over the ensuing days or even weeks.

I went back to Spain for just a week during the early summer and I decided that I would like to spend a few years there. At the time I thought that if it was not to be a totally permanent move, at least a good long stay would allow me to really explore my roots and pick up again where I had left off previously. Jenny was still working at Cortijo Romero and in fact she now had a permanent room there so her house was up to let most of the time. She had a slot of three months or so towards the end of the year when it would be empty so I asked if I could stay in it from around mid September for a few months. I knew that she had people definitely booked in for some time in the New Year of 2004 but I thought that would give me time to look around and find somewhere else.

So I was on the move again. I booked a ferry ticket and began to put things in order. Just a couple of weeks before I was due to sail in mid

September I took a drive up to see my parents in Buckinghamshire. As well as going to say goodbye I had promised to do a minor repair on a low roof they had at the end of the house. Then life changed dramatically as I fell and broke both my feet. I have never done things in half measures. Breaking both was more of a challenge than just one. And oh boy was that one of the most powerful experiences I have ever had, with lessons and echoes right down to the present day.

My father came round the side of the house to tell me lunch was ready only to find me in a crumpled heap on the ground, with my legs tangled in the rungs of a ladder. *"Are you OK?" he asked. "Call an ambulance, I've busted my feet."* Actually my language was a little more colourful than that. I knew instantly what I had done and I ripped my boots off before my feet started to swell. In fact I later learned I should have left my boots on and allowed the professionals to do that. Whether doing that caused more damage I don't know. The ladder I was on had collapsed and though I had only fallen about six feet, it was onto concrete slabs. I was unable to roll and break my fall as my legs were through the rungs of the ladder. I was whisked off to the West Herts Hospital in an ambulance that arrived very quickly. Thereafter proceedings slowed down somewhat.

I was pretty hungry, not having eaten since breakfast, but they told me in the A and E department that they would have to x-ray me before I could get any food or painkillers. Nurses kept coming to ask me if a doctor had seen me yet and each time I had to say no. When something like that happens shock kicks in and bodily systems prevent you feeling the full level of pain. More than anything I felt numb, physically and mentally. Part of me could not quite believe what had happened and I kept thinking that maybe it wasn't real and I could wind the clock back. Eventually I was seen by a doctor and he delivered a pretty grim prognosis. His initial words were *"Well, your injuries are pretty serious."* He confirmed that both feet were broken. The left heel was shattered into several pieces. The right foot had been dislocated and pushed up to split the tibia. 'Ouch' was about right. So I then asked him how serious was serious? He told me that the likelihood was that I would spend the rest of my days on sticks. I swore under my breath and told myself that there was no way I was going to accept that.

I was still in shock and feeling pretty grubby in my overalls. I had no change of clothes. Then I was taken to an orthopaedic ward. Working in hospitals which are largely understaffed is not something I envy. By that time my emotions were changing from numbness to anger and frustration. The questions I had to answer for the registration procedure, when I was exhausted and in pain, really bugged me. Yes, I'm afraid I did take it out on the staff. I was obviously confined to a bed; my right leg was put in traction and the harness and weights would not be removed from the foot for over a week, for any reason. I had to do everything on the bed: wash, use a bed pan and so on. Well, I let rip. At least I did apologise later to the poor young girl who had taken the brunt of my anger. My parents came to visit me during the evening and they were really upset. It took me about a day to come to terms with the fact that I was in a hospital and that I would be there several weeks.

Once that happened, things began to change. I made a few calls and one was to my friend in the house near Exeter to tell him what had happened and that I had no idea when I would be back. The other was to Jenny in Spain to tell her I would not be coming out just yet. The whole thing became a test of how well I was truly able to live the beliefs that were part of my spiritual training of so many years. Concepts such as acceptance of what life gives you; surrendering to the present moment; seeing everything in a positive light no matter how hard that might seem. It is very easy to say those things are what you believe when life is OK or at least the misfortune is not too bad. When the chips are really down, it is different.

This was on another level. It was similar in intensity to my experience in the hospital in Calcutta but different in that then I had been so sick that I was almost beyond thinking or caring. Then as well, all that resulted was that my trip was curtailed by a few weeks. In this case I had no idea what the outcome would be, despite my determination to overcome it. My move to Spain, which was about ten days hence, was obviously not going to happen, and this should have been the start of a whole new chapter of my life. I was not quite sure what might happen with my room in the house in Devon. It was unlikely that my possessions would be thrown out onto the street but there were big changes afoot with the house, though that worked out fine in the end.

I had two choices. Either I kicked against what had happened and made myself and everyone around me miserable or I accepted it and looked for the silver lining. I chose the latter. My parents were amazing. At the age of eighty and seventy-seven, one or both of them drove over to see me almost every day for the five weeks I was there. They were consumed with guilt because the ladder that had collapsed was theirs. But the fault was entirely mine.

Friends and family phoned and a couple of people asked how I could be sounding so cheerful. Well, as I said to them, it was a choice. When you truly accept a situation, it is possible to find the good in it. Well perhaps not in the situation itself, but in the people I was with, both staff and patients. Until I was allowed off the bed I could really only chat with the two or three people near me, though I did have shouted conversations with a fellow several beds away. A hospital ward is a funny place. You are stuck with people you don't know yet certain things, such as what you are suffering from and the likely prognosis, are common knowledge amongst you. It builds camaraderie. It was obvious that the lady in the bed opposite was very ill and probably dying. I believe she did after being moved. The old boy in the bed next to me had been given a double hip replacement in one operation. He had been looking quite strong before the trip to theatre but afterwards the doctors had a real battle to keep his blood pressure stable. It looked as if he might succumb. He was moved in the end but I think he did survive. Everyone there had a little scenario that you became part of.

Meantime I became quite expert at doing everything on my bed with one leg in traction. They refused to release my foot for even five minutes. Washing, eating, all ablutions; my life was entirely on a small six foot by three foot rectangle. I might not go as far as to say that I enjoyed it but there was a considerable sense of satisfaction after I went through the morning routine and they had changed all the sheets, with me still on the bed of course. I had made peace with the nurse who suffered my angry tirade and she proved to be a great character.

Even though I had begun to develop a Tai Chi practice I still found it valuable to sit in silent meditation. I still practise daily meditation. The early morning hospital routine is strictly imposed. We were woken with breakfast just after six; then there was the washing and bed changing procedure. After that, however, there was a lull during which I requested the curtains be drawn around my bed while I meditated. It was my rock; my still place.

I had some crystals with me as well. I had taken just a few when I visited my parents as I often did some work for my mother, who experienced a lot of physical pain due to various injuries she had suffered during her long life. So my parents brought them in to me and I placed them around my feet to help with the healing. Several of the junior staff were quite open minded and interested to know what I was doing. It was good to share with them. Perhaps they went on to look further at healing or at the least maybe they went away with a more receptive attitude. I didn't talk to any of the doctors about what I was doing. Perhaps I was making an unfair judgement but in my experience I have found most doctors are not receptive to such things. Mind you, even that is changing as there is a very small number of hospitals where hands-on healers are called on to complement what is being done by regular staff. I would turn back the sheets, place certain stones around my feet, replace the sheets and then just lie back. Some of the more curious nurses would ask which stones I was using and why. Perhaps I should have offered a basic introductory course in crystal healing.

I was lucky to have a bed by a window so that I could see something of the sky and though the view was largely of hospital buildings, there were trees that I could watch gradually turning with autumn colours. I exercised with my upper body on a frame above my head where I could do 'pull ups'; I read a lot; I meditated and I kept in touch with friends as

I had my mobile phone with me. I even had a visit from a long lost buddy from college days who lived not far from my parents. I had met him again when he visited the house in Devon and he and all his kids turned up in the ward. Of course they insisted that I tell them in graphic detail what had happened. Youngsters can be quite ghoulish in their fascination with blood and guts.

The power of our mind is immense and it can take us beyond physical limitations. So often we think that it is the physical that sets our boundaries and limitations. Everyone in the ward was there for some limb problem: damage following an accident, hip or knee replacements and so on. When patients asked how long they might expect to be there, what they were told seemed to fit a formula. If it was an elbow, it might be three weeks. A knee job could be six or seven weeks. With that information they would then lie back and wait the specified time. Oh dear! It doesn't have to be like that. Unfortunately the doctor is seen as the authority with whom you cannot disagree. I saw people doing just that and at the appointed date they would get out of bed.

Well, there was no way I was going to accept any limitation like that. The damage to my right foot was pretty bad. It needed three operations and in the end I had on an external fixator, which is a bit like a piece of scaffolding, so I was back to my building days. What they do is to drill screws into the bone above and below the break and then connect a rod to the sets of screws that holds everything firm. I know now why bone cancer is so incredibly painful. Drilling the bone is agonising. Even when done under anaesthetic, the pain after you come round is hell. Still, I should have stayed on the ladder.

Even with this on the leg I was not allowed to put it on the ground for some time. I had to stay on the bed. Then all of a sudden I was told that they wanted to discharge me and I would be sent off in a wheelchair. That was not an option because the only place I could go was to my parents' house and with them being the age they were, being wheelchair-bound was impossible. In the end the registrar, whom I had got to know well, agreed with me. It was he who had delivered me that awful prognosis at the beginning.

So I had the doctor on my side, and the nurses understood too. But the one who had to help me achieve some mobility was the physiotherapist. The formula for how long it would be before I could walk with crutches was firmly embedded in this lady's mind. She saw her job not to be to help me to achieve what I wanted, however difficult, but to impose on me her view of things. She did not work at the weekend so on a Friday afternoon she handed me some crutches, grudgingly gave me some instruction and said that if I could walk the length of the ward by Monday, I might be allowed out. Then she left. She was sure I wouldn't do it.

I love a challenge. Standing upright, even with my right leg off the floor, was agony, just with the blood flow pumping I guess. The left foot was also very painful as the bones were still mending. There comes a point when putting pressure on a break actually helps the bone to mend, but it's not much joy. The first time I tried, I got about five or six feet, dripping with sweat, gritting my teeth, and collapsed onto the end of my neighbour's bed. I sweated blood over the weekend, but had fantastic support from the other patients, in particular a fellow at the far end of the ward, who cheered every step I took. By Sunday afternoon I made it to his bed. He was as pleased as I was.

On Monday morning I did a lap of honour for the physiotherapist without letting on how hard it was, so she was forced to take me through the next stage, which was to learn how to tackle stairs on crutches. My parents' house had steep stairs. But really aside from this one person I had been very well cared for. I had particular dietary requirements as a vegetarian with some degree of intolerance to certain milk products. Hospitals then still did not cater well for this kind of thing but they really tried hard. On some occasions they even sent out for a meal from a local Indian restaurant. We shared a lot of laughs about some of the things I ate and of course about my crystals.

Five weeks in hospital with such a severe injury is not really so long but it had seemed an age. You lose track of time in a situation like that and everything becomes a blur. By now autumn was well underway. My parents had lived in their house for many years. They moved there just after I left school and the view then at the back was of acres of orchards. Most of that was now felled and it was rolling pasture – very different but also beautiful. That was the view from my bedroom. The garden was full of birds and squirrels. Mum and Dad put out a never ending supply of feed for the birds and there was a strict pecking order. A couple of pheasants patrolled the lawn below the bird table and feeder, scooping up whatever fell. Tiny tits and sparrows battled each other on the table, often being scared off by a couple of brightly coloured jays. But as soon as the squirrels arrived, they took over and they could chew their way through almost any bird feeder, so they had to be replaced regularly.

When I was seventeen I was still at school. Over the next few years I left school and lived carefree for a time in Amsterdam and then Israel. I travelled the world. At that same age my parents were conscripted into the Royal Navy to fight in the Second World War, which was where they met. My father was on Russian convoy duty. My mother saw most of her young friends killed. I can hardly imagine what that does to a young person. As a youngster I rebelled against them of course, and objected to things, as most young people do. It was only as I grew older that I really understood what they had sacrificed for us in their early years and as young parents. They had truly done the very best they could and gave me and my brothers a start in life that many never have.

Over the years we had disagreed and clashed, as often happens in families. There were times when our relationship was pretty fraught. My father was a very strong character and not a person to show his emotions easily. In addition his childhood had been tense, as his father was also a very domineering man. Growing up in Spain, as a teenager he saw the horrors of the Spanish Civil War. As a young father he had been a very angry and quite frightening figure. Over the years some of the difficulties I experienced with him came from the classic 'Alpha Male' dynamic that often happens between a father and the eldest son. Now I was in the position of being almost like a child again. I could do little for myself and my eighty-year-old mother was caring for me once more, as if the clock had been rolled back fifty-odd years. My father too could not have done more. What happened was a powerful healing for all of us. I find it hard to explain even to myself exactly what happened. So much of it was on a subtle energy level. That, after all, is where our life and our relationships are rooted. You meet someone and fall in love. There is no logic in what happens. You may have be very different, yet some spark flashes between you.

That is what happened between us. Maybe it was because I was with them for five weeks that I simply observed them more closely than I had done since my childhood. I was quite demanding, in part because I was so helpless and was used to being able to shape my life as I chose. In this situation I wanted the same. At times I did make slightly unreasonable demands. Nevertheless they went out of their way to do things for me, which at their age was a huge challenge. I was able to move around, with extreme pain, but I could do very little else. I could just manage to boil a kettle and make a cup of tea but then one of them had to carry it through to where I was sitting. As I am generally a very active person, the enforced inactivity gave me a lot of time to think. The pain made concentration on reading hard so I was able to just sit and observe both of them and myself in that situation. It showed me just how much they really cared. OK so that might sound silly, as they had born and nurtured me after all. But the dynamics between parents and children are complex. We talked and shared things that we had not done before. It was a precious time; a time of deep healing. If the accident was the price I had to pay for this to happen, I accept it gladly. I have tended to need hard lessons to make me step back and look at things, and it was a hard one.

On one occasion I sat with my mother and tried to talk about a particular issue that had troubled me all my adult life. It was very painful to talk about and in fact I could not share with her fully what I was struggling with. It was not till she died just recently that I was fully able to acknowledge and start to deal with the problem. Nevertheless I had never even tried to talk with her as intimately as that before. Just the act of doing that deepened the bond between us, even if she did not see exactly what I was talking about. I think women find it easier to feel the love their mother has for them. For a man it is more difficult, but we both felt it as we sat and talked.

Gradually I forced myself to walk. I probably overdid things and put too much stress on my right foot. Despite the 'scaffolding' supporting that foot it healed with quite a deformity, with the ankle bone protruding badly. Maybe it was because the break had been so bad, or maybe I aggravated it. I shall never know. I started to take short walks outside. I was desperate to get fresh air after being cooped up inside for so long and it was a change of scenery, if a somewhat brief walk round the garden. After being inside for nearly two months, being able to get some fresh air and just stand watching the birdlife was wonderful.

During this time I had a couple of visits to the out-patients department and the time came when the doctor who had admitted me to the hospital, and with whom I had built a good relationship, said that he thought he could remove the external fixator. He gave me an appointment for that. By then I was desperate to go back to Devon and to rebuild my life, with a view to making my move to Spain.

So my last appointment came. The doctor said he was amazed at the speed of my recovery and at the amount of mobility I had achieved. We chatted about the way so many people accepted the limitations imposed by their accidents; the manner in which they accepted the designated recovery time without trying to move things more quickly. He told me that in his experience we could do much, as I had done, with the power of our minds, our intention, mind over matter. It was unusual to hear someone in his position talking like this. Maybe I should not have been surprised. Recently I have become more willing to share my beliefs, 'my truth', with people whom I would once have thought unlikely to respond well. More and more I am surprised how many people are in fact very receptive to ideas about energy, healing, the power of the mind and the spiritual ideas I explore. I should never prejudge people. If I am interested, then why not others as well? Maybe I should have told him about my work and my use of crystals to help the recovery.

The fixator came off and the screws were removed from the bone. Suddenly my life began to open up again. I called Matthew, who was in the house in Devon, and asked if he could come and collect me. My car, of course, was still parked at my parents' house so he drove me back to the house in it. It so happened that he took me back on the day of the final of the 2003 Rugby World Cup, taking place in Sydney, Australia. I am a big rugby fan and we arrived back just in time to watch it on television as Jonny Wilkinson famously kicked England to victory. After a pretty exhausting car ride, that was a real 'whoopee' moment.

It was a strange feeling going into my room there. Everything was exactly as I had left it three months before. It was frozen in time. I had been in the final stages of packing ready for my move. There were cartons of books and other things stacked up around my bed. Of course the move was on hold. I just pushed the cartons and suitcases aside and collapsed into bed pretty early. I would have to undergo physiotherapy and regain my strength. I would have to learn to walk with as little support as I could. At that stage I was still using crutches. Then my housemates told me that both of them would be moving out of the house shortly.

James was going to spend the winter secluded in Scotland in order to write a book he was working on. Matthew had plans and he felt that his time in Devon was done. Of course I could not expect them to stay around for my sake but this was going to pose quite a challenge. The house was big and rambling. My room was upstairs with difficult access via a twisty, narrow staircase. It would have been difficult to set up a bed for me downstairs and at least there was a bathroom right next to my room. The washing machine was way down at the far end of the house. With such huge rooms, pretty much anything I needed to do involved a lot of moving around. Immediately under my bedroom was a cosy room, which was the office with computers, mine included. It had a big open fire and an easy chair and it led into the large kitchen and dining room. I spent most of the next couple of months in there.

My two friends made a huge stack of firewood outside the back door. They got a good supply of food in and then they headed off on their respective journeys. It was the end of November, cold with short days, and I was alone in a big house. The pain in my feet, especially the right one, was intense all the time and every step I took felt as if red hot pokers were being jammed into my feet. I could move around for ten or fifteen minutes at most before needing to sit and rest, with my legs raised. Well, this was going to be an interesting challenge.

I called Larry, my Tai Chi teacher and asked if he could help a little. He was wonderful. Immediately he contacted some of his other students and they rallied round. They organised a rota whereby three or four took it in turns to drop in. They replenished my firewood in the office from the stack outside. They tidied up generally and went to the village shop to get me food. The people in the shop set up a temporary account for me and they also delivered things to me. One of the members of the Tai Chi group, who had become quite a good friend, organised a Zimmer frame for me. She reckoned that I would find it easier doing things in the kitchen with this rather than on two crutches. She was right. I got pretty adept at leaning on the frame while cooking. I was collected twice a week for physiotherapy. I had the house cat, Smudge for company and that was it. Smudge invited himself to sleep on my bed most nights. It was a double bed but cats have a way of taking up a remarkable amount of room and he usually managed to plant himself right in the middle so I had to find a way to sleep round him. That was tricky, because I had to set up a kind of cage around my feet to prevent the bedclothes from touching them as they were still so painful. But we managed. Well I managed. Smudgy was fine whatever happened.

Many people find it hard to be alone. I have never found that, although I had not been in a situation of long enforced isolation like that before. I was unable to drive so the furthest I could go was to walk around the flatter terrain near the house. It was going to be an interesting couple of months; a time of reflection and meditation. There is something very meditative about sitting by an open fire watching the wood crackle and be gradually consumed in the flames. My old Zen teachers would probably have said that was a good meditation on impermanence, which is one of the central teachings of Buddhism. Getting through the tasks of daily living really took it out of me. By the afternoon I was happy to light the fire and put my feet up, usually with Smudge on my lap.

We spend so much of our lives in hectic activity, often living in the future with all the plans we have. Plans and dreams are good. They keep us stimulated and moving forward. Yet in reality we have only the present moment of which we can be sure. Since falling off the ladder I had had little else to do but to be in the moment. I could make tentative plans but till I reached a point where my legs would allow me to get right out again, there was nothing to distract me from truly being where I was. A faithful animal companion is always a good reminder about living in the 'here and now' and Smudge helped me to be in that place. That is the place they are in all the time.

Gradually I progressed from crutches to two walking sticks. I was able to walk a little further and I went to see a neighbour across the road, about a ten minute walk. The physiotherapist still did not recommend that I should drive but I was getting impatient. Just before Christmas I decided to take the car out for a short run. I guess it was a risk but with the roads being very quiet there I reckoned a couple of miles' drive would be fine. I wanted to see how it would go. It was OK so I decided to book a ferry ticket to Spain for the beginning of February. I had been in touch with my friend Jenny. Her cottage in Bubion was still vacant but things were changing. She had decided to sell it and she said I could stay there but that I would probably only have a couple of months before I would have to find somewhere else. I was sure I would be able to do that so I started to get ready for the second time. As it would turn out, her selling the house would prove very beneficial for me.

When I look back I wonder how I managed to pack my stuff and load the car entirely on my own. The pain in my legs was intense, and would be for another year. I had to rest every ten or fifteen minutes when doing work like that. I did get some help to take cases from my room downstairs but it was simpler, if not easier, to load the car myself as I knew in what order I needed things to be able to access stuff on the drive to Bubion. It was a big car but there was little room left after packing except for me to squeeze into the driver's seat. The roof rack was piled high and I had a bike in a rack on the back. All my worldly goods were in the car.

I managed to get in to a couple of Tai Chi classes in Exeter. I could only do some very basic moves but it was great to soak in the atmosphere and to chat with friends. Because my mobility was still so limited, I had to focus even more strongly on the essence of the work: learning to feel the Chi energy. I could not come anywhere near practising the many movements of the 'Long Form' so Larry gave me a lot of advice and guidance as to how I could turn my apparent handicap into something that would enable me to really go deep into the energy.

James returned from his writing retreat just before I left so Smudge was not going to have to fend for himself. Then I headed off. This was going to be a long drive indeed. During the winter months there are no boats on the Santander crossing as the sea can be too rough. Instead I took a boat from Dover to Dunkirk, which made for a lot more driving through France before reaching the Spanish leg of the journey. All loaded, farewells made and off I went.

Chapter 10: Discovering Horses

I felt a bit like Douglas Bader – the RAF pilot who returned to active duty flying Spitfire fighter planes after losing both his legs – must have felt in the Second World War. He had to ease himself into the cockpit, lifting his tin legs into place. I had to do much the same getting into the driver's seat. Once in the car I had to pump the pedals by moving my whole leg up and down. There was not enough flexibility in my ankles to work my feet normally. I could not cover the same mileage in a day that I normally would and even then I was completely exhausted when I stopped to find a place to sleep for the night. But it felt mighty good that I was heading off to Spain.

It was a grey crossing to Dunkirk in heavy rain. Ferry ports are not the most attractive of places and with the weather, France offered a pretty bleak welcome. Although the crossing had not been rough I think I must have looked a funny sight as I hobbled around on two sticks trying to balance against the roll of the boat. I had never used that route before and at first I drove in circles trying to get out of Dunkirk to the main road. I arrived in the afternoon so I didn't go far before finding somewhere for the night.

It was wonderful what helpful reactions were elicited from many people when they saw me in obvious difficulties on two walking sticks. Café staff ushered me towards disabled toilet facilities even without my asking; they carried my bags in little hostels. I know that people who have a permanent disability of some kind often feel resentful if they are offered too much assistance. I do understand that and of course mine was not a long term affliction. Yet I believe there is a good heart in us all and people do want to help others. Sometimes I think that 'political correctness'; some kind of over sensitiveness about how we should show respect, has made folk afraid to offer a helping hand. I was grateful for the love and concern I was shown and I was happy to show that I was grateful.

I had not really begun to explore my roots in Spain till I went there to the Alpujarras for the first time. Yet by now, each time I crossed the border into the country I could feel a subtle change come over me. Of course I am fundamentally English, having been born and brought up here. But a different side of me seems to emerge when I am in Spain and when I am speaking the language. I had been doing some home study while I was in Devon and I was beginning to feel more relaxed speaking it. So I kept going steadily for the Spanish border. Considering how tough it was behind the wheel, the trip did not take too long. I was so stiff by the end of each day I could have done with a crane to lift me out of the car. But I made it to the Alpujarras. As soon as you reach the edge of this mystical and magical mountain range, you cannot help but feel the different energy. It is both ancient and timeless. The inhabitants move at a different pace. There are flocks of goats on the hillsides and wandering across the roads. When I arrived the almond blossom dotted the lower mountain slopes like fluffy pink cotton wool. Spring flowers in the south of the country are very colourful and varied till the heat of the summer burns the landscape to brown. Even then bright red poppies survive quite well.

Orgiva is a gateway and beyond it you drive up to the 'Altas Montañas' (the high peaks); up to my beloved white villages. Getting the car down the narrow cobbled lanes to the house took careful driving. There was barely room to turn it at the bottom but I managed and backed up as close to the house as I could. Then I went in search of the people who had the key. It was late afternoon and the temperature was dropping so my first priority was to get some heat on. There was no central heating, just a portable calor gas stove (the norm in Spain) and the wood burning stove. The water was heated by a boiler fired by a gas bottle as well. That

MY HEALING JOURNEY

caught me out a few times. You never know when the gas bottle is going to run out. Of course you could check before taking a shower to see how full it is but it is not always easy to tell. A few times I was in this very cold and pretty basic bathroom downstairs, just soaped up when the gas ran out. So the dilemma was whether to rinse off in freezing water or head upstairs, dripping wet, to where the gas was and change it. I usually opted for the latter and then I could finish off with a long hot soak.

Arriving as I did in the late afternoon, shops were re-opening after siesta so I had stopped before going to the house to get some basics, and Jenny had also left a few things for me. Wow, I was there at last! At times over the preceding few months I had wondered if I would ever get to Bubion. I took just a few things in from the car, enough to wash and change. I lit the stove and had a basic meal. The view from the balcony upstairs was stunning. You looked down the great deep chasm that formed the Poqueira Valley. The road twisted and turned as it made the steep drop down towards Orgiva, though that was well beyond view. With the sun setting, the upper slopes were orange while the lower slopes and the next village down, Pampaneira, were disappearing in deep dark shadow. Sometimes in the early morning the valley would be filled with a white mist so thick that it looked almost like water. The hill tops pushed up out of it like islands dotted around. It was a view I knew well and would come to love even more over the next couple of years.

I knew the nights would be cold. The temperature plummeted at that altitude and it was a very cold house. The back of the house was sunk into the rock of the hillside and the main bedroom upstairs was partially dug into the rock, though it also had one wall with a window. I piled every blanket I could find on the bed after making my 'cage', which I still needed to keep any pressure off my feet. Then I added socks, a woolly hat and a jumper on top of my nightshirt and dived under the covers with a hot water bottle. I certainly needed that lot. I was fine in bed but getting up in the morning and making it to the calor gas stove was a challenge. The thing is that I could not move at any speed. I still needed my two sticks and it took a while in the morning to get my circulation and joints moving. But when I threw open the shutters, none of that mattered. I was truly blessed to be there.

Once I was settled in, I started to re-connect with the many people I knew. Paco in the bar was delighted to see me, though he no longer had his English assistant. Jenny was living down in Orgiva and there were other friends there whom I had met before. The area attracts a lot of people from other parts of Europe who are into alternative New Age ideas and lifestyles. There were several energy healers, acupuncturists and homeopaths.

I met up again with an English woman I knew who did energy healing work and she helped me with my feet. Sometimes I went to her house; sometimes she came up to me in the mountains. She and her partner had built a straw bale house in the river valley near Orgiva. They had started planning the project during my first visit and now it was complete. Many people have the idea that a straw bale building will not withstand wet conditions. In fact it is weatherproof in many climates, not just hot Mediterranean areas. The outside of the walls is plastered with a lime or clay render. Once that is set and painted it will cope with adverse weather. There are examples of such buildings in North America that have been up for sixty years in northerly parts of the country. Where my friends lived down in the valley below Orgiva temperatures could really soar in mid-summer but the straw bales helped to keep the heat out in summer or in during winter.

She introduced me to her dogs, Leo and Pitou. They were both a little difficult in their behaviour and were causing some problems with the neighbours. A lot of folk were into barter as a way of trading so I was happy to fall in with this and I worked with the dogs in return for her work with my feet. Leo proved a difficult client but Pitou did respond and became calmer. He loved coming up to my house and would lie patiently while I had my treatment. Then I gave him his. I had never had a great deal of contact with dogs but they seemed to be coming into my life more often. I was more used to cat energy and I enjoyed exploring the much more exuberant nature of dogs. Most of my friends in the village who had an animal had a dog.

A chance meeting introduced me to a couple who became very dear friends. Well, nothing is chance really. I decided to take some Spanish lessons and I was told that there were classes organised in Orgiva by the municipal council which were quite cheap and would be a good opportunity to meet people as well. They proved not to be very good and I only went to three classes. However, at the first one I met Moshe. It was the only one he attended. Moshe and his wife Orah were from Israel but they had settled in the Alpujarras. They were a truly amazing couple. Both were gifted healers. Both had trained in different disciplines. He was an acupuncturist with a difference and Orah was a reflexologist. But in my experience true healers go way beyond the constraints of a particular modality or methodology. A training of some sort is valuable as a discipline. For example, it can impart knowledge of anatomy and physiology, which is useful – though few healers use that as a medical doctor does. Of course it gives confidence to clients that the person has not simply set himself up in practice on a flimsy basis.

In Moshe's case his training in traditional Chinese acupuncture was very rigorous. But within the framework of acupuncture he employed additional diagnostic techniques that were based on pure energy. In fact he could see a person's aura and use what he saw, as well as reading the traditional Chinese acupuncture pulses, to make a diagnosis.

We got chatting after the class and he invited me to their flat, just nearby, to meet Orah. The classes did not last long for either of us but they had brought us together. There are some people who you know at a first meeting will become very close friends. That's how it was with them and we are still in touch. Moshe had a thriving practice and they had also bought land some way out of town in the country and they were planning to build a house there. They were excited about the house and the land. Their young daughter, Eilona was not quite as excited as she saw the downside for her of being there. She would have more difficult access to her friends once she was several kilometres out of Orgiva, down a long dusty track leading into the wilds.

But what a vision they had. They would build a house for themselves.

They would erect a couple of yurts so that they could run retreats for yoga, healing and relaxation in stunningly beautiful surroundings. Their dream was to have everything as ecologically friendly as possible. Their water would come from their own well. Solar power would provide their electricity and heat the water. There would be a composting toilet for the yurts. They'd grow a lot of their own vegetables and their extensive land would provide an excellent crop of olives. Early in the year there is an abundance of wild flowers before the relentless heat scorches the ground. Glorious poppies create crimson carpets with soft heads rippling in the breeze. Over the decade since we met I have watched their vision become reality. They even built a swimming pool, which is also ecologically maintained. I always stop a night or two in one of the yurts when I visit the Alpujarras.

Orah is especially gifted artistically and her choice of colour and decorative tiles is very special. There are colourful tiles everywhere: bedded in walls and pathways; on the sides of the house; by the pool. It is exciting to visit as there is always something new for them to show me. I know many people who have made the decision to live as lightly on the earth as possible. I think it is no coincidence that many of them reach a place of harmony and inner peace after going through a lot of challenges. Both Moshe and Orah were conscripted into the Israeli army before they left the country. They had experiences that fortunately most people do not have but it contributed to the strength of their belief that they should find a way to live in harmony with the earth. They met when studying in California and after their daughter was born back in Israel, they knew they had to find another home. Their home is called 'Armonia Alpujarra' – 'Alpujarran Harmony'. Whenever I am there, the peace of their beautiful cortijo fills me and washes away any tension I might have.

Moshe and I decided that we would give each other treatment sessions. His acupuncture helped the healing of my feet and I continued my exploration of crystals in the work I did with him. In fact not long after we met I decided to undertake a formal study course in crystal healing with the Institute of Crystal and Gem Therapists in the UK. The theory was done by distance study, sending modules of work in to my tutors.

The practical side required me to find willing test clients on whom I could work. I had to keep detailed records of my work and submit them as well. Moshe became one of my subjects. It was a great help to get feedback from him as he was so sensitive to energy.

Having been working with crystals for a couple of years already I took a lot from the course. There is a basic crystal theory to use as a starting point. Certain stones may help certain ailments. But you soon develop beyond that to a level where your intuition becomes the guide in selecting a stone to use with a client. You need to build a relationship with your crystal collection. As I discovered when I did my first Reiki training, I have an especially strong connection with Lapis Lazuli. This is a predominantly deep blue stone, often having inclusions of Pyrite and White Calcite as golden and white specks. In Mahayana Buddhism the Healing Buddha is often called "Medicine Master and King of Lapis Lazuli Light", which may account for the connection I have with it. The relationship with your crystals, trust in your intuition and an energy connection with the client allow you to choose what will be best for them. This will often be far from what the textbooks teach as a starting point. I use Lapis in many situations due to the strong connection I have with it.

All the people who volunteered to be test clients were very generous with the time they gave me and also in being very willing to articulate exactly what they had experienced during a session. None of them had experienced crystal work before so it was enlightening for them as well as instructive for me.

One of these was Ramon. I met him through his partner, Maria, who worked at Cortijo Romero. They had a cortijo up in the mountains just a twenty minute drive from where I lived. I first met him when Maria invited me to visit them at their home. They had a very large piece of land, perhaps fifteen or twenty acres in an isolated spot, and again everything was solar powered. They had built the house themselves and now they wanted to get the land in order. It had been wild for many years and the rampant woodland needed managing. I was still using two sticks when I went to visit them and my movement was very difficult and painful. Ramon shared with me what they wanted to do with the land. Much like Moshe and Orah, they wanted to live in harmony with the land and to be as self sufficient as possible. The difference was that their finances were much more limited and they had a huge piece of land to care for. I looked around the place and I was struck by its harsh beauty. Whereas Moshe's place was deep in a soft valley, this was high in the mountains. The land was much drier and quite rocky. The main tree growth was a variety of Spanish oaks, which are smaller than the English ones. It was also much more exposed to both sun and wind.

When I got home I began to think. I had been used to and had loved physical work all my life. I was hardly in a fit state to do much and yet….. amongst other things Ramon was a trained Spanish teacher. I needed to improve my language. He desperately needed help on the land as Maria was still working down in Orgiva. Both of us were on a fairly tight budget. How about some barter? So I gave Ramon a ring and drove over to visit. Years later he told me that he just could not believe I would be able to do what I was offering but to his great credit, he was prepared to agree and give me a chance. I suggested that I would help him with whatever tasks needed doing and in exchange, after we had finished work, he would give me a Spanish lesson. The arrangement was that I should go there early in the morning; we would work till late morning; then we would have a lesson and lunch.

He was not the earliest of risers and more often than not, when I arrived, he was still organising breakfast. At any rate, it didn't take much excuse to start with a good strong coffee before anything else. At first we worked on small jobs round the house. They rented the house out in the holiday season and moved into a small caravan in the woods. So there were quite a lot of minor building repairs to do to get it ready. I was beginning to move with just one stick now but still I must have looked a funny sight as I limped over to where I was working and then half sat or leaned against a wall while I was re-pointing the mortar. At that stage the best bit for me was when we sat down to lunch and started our lesson.

I have always found that being an observer never connects me as strongly with a place as when I can work physically. Work connects me with the earth. A bond is built with the land when I share my sweat with the soil. So many people in the modern world have lost this connection. Of course there are many jobs to be done that are separate from the land and sadly people doing them seldom have any other way in which to make that connection with Mother Earth. Just being on the cortijo was a joy. The view from the house to the south was over the deep valley that led to Orgiva, though that was well out of sight. Behind the house the land rose steeply and was heavily wooded with the oak. From the higher parts of the land you could see some of the high peaks of the Alpujarras. It was getting hotter and it was very dry. In the south of Spain there is little rainfall for most of the spring, summer and autumn. Forest fires are a constant hazard and any bonfire is strictly prohibited, except in winter.

There are always little creatures around but they generally avoid us successfully. I could hear scuffles and the dog would chase after things but usually lizards were the main animals I actually saw. Occasionally there were tracks of wild boar to be seen but I never caught a glimpse of them at the cortijo. Mind you, I saw one just outside my house in Bubion one night. I disturbed him with my torch and he hurried off very indignantly. There were often eagles floating high on the thermals above the cortijo. On one occasion I spotted one with a snake in his talons. It must have been still alive as it was writhing furiously high in the air. In the end the eagle dropped it.

Together we completed the jobs in the vicinity of the house and the first holiday makers would be arriving soon. So the next job was to start clearing and felling trees. That was a whole big step forward for me. There were two main jobs to do. There was a lot of rough ground to be cleared with a strimmer and there were trees to fell. We reckoned that using the chainsaw would be the easier task for me. After working my own land in Scotland I was used to a chainsaw but back then I had had two perfectly serviceable legs. The other advantage of the tree felling was that I would be working in partial shade. With temperatures in the high thirties, that was appealing. It was quite a landmark in my recovery as I abandoned my other walking stick then. With a chainsaw in one hand and a can of spare fuel in the other, I limped up the hill and started felling. It didn't matter that I was in pain. It just felt so good to be doing some hard work again. In fact when I got home at the end of the day, I would take the rest of the evening and sometimes even the next day to recover. I worked on alternate days with Ramon. It was a demanding schedule but it gave me structure to my daily existence and it encouraged me to work on my studies.

When it came to Ramon serving as a subject for my crystal course we kept that completely apart from the land clearance and the Spanish lessons. We did it in the evenings. I would go over at around eight. To save loading my heavy couch into the car, we put a couple of thick blankets on a big dining table they had. The table was by a large window that looked to the south over the valley. It was a beautiful setting at dusk, still very warm; their dog also mooched around and tuned into the energy. With the number of my friends who had dogs I was beginning to see how animals know when healing is happening. They often want to be a part of it. Before starting a treatment session I would stand in silent meditation with my hands on Ramon's head. The setting was especially conducive to meditation and although we were at the end of a large open plan room, it was as if there was a bubble of stillness in which we worked together. Even if Maria was busy at the other end, it didn't matter.

I find that whenever I work that bubble of peace and calm manifests. Some healers like to have music as an accompaniment to their work. I prefer the rich fullness of silence. It affords me no distraction and I have always found that my clients go more deeply into the experience that the healing energy creates in their bodies and hearts. It is preferable to be in a quiet place but the protective space that is created by the universal energy seems to shut out most noise that is not too loud.

By now Jenny had secured a sale for the house I was renting. I put a couple of advertisements up in local shops asking for accommodation. I was surprised to get several calls. All of the houses were in Capileira, the village just a couple of kilometres up the mountain from Bubion. I had a look at one but it was bigger than I needed and it was way out on the edge of the village. The other one looked good. I went to meet Javier, the son of the matriarch of the family that owned this and several other properties. My Spanish was improving but here I was chatting with a local villager who spoke the real thick dialect of the mountains. Culturally there was also a huge gulf between us. Yet somehow we just clicked.

The family owned a 'bodega'. What is that? Well I guess it could be described as a wine bar of a sort. Every bodega is a little bit different. They served wines and beers, accompanied by a small 'tapa', which is a little snack. It usually consisted of a couple of slices of bread and some cheese or ham, maybe 'chorizo' (spiced sausage), perhaps with olives. There are different ideas about how the tapa originated. One is that in days past the sherry drinkers in Andalucia used a piece of flat bread to cover the glass between sips to prevent flies from being attracted to the sweetness of the sherry. Another is that in the sixteenth century, Felipe III decreed that when one bought a drink, the bartender should place a cover containing some small quantity of food over the mouth of the mug or goblet as part of the purchase of the drink. The hope was that the food would slow the effects of the alcohol and fill the stomach to prevent over imbibing, thus curbing rowdy drunken behaviour. I think that one sounds more fun to me. But whichever is the origin, the custom still survives in Andalucia, certainly in the villages. The snack is included with your drink. In other parts of Spain you can also get a tapa but generally you pay extra for it.

They also sold a range of local cheeses, wine, hams, sweets and produce from their own cortijo. From the steep, cobbled street, stepping through a great thick and ancient wooden door there were a couple of steps down into the bodega, which had low beamed ceilings. To the left was the little counter behind which stood Javier or his wife, Florencia. The ceiling positively dripped with dried gourds, bunches of herbs and cured hams, mostly from the local area where they are cured in the dry mountain air. The walls were stacked with all the cheeses, wines and sweetmeats. Round a corner in the adjoining room there was a great open fire and rows of simple wooden tables. They didn't serve full meals but rather plates of cheese or ham and sliced tomato in rich pools of olive oil, accompanied by fresh bread. In the dimly lit interior you felt transported back many years to the Andalucian past.

Just beside the little counter there was a door leading to the stairs to the upper floors, where Javier's mother lived. She was about my age and periodically she would appear just to see how things were. She never served in the bodega but she was the rock of the family, a strong matriarchal figure.

So there I was, sitting with Javier at one of the tables, being grilled about how long I might stay and indeed who I was. I tried my best to explain what I did in terms of healing. That was a tough subject to tackle with my command of the language. In addition I had to try and explain the accident I had suffered. I was still limping and the access to a house was an important consideration for me. But right from the beginning there was real warmth and trust between us. I met his wife Florencia, their two girls aged around two and five, and their little dog, Chipi. Such was the trust and friendship we built that later Javier asked me to do some healing for Chipi when he was unwell. I felt quite privileged to be so well accepted.

My house was just round the corner from the bodega, near where they and the children lived. There was a little shop a two minute walk from the house. It was perfect. I moved in and we became firm friends. Whenever I visit the Alpujarras now I base myself in Capileira and usually continue the tradition we established back then of much chatting in the bodega, sitting by the fire if it is winter. Now I can communicate very well with them.

The little house I rented had wonderful views, of course. What house up in those mountains doesn't? The front door was on the street but the balcony at the back was two floors above the ground. I looked across the chasm that was the Poqueira Valley to the high ridge opposite. There were isolated cottages and cortijos and one in particular that I could see would soon become very significant in the development of my healing work. To the right the higher peaks reached up to the sky. Everywhere I looked and everywhere I walked in the village there were great splashes of colour. Most balconies had flowers in pots or hanging baskets. There were large pots of flowers standing in nooks and crannies on the narrow cobbled streets. Javier's mother had one of the most spectacular displays on her balcony. I sometimes thought that there might be a certain rivalry amongst the householders to produce the best display.

I was lucky to have a small room that I could dedicate entirely as a healing room, which I had not had before. Gradually I was becoming more mobile. My crystal course was completed so I began to promote my work more actively. I was getting on very well with Javier and Florencia and I felt that partly through their friendship I was becoming more accepted in the village. What a change from a year before.

During this time I adopted a couple of young cats. One of them managed to have a serious fall at the back of the house and broke his leg quite seriously. It was a complex fracture that the local vet could not deal with. I took him to the animal hospital in Granada, where he had to stay in for a couple of days. They fitted his leg with pretty much the same fixator I had been fitted with. It struck me as quite an amusing coincidence. When I retrieved him I had to keep him inside until the fixator was removed. He hated it and the only secure room was my healing room. He took up residence there and I think the energy there probably helped him. Anyway he made a full recovery. Of course going out of my way for a little stray beast and paying a lot of money for the vet bills further contributed to my reputation as a slightly eccentric Englishman. But little Twinkle, as I had called him, was worth any amount of cash.

One day while I was working with Ramon he told me about the English woman with whom he was having riding lessons. It was her cortijo way up on the opposite ridge that I could see from my balcony. The horse that he usually rode was beginning to suffer arthritis. Of course he had experienced my work and he knew that I also gave healing to animals. He asked if I would be prepared to work with the horse, provided that Alice was open to it. He had no idea what she might think about energy healing. I had shared some healing with the little donkey I met when I was doing the colour healing course in Exeter, but a horse would be new for me. In principle there is no difference in working with any living creature. I went to meet Alice. I had to go back down the road to Orgiva, turn off as if going to the Buddhist Retreat Centre, and then strike off the road higher up. What followed was a long, rough and dusty drive for at least four or five kilometres. As the road got higher I could look across and down at Capileira. From that perspective it was also possible to see round to the peak of Mulhacen. Every time I went my car changed colour from dark blue to grey. It was like driving through a dust bowl.

Alice knew nothing about healing but she was open minded and agreed to let me do something. Then we discussed payment. I had often thought I would like to learn to ride so I suggested a barter arrangement. She would teach me to ride and I would work on the animal. Once we began to see good results with him I could extend my work to others in the small herd if they were in need of healing.

His arthritis improved a lot and then I helped some of the others; some with minor physical ailments and one with a certain emotional insecurity, stemming from when he was a foal. In the intense midday heat, the horses were brought in to the stables, away from the flies. I would go in with them and just hang out for an hour or two. With some there was a particular thing needing attention. With others I just bonded, often sitting beside them and leaning against their flanks as they rested in the relative cool of the stable. Ramon's chance request triggered in me a passion that has finally come to fruition in my work today. I made this instant and very strong bond with horses as a species, as well as with them individually.

They are big powerful animals and yet they are very gentle. A horse is easily spooked and through fear it can accidentally step on you and break a bone because of its weight. An occasional horse may be difficult due to past trauma or maltreatment. That can cause them to be hot headed and maybe a little aggressive. Very rarely one hears of one that is dangerous. But one has to remember that they are prey animals, so every strange thing or unknown creature may be out to attack them. At least that is the horse's view. Yet think how they have served us over thousands of years. The fact that, as a prey animal, the horse allows us to sit on it is quite something. Generally something on its back would be a predator trying to eat it. To have overcome its instinct in this way speaks volumes for the service that it gives us. Too few people really understand this. I always take essential safety precautions when I work with a horse. I wear steel-toed boots. I am aware where I am standing in relation to whether I could be pushed against a wall, for example. Yet I have never felt fear with a horse and once I have established a bond with the animal I feel confident in the physical parameters within which I can work.

There was something else that I began to feel, and that was the amazing power that horses possess as healers in their own right. I knew something, but in very little detail, of the work being done with horses helping children with emotional difficulties. Spending time in Alice's stable allowed me to feel their healing power working on me. I always experience a healing situation, with person or animal, as a circle of energy and love that flows through me to the client and back to me. With the horses this happened at a much higher level.

It was quite obvious that Rod, Alice's husband, viewed what I did as hocus pocus but it didn't bother me. At one point Alice asked if she could have a treatment because she wanted to experience what she saw her horses receiving. She was very surprised at what she felt. Rod probably imagined I had hypnotised her in some way – but no matter. He was a nice chap and we got on well. He used to invite me to watch the international rugby on their television as they had Sky TV, so I forgave him. As well as working in the ring to learn basic riding techniques we often went out into the hills above their property. Although I am not a particularly skilled rider I loved being on the horse. It gave me another way of connecting with the animal.

There are no coincidences, just events for which we cannot see the connecting threads at the time. Not long after starting to work with the herd I saw an advert in a magazine for a course in South Wales entitled 'Healing with Horses'. It was over a long weekend in the autumn and I thought it would help to deepen my new work. Maybe I didn't look closely enough at the website but I went on the assumption that it would be all about how to do healing work with horses, as a practitioner. Not so.

I left the heat of southern Spain and flew into Bristol airport, where I hired a car to drive to South Wales. It was typical wet and dark late autumn weather. That was the first shock. The second was the course. It was all about horses healing us. It was a small group of six and there were three horses that were our mentors for the weekend. I was completely blown away. I had never experienced anything like that with an animal. Going on meditation retreats had been soul searching processes. Many things I had done in the company of coaches, mentors and human therapists had turned me inside out and made me confront often difficult things. To have a horse be the mirror to my soul was totally new. It was very powerful. It changed me. It showed me beyond any doubt that I was embarking on a whole new chapter in my healing journey. It was also challenging. Coming face to face with raw power, however benevolent it might be, is scary.

I returned to the Alpujarras deeply changed. I went to see the herd and viewed them with different eyes. Now I was really open to what they could give me during the healing process. It is hard to explain to someone who has no concept of what it is. Least of all could I tell Alice, but that was not important. As far as she could see I was still offering the same service to her animals. Yet once I understood what a hugely powerful circle of energy I had tuned into, it seemed to enable me to channel healing energy even more. At that time I didn't realise where this would lead me. All I knew was that being in the company of these noble creatures was a transcendent experience. I had always known, from the outside, that a lot of horse people were really hooked on the whole thing around their animals. I had never felt it from the inside and though I didn't actually have my own horse, I was beginning to feel what so many equine people do.

Then the mountain winter arrived, and it was a harsh one. Fortunately my house was a lot cosier than the one in Bubion had been. One night the temperature began to plummet when I went to bed. I woke up in the morning to find nearly half a metre of snow had fallen. Quite a lot of that may have been drifting snow but even so, I had never seen the like. It transformed the village into a fairytale scene. It snowed steadily through the day so any footprints were immediately wiped out. It was beautiful. No cars could get in or out of the village for several days. The village school was closed, which was great for the kids but a bit more hassle for the parents.

Javier was wonderful in keeping an eye on me. The gas bottles used for heating, cooking and the portable stoves are pretty heavy when full and getting them out ready for collection and replacement was harder with snow and ice on the ground. I didn't even need to ask him. He just turned up with a big grin and changed bottles around for me. My previous short stay had certainly enabled me to meet a few folk but living somewhere on a longer term basis is rather different. All in all it had not taken long to build a network of friends and acquaintances.

Through Moshe and Orah I met an English couple who ran a yoga retreat/holiday centre down in the valley. Part of what they offered their guests was the opportunity to book sessions with local practitioners during their holiday. I offered my services as a crystal healer. At that time I was using crystals as the main tool in my energy work, even with the horses, though not as much as with people. After I had given them a treatment so they could experience what I did, I became one of their peripatetic practitioners.

The centre was down in the valley so it was much hotter, even during spring when the centre reopened after the winter break. It was well off the beaten track, quiet and quite flat with gentle views over olive groves, though the backdrop, as anywhere in the area, was still that of the majestic towering peaks that make the Sierra Nevada. The guests would sign up for different sessions when they arrived and I would get a call to let me know how many guests had asked to see me. It was very different to how I had worked before but it was enjoyable. I was going in 'blind', as it were, to each client. Some did have particular ailments they wanted me to address. Others simply wanted a treatment as relaxation during their holiday. Healing can be just that, and I really enjoyed approaching it in this way.

I set up my couch in a big tent that had the side walls rolled up so there was a pleasant breeze. It was near the pool where a few guests might be lazing in the sun. Once I was ready with my crystals laid out I would call my first client over. It was almost certainly the first and only time I would see them so I had to establish a rapport very quickly. It seemed to happen every time. I'm sure some benefited more than others but I did get excellent feedback about how much they had enjoyed the treatment. With energy healing one has to be quite detached about the results. Energy will go to where it is needed. The client's higher self, if you like, knows what is needed; where and how to absorb what is being channelled. Though they too are working with energy, an acupuncturist and a homeopath, for example, will focus more directly on a particular physical or emotional aspect. There will often also be effects registered in unexpected ways; I have experienced that myself. With pure energy work, however, it is much more often like this.

Working in this way with people whom I would not see again taught me to be very detached from seeing anything specific. After the treatment they always told me how they were feeling and what they had experienced. Hearing later in the week how things had gone for them in the days after the session was very rewarding.

I had developed an unexpected and interesting source of income through Jenny's house in Bubion. She had sold it to a small private syndicate of English people who planned to use it on a time share basis. They lived in the UK and none of them spoke much Spanish. They contracted me to find a local builder and to oversee the renovation of the house. I found a great builder, originally from Madrid. I had to liaise with the town council, pay and supervise the builder and ensure the work was done to requirements and to a good standard. I got to be good friends with Manolo the builder and his family and I learnt a lot about the unique building techniques and materials used in the Alpujarras. The flat roof construction is interesting. The ceiling beams are boughs of chestnut. That's now a carefully protected tree in the area though previously when the old cottages were built it was much more plentiful. On top of the beams there are thin strips of chestnut laid crosswise. Above these strips are placed flat stones which form the base for the river clay that makes the top, waterproof layer of the roof. Once set, the clay is hard as iron and impervious to rain. Knowing my building background, Manolo was keen to instruct me in the technical side of the work. He was something of a rogue but very warm hearted. He was also very concerned for my recovery from my fall.

A short while before I met him, on the anniversary of my accident I had made a climb of Mulhacen, by way of a symbolic recognition of my recovery. I had done it solo, in intense pain, but I made it. I mentioned this to Manolo and I said I was planning to do it again. Although I had managed on my own before, he insisted on accompanying me the next time. I think he was concerned and probably thought I was slightly mad. We had a great time together. He was a little overweight and not very fit but then I was hardly moving at a sprint. We made a good pair and he was excellent company, talking almost non-stop most of the way, as was his wont. He had a never ending fund of stories and anecdotes and it was good for me that he spoke no English, which really sharpened up my language skills. From some of the things he told me I did sometimes wonder if he was using the Alpujarras as a bolt hole; that he might be getting away from something in his past in Madrid. He was that sort of character. But rogue or not, he was one of the most generous and warm hearted people I have ever met. I could never fault the way he treated me.

After the house renovations were complete I continued to act as the caretaker. I cleaned the house and did laundry in preparation for the incoming people; kept wood supplies up to scratch and generally made sure all was fine. I knew several of the joint owners so it made the work more personal. Because none of them spoke much Spanish it fell to me to do quite a lot other than just cleaning. Any liaising with the council was my job. I helped a couple of them set up bank accounts. Added to what I was earning from my healing work, it made for a fairly secure income. I also had to be something of a diplomat with the neighbours. They were a Spanish couple who lived in Granada who had bought the next door house also as a holiday property. The idea of foreigners buying up property as a holiday escape did not sit too well with them. As was the case with many Spaniards there, they also resented the fact that none of my employers spoke other than extremely basic Spanish. I must say I sympathise with that. Still, after a few months I managed to smooth the waters and when my folk started to learn the language, the atmosphere changed somewhat.

Considering that I had been living in a foreign country for quite a short time I had managed to establish a good network of friends; my healing work was growing and developing; I had an income from the house in Bubion and all this was in the most beautiful setting one could wish for. Then I had a stand at an alternative health festival down on the Costa del Sol. There was a wide range of practitioners of several nationalities from all over Andalucia. I talked to several who were based around the general area of Malaga, Marbella and further west, including the area on the mainland just north of Gibraltar. I took a trip over there and explored while basing myself in a place called Jimena de la Frontera. Scenically it was not quite as dramatic as the Alpujarras, although further north still towards the historic town of Ronda there are very beautiful mountains. I met a woman who had a healing centre in Estepona on the coast and she offered me the chance to work there as an independent practitioner.

I decided to move to Jimena de la Frontera and I found a place to rent very easily. It was one of those headstrong moves I tend to make though I am becoming just a little wiser as I get older - not before time! In fact working at the health centre was a disaster. I had to pay quite a lot per month for the use of the facilities and then through my own marketing efforts I had to find the clients to cover that cost and turn a profit. It never happened and I lost a lot of money. My rented house was also very expensive so I was eating into my funds. However, what came out of being in this new place was a phenomenal development of the work I had started doing with horses. It enabled me to take the work to a much deeper level. I met an English couple, Clive and Jane who lived quite close to me. They had a lovely house that they had built on a good spread of land with stables and a dozen or so horses. Some were their own and some were liveried there. They gave riding lessons and also took people out on short treks into the surrounding countryside.

Clive really knew his horses. He had been involved with them for many years in the UK before moving to Spain. As well as having an extensive knowledge of equine care in general, he also had a very detailed understanding of their anatomy, the ailments they suffer and so on. He introduced me to something else that was totally new to me, which was Natural Horsemanship. Colloquially this is often described as Horse Whispering. The training of horses in the past has sometimes been quite harsh. The need to train these animals for warfare or for the heavy demands of the American cowboys has encouraged methods which focus on control and the use of fear. Of course there have always been people who have worked in a more harmonious and gentle way with their horses. In fact as far back as the ancient Greeks there were trainers who espoused more gentle methods. In recent years Natural Horsemanship has come to be associated with people like Monty Roberts and Pat Parelli. They have become names that many people know of through their clever marketing. The film The Horse Whisperer, released in 1998 and starring Robert Redford, was based on this approach – although in that case Buck Brannaman was the man who was the inspiration for the story and he also worked on the film.

Horses have served us for thousands of years and yet it is still unnatural to take a wild animal and teach it to do things that are really at odds with its fundamental nature. Although fear and cruelty is no way to build a relationship with any living being, there are good and bad ideas on both sides of the argument. A natural approach to animal training must be preferable but it would be foolish to criticise people out of hand who are traditional in their approach. Most people working with animals have good hearts. Unfortunately so many people want to make out that their 'new' approach to something is the best and only way to go. Nevertheless, hearing Clive talk about the principles of natural horsemanship resonated with what I had begun to feel in my growing connection with these animals. I felt that if the principles were more widely understood, good trainers could become even better and the horse would benefit.

Clive and I met through someone else, and it was not in the context of either horses or healing. Those things came up in later conversation. He was open to what I did because of an experience he had had with a previous horse when he used a Radionics practitioner. So he introduced me to Diablo. He was a noble and handsome animal: a big Friesian. He towered above me. Clive wanted me to look at him because he was getting on in years and he was in some pain with arthritis in the legs. But I was warned that Diablo could be very aloof. He would ignore you if he felt you were unworthy of his attention. With that warning ringing in my ears I went to meet him. I meditated quietly outside his stall and when I felt it was right I went in to be with him.

I think there were a couple of reasons why he made such an impression on me. He was by far the biggest horse I had met and his presence was very imposing. But more important was the way that he accepted me and really invited me into his space. He was a big fella! I could stand upright under his chin. He ignored me at first and even moved to the back of the stall. I just stood in meditation, quietly waiting. He then turned to look at me, came over and stood beside me. I asked him if I had his permission to place my right hand on one of his chakras. I clearly remember I was standing on his right hand side. He let me know it was OK. Then we bonded very deeply. He was motionless as I focussed healing energy into his being. His mouth began to quiver; his lips relaxed; his eyes closed; his head dropped – all signs that he was accepting what I was giving him. Energy work usually does that to a horse when they respond to it. We stood like this for quite some time. I spent a lot of time with him for the period that I lived there. He could never be ridden again but his movement became much freer and he could be worked to the lunge. His quality of life improved a lot.

Every time I saw him, he opened his heart to me and though he has now passed on I shall never forget him for the noble soul he was and for the love and teaching he gave me. I often say that horses give me as much or more than I give them. They really are very powerful healers and I am blessed to have them in my life.

In the Alpujarras I had established quite a full and rounded lifestyle. Things did not work out so well in this way while I was in Jimena de la Frontera. There were fewer Spaniards there who were into alternative ways of thinking – at least in the immediate area where I was living. I think that is why I found it harder to make Spanish friends, or perhaps I just missed finding them. At any rate my work with horses deepened a lot. I met an Irish woman who rescued polo ponies. Polo certainly does place a lot of physical strain on a horse and sometimes they are cast off if they become injured and unable to continue in the sport. It was interesting to meet someone who had not had any kind of training in the healing arts, yet who had an instinctive feeling for what the animal was suffering in terms of pain or injury. In addition she also had a good grasp of the animal's anatomy and physiology. She would ask me to 'read' a horse's state of mind and its physical condition. Then we would compare notes. At any one time she had three or four ponies on her land, and she spent a lot of time and money caring for them. I learnt from observing her instinctive connection with them, and it gave me yet another chance to be with an animal that was fast becoming the focus of my work.

I flew to the UK to attend another course with the woman in South Wales. I began to see that I really did have a special connection with these animals. I had always loved working with people and other animals but with horses there was something special; something different. They responded to me very strongly.

By then I had moved from Jimena to San Pablo de Buceite, a little village a few kilometres up the road. The house came with a beautiful garden filled with various citrus trees, several large pomegranates, a Sharon fruit tree, a custard apple and the most wonderful strawberries that I was able to pick for breakfast every day for several weeks. In the back garden at the bottom of the steps leading to the garden was an enormous cactus, standing over twenty feet tall. During the flowering season it had huge white blossoms that came out at night. They gave off a rich scent that I could smell from inside the house. Cactus is often thought to be slow growing but this one had not read the rules. I swear it seemed to grow before my eyes. There was a point when one stem was hanging precariously over the steps. I borrowed a ladder. Balancing on top of the ladder, trying to avoid the vicious spines, I hacked off great sections. Then I had to avoid being speared by them as they fell.

For many years – in Bristol, Scotland, Exeter, Capileira – I had shared a house with cats. They had been a natural part of my life. When I was in San Pablo I adopted a handsome white cat called Mateo, whose owner was going away. He was good company and what I like about cats is that they simply do not obey the rules you set. Dogs can be trained to a greater degree, but cats rule. That is good for me as being on my own I can become somewhat rigid in my lifestyle and habits. That is not such a bad thing but it is good to share the house with another being who just does things without my permission.

Unfortunately the economic downturn that was engulfing Europe towards the end of the first decade of the twenty-first century was hitting Spain particularly hard. I had been doing some building project management for an English woman on a house in Jimena, much as I had done in Bubion. The recession was biting all round. Her money dried up so my work stopped and I had little else. I found it impossible to survive so I decided that I would have to return to England. At the time I did not want to, even though it was an economic necessity. However, as always it proved the right thing in the end, though it took me a while to see it.

So once more I loaded my trusty car with my worldly goods and set off to drive up through Spain and catch a ferry to England. I was returning with nothing to go to in the way of work and without a clear idea of how things would turn out. There were many parts of the country that I knew and had lived in but I have never returned permanently to a place where I have been before. That has always felt like trying to recapture something that will have certainly changed. I knew Cheltenham a little, having lived in Bristol only a short distance away. I also had an aunt living there who had always been a very good friend as well as a relative. She agreed to let me use her spare room till I found my feet.

Chapter 11: Death and Healing

Returning to the UK after five years in Spain was a real culture shock. I noticed many changes in the social fabric. When you live with changes as they gradually occur, you don't notice them so much. Plugging back into the country was different. People here grumble about the European Union bureaucracy that leaks out of Brussels. The same rules apply to Spain yet to a large degree things there are not enforced or they are simply ignored. I heard considerable objection to such things as the plethora of wheelie bins foisted on householders; the sometimes ludicrous division of waste; possible fines if a bin is left on the road after it has been emptied. Without getting into discussing the 'green' issues involved, it is indicative of a very different mentality here and I found things like that very hard to adjust to. Life in the mountains of Andalucia was one of freedom, a certain anarchy and a very laissez faire approach to things generally.

It was financial circumstances that had forced me to return but I was struggling to accept the very different reality of my situation. From the wild of the mountains I had plunged back into a suburban location in Cheltenham. It had been ages since I had lived in that kind of situation. For a long time, I had been used to wide open spaces and rugged scenery. My aunt went out of her way to accommodate me, even giving over her dining room for my use as an office cum computer room. At that time I was trying to develop a home based business, working online. I felt uncomfortable imposing on someone else's personal space, even though we have always got on very well. She too had been used to her independence for a long time after being widowed so I was very grateful for her forbearance at my invasion.

I had had pipedreams of the day when my online business would bring a big enough income to enable me to buy some land and set up a horse sanctuary. I had seen many such ventures and I thought it would be a wonderful thing to do. It would have been but it would also have been a massive financial undertaking with many responsibilities I had not really considered. The most important thing was to use the gift I have; to do the work that was probably right in front of me, had I but looked. In short I was just not living in the moment. Of course dreams are important. They keep us inspired and alive. Too many people do live sad lives of mediocrity, despite harbouring things in their hearts that they long to do. But if we live too much in those dreams, especially if they are totally unrealistic and even making us live in a way that is not true to ourselves, they become destructive.

I had been trying to build an online business, alongside other things, for about ten years. It simply had not worked. For many it does work but it was just not me. It was costing me a lot of money – a home based business is not free of costs. I desperately needed an income. Finding work once you are over sixty is not so easy, but things began to change. Through undertaking some voluntary work I found an opportunity opened up to work with the Probation Service as a Community Service Supervisor. Looking after people who have been to court and given a sentence that includes a certain amount of hours of unpaid work to benefit the community is a challenge. You are dealing with a wide range of people. Some have just slipped off the rails, committing fairly minor offences and they accept their retribution. Others may be serial offenders with a more cynical attitude to life and the judicial system. There are many shades in between. But if I truly believe that all people have a good heart then to judge these fellow human beings is wrong. Nevertheless, the reality of supervising a group of up to eight people single-handedly for a whole day was a big challenge. For over two years I worked full time. I didn't always get it right in the way I handled them but overall I got on well with most of the offenders. Later I changed to working on a relief basis for perhaps four or five days per month. This was less stressful and has enabled me to do a better job. I always tried to be true to my beliefs in discussions that took place in the groups regarding morality, spirituality and alternative ways of viewing life. Some of the offenders who had come from a very difficult and oppressive background, with little opportunity to question life, thought I was at the least eccentric and possibly completely off the wall. Others did respond. I never preach to anyone but it is important to speak one's truth. People respond well to that. I learnt a huge amount about the deprivation under which many people live. It's one thing to read about it. It is quite another when you come face to face with someone whose life has dealt him a lousy hand of cards.

Hitting sixty-five, the official retirement age, was a wake up call. It is not that I fear old age. But I saw people around me dying – one being my father, just before my officially becoming a pensioner. It was sobering because I realised that I was not feeling deeply fulfilled in my work or my life. I had allowed my healing work to slip onto the back burner. My excuse was that I needed to build a substantial income to follow my dream, clear my debts and set myself up for my old age. Would my life slip away with the music inside me still unsung? What a sad mistake that would have been.

Then I had my epiphany in January 2013. I was not feeling in a very good place; I had a lot of financial worry weighing on me. I went to a talk in Cheltenham on the subject of money, exploring the blocks we have about money and riches, the conditioning that locks us into poverty or at least into 'just getting by'. With about twenty people in the room, we were sharing some of the things that held us back from embracing the idea of being wealthy. Money is so often seen as rather sordid; a necessary evil. The speaker asked me what I would be doing if I could freely follow my passion. Immediately I spoke about my horse healing work, which had developed so strongly in Spain. I could feel my whole vibration change. Everyone in the room felt it and remarked on it. Then the lady asked me why I was not doing it. I mumbled reasons about needing to earn a living and that it would be difficult to generate an income like that. Very bluntly, she told me I was making excuses – and she was right. Several people in the room said they would like me to see their horses. It was stunning. One of them was a lady called Rosalind who lived nearby in Gloucester. We struck up a friendship and started texting and phoning to support each other in making the changes we both felt were needed in order for us to become more fulfilled.

I left the talk knowing that I had to follow my passion and purpose first, after which money would flow to satisfy my needs. I am a horse healer. Really acknowledging that to myself was a huge turn around. A few months before I had met some great people who do web design. I contacted them, had a meeting and set about designing my new website with them. As the eighteenth century German poet Goethe said: *"Whatever you do, or dream, begin it now. Boldness has genius, power and magic in it."* Once you know and understand your true purpose in life – the thing that is your gift to the world – it is worse than foolish to delay in its execution. It is a betrayal of the universal energy that gives us life. I felt over the moon when I made the decision, though I was also pretty nervous.

I had no idea how I would really develop my work as a viable business. Something many healers struggle with is the issue of charging a fair fee for their work. I had inner work to do on just that. My web designers were fantastic. They tuned in to my wavelength. They understood what I was doing and gave me great encouragement as well as designing a great website. Rosalind also proved a good friend. Her daughter Sarah had a horse and she allowed me to shoot a video with the horse to put on my website. Very kindly Ros' partner handled my video recorder for that.

Finally after nearly forty years of apprenticeship I was taking my healing to the world. Well, it is all in the timing, as they say. In May 2013 my website went live. One challenge that loomed was the business networking group to which I belong. For six or seven months I had been promoting my online business, largely unsuccessfully. What would the members think if I suddenly appeared 'wearing a new hat'? At the first meeting at which I announced my new venture I said, *"Do you know the old saying about a leopard not changing its spots? Well, this leopard just did."* Most of them responded very positively to my passion and the fact that I was finally speaking my truth. That is what moves people. They might not understand something but they respond to real integrity. In actual fact, many more people did understand than I had thought would be the case. Simply, that is because healing is completely natural, and on a deep level most folk can relate to it.

Continuing the work with horses that had begun in Spain was the most fulfilling thing I have ever done. Wolfgang Goethe's quote is so true. When you take a bold decision that is truly aligned with your purpose, your soul's calling, things begin to happen. What seem to be difficult challenges are not so difficult; unexpected openings appear; the right people come into your life. Although the Cotswold area in which I live has a big equine presence, I knew nobody in that world. I had my contacts through my networking group but I was not aware that any of them had horses or knew of people with them. I was amazed at the speed with which possibilities opened up. It transpired that there were people in the group with contacts and they really wanted to help.

Ros and I were supporting each other. She gave me so many ideas. Her daughter was very kind in allowing me to spend time with her beautiful horse. My friend Clive from Spain had remarried and had also returned to the UK. He was living in Cornwall. I got in touch to let him know about my plans. He was very generous in his support and very kindly he gave me a testimonial to put on my website. I often say that *'Life is a team effort'*. There are loners, of course, but I believe that real success only comes through working together, even if the nature of what you are doing is fairly solitary. People rallied round. All of this boosted my confidence in knowing that I had made the right decision. I began to build my own 'tribe', as Seth Godin often talks about. He is an entrepreneur and a marketer with some very interesting ideas. He believes that the way to success in life and business is to build around you a tribe that shares your beliefs and ideals. That may sound obvious yet many people miss it. In business they focus on blanket advertising; they spread themselves all over the internet quite indiscriminately. It is far better to work from oneself outward, rather like dropping a stone in a

MY HEALING JOURNEY

pool. The ripples gradually spread and as they go, they move things on the surface of the water, thus having an effect on them.

I needed to look at marketing but as the nature of what I do is a little esoteric in some people's minds, that was quite a challenge. During my short stint in the Life Assurance industry in my thirties, one of my managers had said that what we earned was the reward for a job well done. That really stuck with me. I applied that principle when I was running my building business. I had to apply it now. I knew that word of mouth recommendation would be the best way for my work to develop once I had made a breakthrough with one or two clients initially.

Suddenly I received an unexpected email. It was the summer of 2013. My website had been live for just a few months. I had had leaflets printed, some of which I had put in a shop in Cheltenham. It was an organic whole food shop that had a rack for leaflets and advertisements. It was obvious that most of the people who put things there were the kind of people who might well be open to what I was offering. The email was from someone who was a presenter on local Radio Winchcombe. He had found a leaflet and he wondered if I would be interested in coming on his show as a guest and talking about my horse healing. He had contacted two other people who also worked with animals as he thought the combination would work well. I agreed, and I accepted his offer. In the end neither of the other two joined us. We established an immediate rapport, finding we had a lot in common. He suggested that I might like to have my own show. Initially I was hesitant as I wondered what its purpose could be. Obviously one does not have a radio programme simply to promote oneself. However, I am passionate not only about horses themselves but also about the many ways in which they are used to help and heal people. For example, there is a lot being done now in equine guided work to help emotionally disturbed children and equine guided leadership development. There are also different approaches to caring for them, such as barefoot work, i.e. not being shod.

This was a golden opportunity to promote awareness of these ideas. I could showcase local people working in these many ways. It would enlighten both horse and non-horse people; it would help my interviewees in increasing their profile and it would be fun. That last is an essential ingredient for me. I decided on a one hour show on a monthly basis, which would be an interview interspersed with three or four tracks of music. I called it 'All Things Equine with a Twist'. I submitted my proposal to the radio station and it was accepted. In quite an amazing way this started to build my tribe. Once the word got out that I was doing it, people wanted to help with suggestions of possible interviewees. I approached people I did not know and they were very responsive, and some have become friends. Other people have asked me if they might be a guest. My mentor at the station who had encouraged me to do this took me under his wing and gave me a lot of time, energy and advice. He is very experienced in the field and he was and still is very generous with his time. Aren't people amazing? They really do want to give, to help but so often they cannot find ways to do this. I do believe, however, that it is a trait common to most of us. So within a few short months I had taken my healing to the wider world, I had become a radio presenter and I had decided to write this book. It was a momentous year.

Most people see the human race as superior to animals. This belief is usually based on the fact that we have a whole range of physical and technological tools. We can make things whereas animals cannot or do not. Many also say that animals have no emotions, no consciousness nor souls. I disagree with that. I think that this misconception comes from the fact that many of us find it hard or impossible to communicate with an animal. This belief causes confusion because it prevents us understanding what an animal is 'saying'. If it were a person, we would understand. When people say that ascribing human emotions to an animal is anthropomorphic, it is usually meant as a criticism; it is something foolish. Of course there are many dedicated pet owners who do see the complexity of character of their companions but overall it is a minority. However, in my view, and in the view of other animal healers and communicators I know, the members of the animal kingdom have the same range of feelings and sensibilities as us.

In their simplicity, children often connect to the world around them far better than we do as adults. We allow our intellect to make things complex, and in that complexity we lose the ability for heart to heart communication. Heart to heart is how animals talk to us. In recent years I had begun to see the emotions and individual characteristics that they display but still I think that I was not approaching them with the heart of a child. Just after I launched my website I went to Germany for a workshop run by a well known American animal communicator. No one has a magic formula for inter species communication but I knew I would learn by simply being with someone more experienced. I was not expecting to be handed a secret formula; rather sharing experience and ideas would open my abilities a little more. Some of the participants brought their dogs so that we could work with them. We visited a large horse yard nearby and we also went to Frankfurt Zoo to work with some elephants. The most important thing I took away from the course was that I needed to work on a true heart to heart connection with the horses that would be my clients. In fact I probably learnt more from one of the other participants, Catrin, who lived in Frankfurt. She recognised the ability I have and gave me a lot of encouragement and help. I did some distance healing work and diagnosis with her cats and dogs. This proved very effective and accurate and further helped my growing confidence. I met her dog on the course and Catrin sent me photos of her other animals, with various questions. I meditated with the photos and allowed my intuition to kick in. Then I phoned her and we discussed what I had intuited. It was very accurate and insightful. She loved helping and I kept learning.

Exploring many different healing modalities has always kept me stimulated. It has also reminded me that I am constantly a beginner. I am always learning. It has been said that the wise man admits he knows little and the fool claims to know everything. Whenever I have spent time with a new mentor or done some kind of training I have come away with a new insight. It is not so much a case of learning new techniques, rather something inside me shifts on an energy level. Then this is reflected in the deeper contact that results between me and a client. I love working with crystals, both for their energetic properties and the beautiful artefacts that they are. Yet there are periods when I hardly use them in my work. At other times I use them more. For a long time I had begun to feel that the key to healing was something much deeper and more subtle than an array of techniques or methods. After my experience in Germany, and after more contact with my equine friends, I began to see that, for me at least, the key is simply 'love'.

That may sound rather 'woolly', yet is it? The love between two people can be so strong that they may do rash or dangerous things. The abdication of Edward VIII in England in 1936 for the love of Wallis Simpson was a huge constitutional crisis. In the climate of the time it was a momentous thing to do. A mother's love may cause her to make immense sacrifices for her child. The world's great spiritual leaders such as Jesus and Buddha were famed for their selfless and powerful love.

Richard Gerber, M.D. wrote a book called 'Vibrational Medicine' in 1988. He wrote about many of the subtle energy therapies and he made a telling comment about love:

"Over the years, as I have researched healers and healing, I have been impressed by the commonality of loving intent amongst healers. They work primarily from a position of heart-centred, unconditional love when they work with another being's energy field. It appears that love may actually be a real energetic force, not merely a catalyst for action, transformation and healing."

So the challenge facing me was how to nurture that love within me and how to focus it in the healing situation. As I have said, meditation is for me an integral part of my healing work. This is because it connects me with the source of healing – universal energy, or God – which by its very nature is pure love: unconditional, non-judgemental and all accepting. By making meditation a part of my daily life and by meditating before and during a healing session, I can stay in contact with that energy. I am part of that energy, as we all are, but it is more than me. My preparation immediately before giving and during a treatment includes telling my client, non-verbally, that I love them. I invoke love from God for that being. I focus within my own heart chakra area in order to feel and merge with that pure love energy. I visualise a connection, maybe a tunnel, between my heart and the heart of the animal. I send loving energy down that tunnel and it connects us on a subtle level.

The power of intention and visualisation is immense. In fact it was the Russians who first started to do research in this area before the fall of the Iron Curtain. They worked mainly with sportsmen but with other people too. They found that athletes who visualised and mentally recreated the actual feelings of a race gained almost as much benefit from that as from an actual physical training routine. It is sometimes called mental rehearsal. By feeling love inside me, smiling, creating a feeling of warmth, stimulating care and compassion, a very strong bond is made with an animal. Although there are situations with a horse when healing happens almost despite me, an infinitely more powerful energy manifests when I come from a place of love in this way.

With horses in particular there are signs that indicate how well it is receiving the energy. Their heads will drop; their eyes close; their mouths quiver; they become very still. Sometimes I stand in front of them, supporting them under the mouth as their heads drop. Our heads often touch. Sometimes we look deep into one another's eyes. Sometimes we both have our eyes closed. We are both motionless. We seem to merge together for fifteen minutes or more. Bearing in mind that it is normally quite a skittish, nervous prey animal, that is quite remarkable.

Healers often say that energy goes to where it is needed. That does not mean that I ignore a presenting symptom. If there is a particular injury or area of pain to deal with, I will place my hands there. At this point it must be said that healing should not be considered as a replacement for veterinary care. People are obliged by law to consult a vet and they need the vet's permission before calling an 'alternative' equine practitioner, such as an osteopath. The exception to this, not requiring permission, is energy healing or the laying on of hands. Often I deal with behavioural or emotional problems. These may result from past trauma, sometimes unknown by the present carer, which is a word I prefer to owner. In this situation it is likely that I will work mainly around the heart, the head area or the central chakra of the horse. I am simply making a deep connection and healing energy flows into the whole being of the horse: its body, mind and emotions.

Quite obviously none of us is immortal but because both my parents lived till I was well over sixty, they gave the illusion of being around forever. When my dad died quite suddenly just before I turned sixty-five, it came as a huge shock. He seemed to be in good health. I had been due to visit them at Christmas but due to heavy snow I had cancelled driving up to see them. On New Year's Day I phoned to have a chat. Dad was in bed, feeling unwell, and he answered the extension phone by the bed. He told me how deeply tired he was feeling. I knew then that I would not see him again. Just a few days later I had a call late in the evening from the ambulance crew that was at my parents' house to tell me he was dead. He had stayed in bed in the morning and later in the day Mum had found him as he had passed on.

It is the natural order and he had lived to nearly eighty-seven. He had not suffered and he died quickly. I am not frightened of my death but all of a sudden it made me look at my life and consider things in a different light. I was so grateful that we had healed our difficulties when I stayed with them after my accident. I realised even more deeply what a fantastic man he was, how much he gave me and how much I loved him.

At the end of September 2013 my mother died. At ninety-one she had lived a long life and she never really recovered from my father's death. It was not unexpected but still it was very difficult. In fact it triggered a lot of things for me. I read once that in some way we do not fully grow up till both our parents have passed on. That seems a strange thing to say. After all, with medical science now able to prolong people's lives so much, it is common for people in their sixties to have one or even both parents still alive. Are we still so immature at the age of sixty? On some level I think there is something in that notion. It was as if I was finally released from my past, or at least I had the opportunity to be fully released. The subtle energy connections that bind us to our ancestry are very strong. There are many societies that honour and revere the ancestors with good reason, amongst them the Japanese, the Chinese, American Indians, most African peoples; indeed the majority of the world except for the western nations. Why might that be, I wonder?

Shortly after my mother's death I went to my doctor to find out what might be behind some health issues I had been experiencing for several months. The symptoms could have indicated lung cancer. I was going through some challenges and Mum's death had hit me quite hard. I was in the state of mind where I assumed the worst and I thought cancer might be a reality. On one hand I was not frightened; I just wanted to know. Not knowing till the test results came through was what affected me badly. The test results were negative with regard to cancer, but there was something amiss in my lungs.

In the meantime I had decided to make radical changes to my diet on the assumption that it would prove to be a tumour. I believe that it is possible to cure cancer almost entirely with diet. Of course the mainstream medical establishment disagrees violently. Their reaction to anyone who refuses chemotherapy and who adopts alternative health strategies is one of scorn, sometimes verging on threatening. I believe there is no solid evidence to support the use of chemotherapy. In rare cases it seems to work. However, in general, at best it gives some short term relief but cancers then return far more aggressively and kill in a short time. The side effects with the consequent drastic reduction in quality of life make it, in my view, a complete non-starter. Unfortunately the cancer industry is a huge and lucrative one for the pharmaceutical conglomerates.

Cancer thrives in an acid environment. One of the first things should be to change the internal environment of the body, as most of us have a very acidic one. Eliminating meat and dairy produce from our diet helps do this. I had been a vegetarian for over thirty years but I had started to eat meat again just after I broke my feet. My body seemed to tell me then that I needed it. Now I decided to become vegan overnight. The other poison that most of us consume is sugar. I eat almost no tinned or processed food so I don't get it from those sources. I do not take sugar in drinks. However, after an honest appraisal I realised that my consumption of biscuits, chocolate and cakes was way over the top. They went as well, as did fruit juice. This latter is effectively a huge sugar hit, having had all its good fibre removed.

When I was in Spain I had met someone who used, sold and swore by a liquid, stabilised oxygen product that you take in water. He had used it for many years and he had cured his diabetes with that and with dietary changes. The product raises the body's alkaline level, cleanses the system, promotes healthy gut bacteria and really strengthens the digestive system. I tracked him down and after finding out more, I added it to my regimen. In just a few weeks my energy level increased immensely. My digestive system, which has always been delicate, improved even more than it had with the aid of other supplements. All in all I felt very much better.

Further tests suggested that I had developed asthma. At my age I was surprised, but that can happen apparently. There is asthma in my family; as a builder I was exposed to all sorts of unpleasant dusts; I had smoked as a youngster: it had all caused scarring on my lungs and breathing obstruction. Again, giving up dairy produce has helped that. I also got hold of a Himalayan salt pipe. I researched this widely and I found a lot of information to suggest that it could help and would be preferable to NHS prescribed inhalers containing unpleasant chemicals. Using that for twenty minutes a day has begun to help.

How the misdemeanours of our youth come back to haunt us; puffing away as I did a way back was never going to cause me problems. I was indestructible! During the early stages of finding all this out, I did get somewhat downcast. Once I knew what I was dealing with and I could take positive action, I began to see it as a good wake up call. Over recent months I had not been eating well and I had slipped into a lazy routine. The changes I made have not only helped the immediate challenge but they will be beneficial as I get older.

With my mother's death all the older members of my family – parents, aunts and uncles – who were adult when I was born were gone. My aunt in Cheltenham was very much younger than my mother, only eight years older than me. So although she had watched me grow up, in many ways I view her almost more as a big sister. She has always been very supportive of all that I have done but somehow the energy connection in her case is different. With the last severing of these ancestral connections something inside me changed. In a strange way I was now free to be who I am with nothing projected on to me from older relatives who still viewed me as a little boy, even if I was grown up.

There are so many subtle forces that impose on us through our lives. The expectations and views of us from others, especially family members, exerts a profound influence. We might not think they do; we might try to deny them; and yet they are there. This seems to connect with the idea that we do not fully grow up till our parents have gone. Even as I say that I can hear many people saying it is nonsense and that they are fully grown up. Maybe, and maybe not……

A direct consequence of my mother's death was that it gave me the impetus to deal with a challenge I have faced for many years. In my late teens I began to suffer from intrusive thought patterns which seemed almost to have a life of their own. I felt compelled to counter them by developing certain habit patterns that were uncomfortable and somehow invasive of my whole life. Just after I went to college I recall going to my GP and asking him about some of the unwanted, yet uncontrollable feelings I was getting. He had absolutely no understanding of what I was really getting at and gave me no help whatsoever. Gradually I began to develop slightly eccentric behaviour patterns that were sometimes noticeable, and on occasions they evoked unkind remarks from people. I began to feel that all was not well with my mental health. Unfortunately back in the early seventies there was still huge prejudice about mental illness. Unless someone suffered so seriously that they were hospitalised, they would often go to great lengths to hide their problems. As was common I developed coping strategies to hide what I was suffering from.

What I was going through is, in part, what contributed to my interest in mental health and made me do some voluntary work with MIND in my twenties. I felt a strong connection with and compassion for the clients we were helping. Unfortunately I saw the considerable prejudice that many felt towards them. This further reinforced my fear of trying to seek help. I simply worked harder to mask what was going on. I realise now that I was suffering from Obsessive Compulsive Disorder. Sadly it was as if a destructive cycle had been set in motion. Things would happen; people would make comments (quite possibly innocently) that reinforced my fears and shame. I would develop more ways to hide the behaviour. Shame is one of the biggest stumbling blocks that OCD sufferers have to deal with. Even in my marriage I was unable to open up to my wife about the full extent of what I was dealing with. Instead, as again is often the case, I endeavoured to bend her to accommodate my compulsive behaviours. That was a recipe for disaster.

When I worked at the psychiatric hospital I saw so much cruel lack of understanding of mental ill health by so many staff that it further put me off seeking help from those professionals. I tried working with a number of alternative practitioners but again I seemed unable to beat it. I tried to talk to one or two other people, my old friend Hugh being one. It just seemed that I was never able to open up fully, though as I now see, more professional help is what I needed. Maybe on some level I was still unwilling to acknowledge fully that I was ill. In a way I was confused. On one hand I was a healer – but how could I be that if I was suffering from OCD? Yet my experience continued to show me that my healing work was powerful. I think I felt, subconsciously, that by fully acknowledging that I should seek help, somehow my work would be nullified. Considering that I acknowledged that the source of healing is beyond me, that was a very self destructive thought.

With my mother gone, I knew I had reached a point when I must deal with my mental ill health. I would not take it to my grave. With great trepidation, I went to my GP to seek help. Of course he was very understanding. Times have changed to a considerable degree. From what he said I realised that it is in fact quite a common problem. Having harboured mine for nigh on fifty years, the behaviour patterns had become deeply entrenched and were becoming worse. The relief at his reaction was immense. Immediately he put me in touch with an NHS group that would be the start of a process of healing. Initially I attended a weekly group session. It was not quite a therapy group so much as a chance to learn about and understand what the illness is. To share the room with half a dozen other OCD sufferers was a great relief. There were indeed other people like me and they were not completely crazy – which is what most of us think. The two ladies running the group were very experienced and deeply compassionate. Finally I saw that healing would be possible. The next stage will be one to one therapy. It will not be easy. It is often said that we hang on to things that are not serving us because on some level there is a payback. What that could possibly be for me I do not know. However, it is certain that I will have to face up to some painful inner ghosts – but I will do it.

During the group work we were told that this condition will always be with us but that it is possible to reduce its severity and intrusion; in other words, to manage it. This I do not accept. As well as undertaking Cognitive Behavioural Therapy, I believe that there is work to be done on the more subtle energy level. I intend to work with two energy healers as well so that I can go really deep inside to cleanse what is there. I know that full healing is possible. Part of the process is to accept that I am OK. It has been said that we are perfect the way we are. That can be misunderstood. It does not mean that we have nothing to work on, nothing to improve or that we cannot grow. Rather it is that basically as a person, each of us is fine. We all have failings, faults and imperfections but they do not diminish our essential being. That inner being is perfect. In other words, I am not a weird person to be shunned. Of course some people will react in that way but then I do not want them in my life. We are all both perfect and imperfect at the same time. Since seeing my doctor I have shared what I am facing with a very small number of people whom I felt I could trust. Their acceptance and love for me has been unconditional and that is a very big part of my healing. It is ironic that I have always accepted the people I have worked with but that I judge myself very harshly.

Though attitudes have improved there is still a lot of ignorance of mental health and prejudice towards sufferers. Figures vary but probably one in four people will suffer health problems in this area during their life. Many of them may go through quite a short period, unnoticed by others, when things are tough. They pull through and may not even fully appreciate what has just happened. That doesn't mean that as soon as someone has a fit of the blues we should assume they are ill. That would be overreacting. Nevertheless, mental ill health is a real problem for many people. The problem may be at one end of the spectrum, such as schizophrenia or it may be at the other end, such as mild depression. Mind you, even this latter can be a time bomb.

For me, living a life of gratitude is a major key to happiness. Accepting that everything happens for a reason allows me to learn and grow and not to wallow in self pity and negativity. I have been able to see the positive in almost everything that has happened to me, even if it has been well after the event. However, I have to confess that I find it hard to see all the good in this challenge. I know it is there. It's hard to explain, but in some way I believe it makes me a better healer, or at least a more compassionate one. Perhaps by sharing it here, some people will realise that they are not alone. I hope it will help to reduce some of the prejudice. If I can use my experience to help in this way then I am happy.

It is funny how most of us tend to think that we have it all right and that everyone else is out of line. I am reminded of an old saying, from Yorkshire I believe:

"There's nowt as queer as folks, except for thee and me. And thee is pretty funny, lad!"

We are each unique, special and beautiful and when we can see that, seeing from the heart to the heart, then, I believe, we will help to build a better world.

Epilogue

It feels appropriate that the thoughts for this Epilogue began to take shape on my birthday, 2nd March. I had a birthday card from my dear friend Sinead, in which she wrote: *"I have a feeling that 2014 is your year."* It is.

In the final chapter I said that I intended to work with two energy healers to get to the root of the OCD that I suffer. I had my first session with them some three weeks ago. Chris and Stephanie work together with their clients. It is usually Chris, who is psychic, who receives the images and the information regarding their client. Stephanie seems to act as the reinforcer. That may not be exactly how they would describe it but no matter, because it works.

During that first session Chris picked up a lot and he felt that the root of my difficulties went back to an incarnation when I had been a young lad during the First World War. Horses were involved as well. It was powerful yet in some way it was incomplete. As usually happens following such work, I was exhausted that evening. Then I was quite ill for the rest of the week. They and I felt this was due to the work being incomplete; the information received was not everything.

We agreed that another session was needed. We all work together in a mastermind group of healers and equine people that meets regularly. They invited Jenny, who is also in the group, to join us. Jenny and I have become good friends and she has proved to be a rock of support for me in the last year. So we all got together a week ago. It was very powerful. I was a young lad living in Cumberland at the outbreak of the Great War.

When I was conscripted into the army I was forced to leave my farm and my beloved horse. At one point during a battle I heard a horse in great distress and I went to try and find and rescue him. I was accused of cowardice and condemned to be shot, as was so common then. While incarcerated prior to my execution I felt terrible sadness that I would not see my own beloved horse again, a sense of failure that I had not been able to rescue the horse I had heard, and paralysing fear at my ensuing fate.

In the week since I have felt a deep inner peace. So much of it makes sense. Fear is certainly part of the OCD. The very special bond I have with horses, developing very late in my life, could well have a root in this past scenario. Just three days after this work I went to see a movie. There is no coincidence as to how it fitted into what had happened in the healing session. My aunt had booked two tickets to go and see 'War Horse'. This was not the movie version but a live transmission, beamed to cinemas, of a stage performance of the play at the National Theatre. She had thought I would enjoy it. As it happens I had no idea what it was about. It is a fictional story about a young boy whose horse is taken from him on the farm to be used in the cavalry in 1914. Eventually he joins up and at the end of the war, when both he and the horse have been wounded, they are reunited. I sat through it mesmerised. It was such a close reflection of what Chris had told me and of my own feelings. This and the healing session have set in train yet another chapter in my journey. There is still much to be done but I feel that I can now move still further on the path.

Then I have to ask whether it is all true. How can I know? Over my life I have read so much and spoken to so many people who claim to have the answer to life's big questions. The Tibetan Book of the Dead describes in minute detail what Tibetan Buddhists believe happens between our death and our next incarnation. Christians swear by every word in the Bible and most of them vehemently reject the concept of reincarnation. Mind you, I believe that the early Christian church did accept reincarnation but the papacy suppressed it in the early centuries after Christ. Then there are the writings of Raymond Moody. He is a medical doctor and psychologist who has studied and written extensively on near death experiences that people have had. It is very convincing. Amit Goswami is a quantum physicist who has written a lot of books to support the notion of God. Though what he says would not accord with a Christian viewpoint, he suggests that there is an energy that is all-knowing, omnipresent and eternal. I remember reading what the late George Harrison's wife said when he died. The famous musician was a very spiritual and God-seeking person; a very gentle and loving man. His wife said that at his death the room was filled with the most radiant, all encompassing light as his soul left his body.

So what is true? People swear by the particular holy book of their chosen faith. They argue furiously that theirs is right and others are wrong. People go to war and kill for this. How can we kill if our faith is about a loving and forgiving God? Not one of these scriptures was actually written by the master to whom they are attributed. In most cases the accounts were handed down orally for tens or hundreds of years before being written down. How can this be the unquestionable word of God or an absolute description of how things are? Most of these writings offer moral guidance and a blueprint for a good life. The modern writings by the likes of Raymond Moody offer serious food for thought. My own experiences are very powerful for me…..but for anyone else?

A part of me does believe in reincarnation but maybe that is not important. That does not mean that I disbelieve what Chris and Stephanie felt they had discovered about my past. Whether that is true in a hard and fast way does not matter. Maybe it is a way for me to interpret and understand what is happening in this life now, which is the only certain one I have. Maybe it is a deep spiritual metaphor.

The only thing of which I am sure is love – which comes back to what my dear old mum used to say about love being what makes the world go round. I try to make that the foundation of all I do and of all my interaction with my fellow beings. Horses and the other animals I work with tune in to that immediately. So do the people for whom I still do healing work. But then so does nearly everyone else with whom I interact. A lot of people might find it hard to acknowledge that, because of the inhibitions we have about showing our emotions or admitting that the most important thing in this often hard world is just love. Yet whether it is the person who serves me in a shop, my colleagues in the business networking I do, or the clients with whom I work in the Probation Service, I truly believe that they respond to love even if they might not realise it or put it in those words.

For me now, that is all there is. I hope that I will continue to go deeper into it and that everyone I meet will join me in that journey. 2014 is my year.

About the Author

After travelling the world on his search, Charlie Holles has finally settled in the Cotswolds in the heart of England. The peaceful ambience of the area reflects the inner peace he has found. It is a perfect setting for the horse healing work to which his life is now dedicated. This work takes many forms. He works directly, hands on, with the animals.

Charlie is also a broadcaster with Radio Winchcombe, promoting the great power and healing ability horses possess. He champions the cause of all animals and through further writing, he will contribute to the growing awareness that all sentient beings with whom we share the planet should be treated and respected equally.

Find out more about Charlie and his healing work, and contact him at:

www.charlieholleshorsehealing.co.uk

or email charlie@charlieholles.com

Printed in Great Britain
by Amazon.co.uk, Ltd.,
Marston Gate.